PAKISTAN AND AMERICAN DIPLOMACY

ADST-DACOR Diplomats and Diplomacy Series

SERIES EDITOR: MARGERY BOICHEL THOMPSON

Since 1776, extraordinary men and women have represented the United States abroad under widely varying circumstances. What they did and how and why they did it remain little known to their compatriots. In 1995, the Association for Diplomatic Studies and Training (ADST) and DACOR, an organization of foreign affairs professionals, created the Diplomats and Diplomacy book series to increase public knowledge and appreciation of the professionalism of American diplomats and their involvement in world history. In *Pakistan and American Diplomacy: Insights from 9/11 to the Afghanistan Endgame* career diplomat Ted Craig, who served twice in Islamabad, offers an insightful and entertaining look at the maladies that have governed U.S.-Pakistan relations in the twenty-first century, along with revealing snapshots of Pakistan's troubled relations with Afghanistan, India, Bangladesh, the United Kingdom, and other "cricketing" powers.

PAKISTAN AND AMERICAN DIPLOMACY

Insights from 9/11 to the Afghanistan Endgame

Ted Craig

An ADST-DACOR Diplomats and Diplomacy Book

Potomac Books

AN IMPRINT OF THE UNIVERSITY OF NEBRASKA PRESS

All rights reserved. Potomac Books is an imprint of the University of Nebraska Press.
Manufactured in the United States of America.

♾

The opinions and characterizations in this book are those of
the author and do not necessarily reflect the opinions of the
U.S. Government, the Association for Diplomatic Studies and
Training, or DACOR.

Library of Congress Cataloging-in-Publication Data

Names: Craig, Ted (Diplomat), author.
Title: Pakistan and American diplomacy: insights from 9/11 to
the Afghanistan endgame / Ted Craig.
Other titles: Insights from 9/11 to the Afghanistan endgame
Description: [Lincoln, Nebraska]: Potomac Books, an imprint of
the University of Nebraska Press, [2024] | Series: ADST-DACOR
diplomats and diplomacy series | Includes bibliographical refer-
ences and index.
Summary: "Through the lens of the 2019 Cricket World Cup,
former senior U.S. embassy official Ted Craig offers an insightful,
fast-moving tour through U.S.-Pakistan relations, from 9/11 to
the U.S. withdrawal from Afghanistan"— Provided by publisher.
Identifiers: LCCN 2023048937
ISBN 9781640126008 (hardback)
ISBN 9781640126138 (epub)
ISBN 9781640126145 (pdf)
Subjects: LCSH: Cricket—Pakistan. | Pakistan—Foreign
relations—United States. | United States—Foreign relations—
Pakistan. | Pakistan—Foreign relations—21st century. | BISAC:
POLITICAL SCIENCE / International Relations / Diplomacy |
HISTORY / Asia / Southeast Asia
Classification: LCC E183.8.P18 C73 2024 | DDC 327.5491—dc23/
eng/20231103
LC record available at https://lccn.loc.gov/2023048937

Designed and set in Lyon Text by K. Andresen.

CONTENTS

MAPS

PREFACE

During the second half of the Afghanistan war, the arc of U.S.-Pakistan relations was shifting. Both nations were grappling with issues of terrorism, counterinsurgency, and the stalemated war in Afghanistan. I was immersed in these issues and in our troubled bilateral relationship as a U.S. diplomat serving in Pakistan and as an analyst in Washington. As America approached its negotiated departure from Afghanistan, the ground shifted under long-standing U.S.-Pakistan problems, opening possibilities for improved ties, but great risks persisted.

Global shifts wrought by the U.S.-China competition, including closer American relations with India, are placing new constraints on U.S.-Pakistan relations. After the drama of the last twenty years, however, it may be that a little restraint is good for Pakistan-U.S. relations. The Taliban victory in Afghanistan will change the equation further, in ways this book will explore. At the heart of the story are policy failures by both the United States and Pakistan. I suggest that much of the trauma was generated by the ideological blinders of key institutions on both sides, strategic misconceptions that poorly served the interests of both countries.

Cricket offered a lively and logical way to organize the manuscript. *Lively*, the American reader might ask? Give it a chance. The sport has its excitements, more so when the protagonists include national teams from Pakistan and India, bringing flare, animated fans, and a national rivalry that has now endured three and a half wars. Cricket itself has a surfeit of scandal, politics, and rivalries among the small group of countries at the top of the sport.

There are also broader lessons from the sport's prominence in Pakistan. In a society bound by class and constrained opportunities, cricket has been one of the few meritocratic outlets. Pakistan for decades sustained competitive teams by recruiting its best talent, regardless of family or geography. Some of its top performers have come from poor backgrounds.

It is a system of opportunity unavailable to most Pakistanis in education, government, or business.

Structuring the heart of the book around the chronological progression of Pakistan's 2019 World Cup matches is an artificial construct but as good as any other method for organizing episodes, maladies, negotiations, and events in U.S.-Pakistan ties and the region. Chapters 1–3 lay the groundwork by introducing three major themes—first, the state of democracy and governance in Pakistan (keyed around national elections held in 2018 and won by cricketing great Imran Khan); second, the rules of cricket and its development in Pakistan; and third, a brief exposition of the highs and lows in U.S.-Pakistan relations, particularly in the 2010s, with attention to Pakistan's other great international patron, China. Chapters 4–12 follow the nine matches Pakistan played in the World Cup competition, with themes built around Pakistan's relations with each country.

I put the discussion of terrorism and counterinsurgency into chapter 6, centered on the match against Sri Lanka, in part because its national team had the closest call with insecurity when playing cricket in Pakistan. Sri Lanka, like Pakistan, had a long history with terrorism after independence. The issues in Pakistan-India ties are enough to fill multiple volumes. In chapter 8, I give attention to recent diplomatic episodes and an aerial dogfight between the two countries.

In chapter 11, I describe the contention between the U.S. and Pakistan over Afghanistan. In 2018-19, Pakistan offered modest assistance to U.S. efforts to broker peace with the Taliban, but this followed almost two decades of sharp disputes between the two countries over war, terrorism, and mutual betrayal.

In part three, the book includes a discussion of the complicated issue of anti-blasphemy laws and militancy, including how Western embassies helped one wrongly accused victim. It concludes with a look at how the United States and Pakistan might build a more effective bilateral relationship in the years ahead.

Although the manuscript includes multiple sources, in part to demonstrate I am not revealing internal knowledge from my government work, many of my insights came directly from Pakistani friends and acquaintances, others from meetings in which I participated in an official capacity. Except where the protagonist's views were already public, I have refrained from naming names. Wherever possible, I use secondary sources and public statements to document U.S. policy and decisions. In some instances I have said less than I could have.

My hope is that the book will be an entertaining and informative read to those unfamiliar with the region and American diplomacy. I trust I have included enough current history and insight to interest foreign policy professionals. Throughout, I have endeavored to draw lessons from diplomacy or cricket.

Anything assessed accurately herein owes a great deal to the work of excellent American colleagues at the embassy and in Washington, insightful foreign diplomats, and the many Pakistanis who shared their lives and took the time to teach me about their country, their culture, and their sport. I am indebted to the many readers and editors who helped me improve this book, and particularly to Margery Thompson and the Association for Diplomatic Studies and Training for supporting this project. I am grateful to the many family and friends who supported me in my tours to Pakistan and in the writing of this book, and above all for the love and support of my son and daughter, Alex and Sofi.

PROLOGUE
Resetting the Relationship

Mohammad Amir was just twenty-five years old when his life arc passed to redemption. Seven years before, a green eighteen-year-old, he had stepped into humiliation and guilt, the youngest of three Pakistani cricket players caught cheating in a British tabloid sting. The promising bowler (a "pitcher" in baseball parlance), in 2010 already a star on the national team and playing a Pakistan-England test in London, bowled two "no balls" at precisely the point in the match promised by a fixer to a bookie. The fixer was a British-Pakistani sports agent, Mazhar Majeed, enjoying far too much access to the Pakistan national team; the "bookie" was really a journalist. Majeed's promises and his comically villainous counting-out of 150,000 British pounds were recorded on video. Amir, not a bowler prone to delivering "no balls," stepped wildly across the delivery line in the third over, twice committing his choreographed fouls.

Amir would join the other two indicted players—Mohammad Asif and team captain Salman Butt—in asserting their innocence before a tribunal of the International Cricket Council (ICC) in 2011. They did not persuade. All three received playing bans, Amir's the shortest at five years. Later that year Amir confessed when facing criminal charges in a British courtroom. He broke ranks with the other two defendants and admitted his guilt. He insisted he had taken no money but confessed to purposefully stepping across the line. He served three months in jail.

This spot-fixing scandal was just the latest dreary episode tainting the sport. Though the crimes in this case were just three no balls, hardly enough to swing a match, Majeed described the poor deliveries as proof that he could engineer future match-changing results. In his videotaped braggadocio, he suggested that an epic Pakistani collapse against Australia in a January 2010 test match played in Sydney owed to such corruption. Defensive after years of scandals in the sport worldwide, players and commentators roundly condemned the guilty Pakistanis.

Nonetheless, Amir had moved from risible claims of innocence to something like atonement. He asked for forgiveness. He would put in the work over the next five years to stay in shape, coming back to cricket in 2016. He had all the ingredients for popular rehabilitation—humble and rural roots, youth at the time of his crime, a confession, good looks, and soon enough a stable marriage and a child. As important, he possessed the skills that Pakistani fans elevate above all others. He was an accomplished left-armed fast bowler.

Most Pakistanis welcomed Amir's return. Foreign fans were less forgiving. Some taunted him on his return to play in England in 2016, and he could expect sharp treatment as Pakistan prepared to contest the 2017 ICC Champions Trophy in England and Wales.

Conducted under the same One Day International (ODI) rules that govern the World Cup of Cricket, the Champions Trophy was then the sport's second most important international competition, conducted quadrennially and two years apart from the World Cups. The Trophy tournament had a smaller field, just eight teams in 2017, the best eight in the world. In its first match, Pakistan looked well outside the top tier.

Opening group play, Pakistan drew the defending champion and tournament favorite: India. India is Pakistan's greatest adversary in geopolitics, its enemy-neighbor, an opponent in three wars and several skirmishes fought in just seventy years of nationhood. India-Pakistan is also a great cricket rivalry, albeit one marred by inconclusive results in the longer multiday "test" format, where teams can play for a tie rather than risk a loss. India-Pakistan matches draw massive television audiences, consistently among the world's largest for sporting events. When contested in the United Kingdom, the matches draw sold-out crowds from the large diaspora communities of both countries.

The much-anticipated June 4 meetup proved a disappointment to fans of competitive matches. Pakistan lost by 124 runs; in ODI cricket the margin was a rout. Bowling against the strong Indian batsmen, Mohammad Amir gave a creditable performance. He took no wickets (outs, in baseball) but kept the Indians from scoring much. His bowling teammates, however, gave away too many runs, and Pakistani batting fell short.

Pakistan recovered from the dispiriting defeat against India with a win over South Africa. In the final match of group play, against Sri Lanka, Amir took a key pair of wickets and made crucial runs with the bat. Pakistan won the match easily, advancing to a semifinal match against England at Cardiff.

If India was Pakistan's greatest rival in all things existential, England was its more consistent rival in cricket. Where India and Pakistan often let years pass without playing due to tensions and conflict, England and Pakistan played regularly. The two countries now have a deep and edgy cricket history to complement the weight of their colonial past. Results between the two sides are balanced. England's team was coming into form in 2017, however, and it was a favorite.

Amir, out for injury, did not play against England, but Pakistan's other bowling talent did fine, limiting England to just 211 runs. England's run rate of 4.23 for every over (six balls) was one of its lowest ever in an ODI contest. Pakistan then pursued the modest 211-run target methodically, using thirty-seven of fifty allotted overs to surpass the total and take the match. On the other side of the bracket, India steadily outplayed Bangladesh to claim a nine-wicket win of its own.

The Trophy final was played at the historic Oval in London, contingents of boisterous Indian and Pakistani fans filling the stands. India was the heavy favorite, but Pakistan's batting emerged to immediately tilt the match.

Pakistan raced out to 338 runs, with only four wickets surrendered. Fakhar Zaman, after a long slog in domestic Pakistani cricket, emerged as a star with 114 runs scored on 106 balls. (The following year, Zaman would become the first Pakistani to score a "double century," 200 runs, in an ODI match.)

In their turn at bat, the Indian batting order was now looking at a difficult and distant target. The Indian batsmen took risks to score more runs, making themselves vulnerable to the Pakistani bowlers. Still, Amir deserves credit for what followed. In a wink, he dismissed India's best three batters. He took Rohit Sharma "leg before wicket" (lbw) after just three balls, for "a duck" (no runs scored). Amir then induced poor shots from both Virat Kohli and Shikhar Dawan (the "batsman of the series"), taking two more critical wickets.

From that point in the match, the result was a given, and after 30.4 overs, Pakistan had bowled out India for only 158 runs. Pakistan's 180-run win was the largest ever in an ICC ODI tournament final.

The win put Pakistan briefly atop the cricketing world, with an eye to the World Cup competition coming in 2019. Mohammad Amir became a hero, the author of a series of balls that would be replayed and remembered for years. As his career began to wobble toward retirement in 2020, many lamented the years lost between 2010 and 2016, when the young pace bowler might well have anchored other epic wins for Pakistan.

Team sport is at best a dodgy metaphor for interstate relations, but Pakistan's briefly successful formula for a return to the top of cricket in 2017 paralleled questions I asked myself as I returned to Pakistan in 2018. Was there a magical diplomatic outcome that could redeem America's necessary exit from Afghanistan? Could Pakistan find a way back from decades of colluding with Islamist militancy? And could the United States and Pakistan chart a successful relationship in the post-Afghanistan dispensation?

Americans in Islamabad

As an American diplomat, I was posted to Pakistan's capital, Islamabad, for assignments at the beginning and near the end of the 2010s. On both of those tours, Pakistan played in the quadrennial Cricket World Cup, inspiring my abiding fandom of the sport. Watching the sport on television was the only way to experience it during those tours, as security restrictions kept us away from large public venues and insecurity prevented Pakistan from hosting matches.

Since the attacks of 9/11, American diplomats serving in Pakistan have been mostly confined to their cities of assignment. Unlike every other tour in my Foreign Service career, where road trips to remote parts of a country were a great attraction, I was grounded in Islamabad while serving there. I made choreographed trips to other cities—Quetta, Karachi, Lahore, Muree—but I carried forward the curse of post-9/11 American diplomats in Pakistan: my view of the country's people and its geography was constrained. Most of the time I could at least move about the city, a freedom not shared by my colleagues in Peshawar, Kabul, or Baghdad.

Islamabad is a spacious city, designed from scratch as the new country's capital and marked by wide boulevards and parks. On a drive around the capital, particularly in the early evenings as the heat recedes, many open spaces are filled with some form of cricket—maybe just three or four boys working at bowling and batting. Cricket is an expansive sport, so balls hit into the road are a hazard. Late at night on the well-lit 7th Avenue, I had to dodge deep fielders standing in the road.

The city I returned to in 2018 was little changed. Although it features a handful of striking, monumental buildings, Islamabad is really a city of uniform neighborhoods. Residential "zones" dominate the city. The walled homes range from the pieds-à-terre of the political and business elite, venues for work and meetings, to the warm, modest homes of civil servants and professors. The model of self-sustained neighborhoods and the security threats meant a quiet city with little urban vitality but plenty of gracious hospitality behind the gates. The capital's denizens socialize in homes, in modest restaurants, and at weddings and Iftars and galas at the bunkered hotels. My social life among that demographic was delightful and full of interesting people, but it was incomplete as country "immersion."

The city spreads south on flat ground at the foot of the Margalla Hills. The founders did well with the capital's location—close enough to the mountains to offer a little relief from South Asia's blistering summer heat. It is the same reason Britain put its regional garrison town nearby, in Islamabad's twin city of Rawalpindi. The city is still headquarters of the powerful Pakistani Army, signified in the vernacular as "GHQ"— general headquarters.

Islamabad can give off a dilapidated air. Decaying concrete buildings, many birthed out of the brutalist architecture of the 1960s, are set against the spectacular flowering jacarandas and crepe myrtles. Heavy monsoon rains and crackling summer heat take their toll on streets, buildings, and the ubiquitous walls ringing most houses.

The strip-mall shopping centers look a terrible hodgepodge: empty, cinder block–exposed caverns next to the hum and flashing neon of electronics and blue-jeans emporiums. The shopping centers look better at night, their blemishes obscured and their facades much improved by the hubbub of Islamabad families.

There was not much new to see in Islamabad when I returned aside from a lightly used "metro" system (bus lanes with stations) and a new mall. Two other changes had come from abroad. One was a new Chinese Embassy, built just outside the diplomatic enclave. It was a low-slung, elegant compound that spoke to China's substantial interests in Pakistan and its long-standing elevation in Pakistani minds as the country's most important and dependable friend.

The other major new landmark was the American Embassy compound. Construction began before I left the country in 2011, a much-needed enhancement to an old and overcrowded embassy. The compound then had the ambassador's home and just a dozen or so apartments. Hundreds of Americans—diplomats, military service members, aid workers—lived scattered throughout the neighborhoods of an Islamabad rated a dangerous place for Westerners. On the compound, the offices were small, divided into insufficient cubicles; meeting space was hard to come by. The main office building, the Chancery, was the same one burned and bruised by a violent protesting mob in 1979 (an attack that left two marines and two Pakistani employees dead).

One thing the old compound had, at least, was plenty of green space, including a remarkable hillside garden of trees and paths. The gardens gave way, and I returned to a compound filled with modern glass-and-brick buildings, including a striking marble mausoleum of an ambassador's residence and a hotel for short-term visitors. Three eight-story apartment buildings had been built, enough for most U.S. government staff. The American Club bar had gotten bigger, changed from a wood-paneled speakeasy to something more spacious and serviceable but with less character, nestled in a prefab building. In all, the compound now has the appearance of a new and well-endowed junior college.

Within the course of months, in 2018, our mission began moving staff to the compound, gutting the Islamabad home-rental market. Some of us were allowed to stay in the city for ease of access to our Pakistani contacts. Some who lodged on the new campus missed the connection to "nearby" Pakistan, but for most U.S. diplomats, Islamabad was a more comfortable and safer place to serve. Aside from the more secure housing, moreover, Pakistan was a safer place for Americans in 2018 than it had been during my first tour. The country's tough fight against insurgents and terrorists, described in chapter 6, had turned a corner, at the price of liberties and lives. The Pakistan Army had come out on top.

The U.S. government had overbuilt the offices, it turned out, as many agencies—particularly the Department of Defense—had drawn away staff in the intervening years. Meeting space was now easy to come by, and our ample political and economic sections' suite featured "collaboration spaces" of all sorts. There were long views across the green city toward the Margalla Hills, to the north, and toward Rawal Lake, shimmering to the south.

Those serving in Pakistan often managed a tinge of guilt for enjoying the experience. It was a country steeped in economic inequality, where coddled religious conservatives nurtured young men who committed violence against minorities, women, journalists, and voters. Our interlocutors could be progressive and friendly but also deeply compromised within institutions that committed abuse or fueled financial corruption. Some of my Pakistani friends noted the same dilemma in dealing with Americans, representatives as we were of a government many viewed as meddling and oppressive. Pakistan is not unique for fuzzy ethics, in any case. What was unique in my circles was the warmth and manners. Pakistanis, I found, are unfailingly polite and persistently hospitable.

Many American foreign policy professionals caught the bug once in Pakistan and worked their careers to manage a second or even third tour. For a political officer like me, it was a propitious environment. Politicians, press, NGO leaders, and businesspeople were often pleased to talk with us, despite the prying eyes of Pakistani intelligence. The conversations were not always direct, but they were usually insightful. For Americans experienced in diplomacy in other regions, where politicians and industry leaders might brush off American diplomats, the access was a treat.

Shaping a Team, Quickly

Given the preponderance of one-year tours of duty for American diplomats in Pakistan—a product of our "unaccompanied" status, meaning no spouses, partners, or kids—teams must coalesce quickly. One of these was the "country team," comprised, as at all embassies, of State Department section heads (consular, economic, management, political, public affairs, diplomatic security, and narcotics and law enforcement affairs), our colleagues from the U.S. Agency for International Development, and representatives of any other foreign affairs agencies operating at the embassy. (In our case, these included but were not limited to DOD, Homeland Security, DEA, Agriculture, Commerce, the Legal Attaché [FBI], and other elements best left unwritten.) Our meetings included our colleagues at consulates in Karachi, Lahore, and Peshawar, tied in by secure video.

Ambassadors and their deputies have a great deal of sway over the atmosphere at country team meetings and the degree of collaboration at a post. Only on rare occasions in my State Department career did I encounter dysfunctional models—one leader who knew little and asserted much, another who was uninterested in the morale of staff and their families. In 2018–19 in Pakistan, I was fortunate to be part of a collaborative, professional, and personable team. There were a few sharp elbows, as always, but we operated effectively across the mission. Typically the greatest sin at these biweekly meetings was oversharing.

The deputy chief of mission, John Hoover, a former ambassador himself, was a great writer and perceptive political analyst, and he kept a huge mission operating smoothly, our multiple agencies all focused on top U.S. foreign policy priorities. He was in charge when I arrived because our ambassador, David Hale, had departed for Washington to prepare for a senior job in the State Department.

A new chief of mission would arrive by the end of that August, a two-time former ambassador, Paul Jones. He was friendly, skilled, supportive, and demanding all at once, a stickler for detail and constantly energized to move forward on key objectives.

The political section at any U.S. Embassy is principally responsible for the standard stuff imagined in the world of diplomacy: managing relations with the "host" country on a range of bilateral and international issues. We might on any day receive instructions to press Pakistan on Afghanistan issues, nuclear proliferation, counterterrorism, religious freedom, or gender rights. Our co-located colleagues in the economic section managed a good part of the rest, including finance, trade regimes, climate change, and the rights of American investors and traders.

Beyond direct engagement with the Ministry of Foreign Affairs and other government offices, political sections are also responsible for reporting to Washington on the confided thoughts of influential persons and providing analysis of political and policy developments in the country. We are foreign correspondents with a more restricted audience. To do the job well, we need to talk—to civil society leaders, politicians, academics, journalists, businesspeople, and fellow diplomats, taking up these conversations in offices, coffee shops, and receptions. Not surprisingly, these conversations get better with time, benefiting from the trust built through successive meetings. In Pakistan, with our diplomats often serving short tours, the timeline was compressed. Good officers pushed the meetings forward as often as possible.

I was lucky to lead an exceptional team of American officers in 2018–19. Most were new to the country, with just a handful carrying over into a second year. In the mix were strong analysts, talented writers, and deeply committed public servants. All of them put in extra hours, and the section would generate a spate of vital reporting to Washington on politics, terrorism, Afghanistan, China, military plans, and human rights.

I had strong unit chiefs and a new-to-country deputy counselor who mastered our broad portfolio and could step into my shoes on any issue. He kept the substantive work of the office on track, juggling demands for coordination across agencies, reporting to Washington, and managing our high-level visitors. I benefited from a crackerjack office manager to keep me on schedule and to track the section's interface with countless areas of embassy management.

The political section also provided an administrative home to political officers assigned to the U.S. Consulate down the road in Peshawar, where they could spend just a fifth of their time due to security concerns. A separate door gave the ambassador quick access to our suite, representative of the close working relationship ambassadors almost always develop with their political and economic teams.

The counselor of a large, energetic section can contribute by giving guidance and stepping aside from the details, using his or her access to senior people to supplement the reporting to Washington and protect the team from missteps. To serve the team, the counselor needs to maintain access and relevancy to the top brass, but he or she can do it without dropping into every meeting. I made it a point to send one of my team to meetings whenever appropriate. Entrusted with responsibility, they produced great reports, organized successful events, and provided sage counsel. Amid an adversarial bilateral relationship and a security-constrained existence, all contributed and moved forward, and we enjoyed the camaraderie—not of the foxhole, but of the weird bubble that was service in Islamabad.

The Stickiness of Institutional Ideologies

Soon after my return to work on the U.S.-Pakistan relationship, the U.S. secretary of state, Mike Pompeo, began a trip to South Asia. With Pakistan he sought a "reset." It was not the first such effort and will not be the last. Much of my tour was consumed by the search for areas in which the United States and Pakistan might collaborate, particularly on Afghanistan. The scope for cooperation was narrow, constricted by the unwavering policies of Pakistan's military establishment. By mid-2018, however, the United States was no longer asking for much.

This book is not written as an academic treatise. If it were, however, it would elaborate a theory of the inertial dampeners of institutional ideology on policy change and the effects of this phenomenon on diplomacy. By inertial, I mean that perceived "strategic imperatives" ruled policy in both capitals and were difficult to change or reevaluate. In its most pervasive manifestation in the U.S.-Pakistan relationship of the early twenty-first century, the controlling ideology was the Pakistan security establishment's idea that its interests in Afghanistan could best be protected by supporting the Afghan Taliban. This undercut the West's efforts to remake that country. It was, to be sure, a "strategy," but the establishment's commitment to it—despite the damage to Pakistan's national interest—gave it the cast of an ideology. It was first rational and then a product of groupthink, consistently impervious to reexamination.

A second, related institutional constraint was the Pakistan Army's conviction that the country's central identity as a homeland for South Asia's Muslims required an unceasing campaign to vindicate the self-determination of Kashmir's Muslim population, even at the cost of war and consistently poor relations with its neighbor India. In this case, the institution's ideology was planted firmly and nurtured among the Pakistani population at large. This policy too had morphed from strategy to ideology, rarely questioned on its merits.

Leaders in the United States faced their own ideological constraints when dealing with Pakistan. The longest lasting was the post–Cold War conception that the United States had the power and influence to change governance in foreign lands, whether through sanctions, democracy assistance programs, or the application of military power. A corollary to this was Washington's commitment to the idea that the electoral votes received by Presidents Karzai and Ghani in Afghanistan, however muddied by irregularities, conferred an authority to rule Afghanistan that the Taliban needed to heed in negotiations. Another institutional ideology was exaggerated counterterrorism posturing. Seemingly any pundit or bureaucrat in Washington could end a cautious feeler toward the Taliban by fulminating that America could make no compromise with terrorists.

President Barack Obama's team fought tough bureaucratic and diplomatic battles to surface the idea of negotiating with the Taliban, despite the evident necessity of such a path out of Afghanistan. President Trump proved more capable of breaking down the institutional roadblocks, for better or worse. That presidency was nothing if not norm-shattering.

Though much of the history recounted in this manuscript lends credence to the thesis that institutional ideologies in Pakistan and the United States have stymied pragmatic solutions to the security dilemmas faced by both countries in South Asia, it can be fairly argued that these institutional worldviews are not destiny. A combination of time and leadership can change an institution's strategic concepts, as can pressure from thought leaders and political movements outside the institution.[1] Foreign pressure might help on the margins but is the least efficacious change agent.

By 2022 there were suggestions of a loosening of the old ideologies governing Pakistani strategy. Certainly, Pakistan's disappointment with Taliban rule in Afghanistan punched holes in the case for its long tolerance of and support for the group. Most pronounced, however, has been the Pakistan military's evident acceptance that national security requires improved economic and financial health and, therefore, a diminishment of its costly support to Islamist militancy. It is far too early to conclude this change will stick, but trends between 2019 and 2022 were positive.

On the American side, the end of the ill-conceived nation-building effort in Afghanistan has freed institutions to set aside the once palpable current of moral outrage directed at the Pakistan state. There remain open wounds among some serving in senior positions of our government, but the policy community in Washington is moving toward a more nuanced and sustainable approach to U.S.-Pakistan relations.

Pakistan and the United States have a great deal of history now. Though that history has often been conflicted, there is a path toward reestablishing that history as a strength, beneficial to the interests of both countries and their peoples.

PAKISTAN AND AMERICAN DIPLOMACY

Part 1

PREPARING THE PITCH

1 PAKISTAN'S ELECTIONS AND AMERICAN DEMOCRACY PROMOTION

On July 25, 2018, Pakistan passed one of the standard tests demonstrating a consolidated democracy—in national elections, an opposition party received the largest number of votes, setting the stage for the country's second straight transfer of civilian authority from one political party—and leader—to another. In this instance, former cricket star and global celebrity Imran Khan had prevailed after twenty years spent building a political movement. He had channeled popular discontent over economic mismanagement and corruption to at last become prime minister. It was, for Khan's truest believers, the emergence of *naya* Pakistan, new Pakistan.

I arrived back in the country the day after the vote, acutely aware that the real story of the country's democratic health was less benign, and Khan's victory was less than what it seemed. Most significantly, Pakistan's powerful military establishment had played its most assertive role to date in orchestrating the outcome of a civilian election. The army had run the country before through martial law, and it had told prime ministers what they could and could not do when civilians formally ran the government, but it had never pushed so hard for one civilian candidate and party in an election.

The election was just one among many challenges to U.S. foreign policy in Pakistan. That America might have an interest in the integrity of Pakistan's internal political processes was an established starting point in our approach, but, in 2018, the foundation for that presumption was as weak as particle board. The neoconservative-liberal internationalist commitment to pushing democratic norms on the world had run out of steam. In the Trump administration, where there was a more selective approach to advocating for democratization and human rights, our concern for Pakistan's governance struck astute Pakistanis as little more than a tool for ratcheting up pressure on the Pakistan military. Still, for a week at least, observers watched for a sign of how American and "like-minded" (i.e., pro-democracy) allies would respond to another flawed Pakistani election.

Dilemmas and Decay in U.S. Democracy Promotion

The enterprise of democracy promotion loomed large for Foreign Service officers of my generation, serving in the post–Cold War decades. In championing democracy, we built strong ties with millions around the world even as the efforts to promote voting and principled governance sometimes soured our relations with the governments in power. The American efforts contributed to great outcomes and provoked other lasting headaches. By the late 2010s, however, clutches of semi-authoritarian elected foreign leaders, nativist movements, and social media disinformation had begun to challenge the work like never before.

The American role in promoting democracy offers several jumping off points, from Woodrow Wilson's quixotic intervention at Veracruz against a Mexican dictator to FDR's "Four Freedoms," to Jimmy Carter's elevation of human rights in U.S. foreign policy. There was a definitive pause in democracy promotion in the early Reagan presidency, although champions of his diplomacy would argue that waging and winning the Cold War against the Soviet Union was the necessary superstructure to allow for democracy's growth.

For much of the Cold War and many of the Reagan years, however, America frequently gave a pass to friendly dictators, whatever their democratic credentials. Washington worked well with military strongmen, from Pakistan to Brazil to South Korea. As the Cold War wound down, however, pressures for a more principled policy emerged on both right and left in the United States. More important, populations in many countries around the world pressed for change.

The spillway had opened with the Reagan administration's tortured abandonment of longtime ally Ferdinand Marcos in the Philippines in 1986 and then accelerated as the Central American proxy wars ended, leaving American officials the leeway to push back against egregious human rights violations by client governments. In my first tour as a diplomat, in Guatemala, I stumbled upon fierce arguments between the ambassador and elements of another agency over how to deal with violent and no longer useful allies from those wars.

Guatemala was also where I had my first on-the-ground experience with the United States' increasing readiness to oppose nondemocratic regime change, when embattled Guatemalan president Jorge Serrano illegally dissolved the Guatemalan Congress to bolster his power. This "self-coup" began in classic fashion, with the executive taking control of radio broadcasts and eerie marimba music replacing contemporary pop. Washington opposed the extralegal move, and within days Serrano's already tepid support in Guatemala vanished. As was the tendency in those years, we took the frustration of this antidemocratic effort as emblematic of an ascendent trend toward more liberal government around the world. In retrospect, Serrano was just a little early and a little clumsy in his use of executive powers to undermine democratic institutions.

The 1990s and 2000s saw the emergence of a small industry built around democracy and governance (DG) assistance overseas. Specializations in academia, in think tanks, and at the U.S. Agency for International Development included elections, anticorruption, local governance, administration of justice, press freedom, and women's empowerment. As our appetite to improve foreign countries grew with our suddenly unrivaled global power in the 1990s, we took it upon ourselves to demand as well religious freedom, internet freedom, and the defeat of human trafficking. Governments determined by the will of the people were just the starting point on our list.

In their modest manifestations, DG expertise and programs were critical to helping dozens of newly democratic countries. When undertaken in response to requests from emerging democracies, Western technical support could be vital.[1]

Despite setbacks, today most of Latin America, much of Africa, and most of Central and Eastern Europe have some form of democratic governance. Compared to 1972, before the "Third Wave" of global democratization, when much of the world was ruled by military juntas, "presidents for life," or totalitarian parties, today's situation is markedly better. Credit goes first to the people of these countries, but foreign DG programs provided a boost, particularly in the immediate years after the Cold War.

Within the State Department, it was accepted wisdom from the late Reagan years through the Obama presidency that the United States could and should press foreign governments—friends and foes alike—to respect norms like elections, free press, and human rights. The "Freedom Agenda" of the second (W.) Bush administration was the apotheosis of this thought, arrogating to the United States the right to define its national security as intrinsically tied to the democratic practice of foreign governments.

At the high-water mark of U.S. power and influence, at least to 2005, governments were drawn to democratic norms as a means of achieving safe harbor in the West. Key institutions, like the International Monetary Fund and the World Bank, pressed "good governance" criteria for the financial lifelines that many developing and transitioning countries had come to need. It was part of a larger web of financial, reputational, diplomatic, security, and commercial preferences established by international institutions.

Already, however, the tide was receding. The struggles of American forces in Iraq and Afghanistan demonstrated limits to unilateral American military power. Soon the Great Recession of 2008 dampened U.S. economic power. China and Russia began to offer robust alternatives to liberal democracy. Finance, military equipment, technology, and multilateral support were available in Chinese and Russian harbors, with no elections required. Increasingly authoritarian populist rulers the world over learned to exploit the mechanisms of democracy to sustain their power.[2]

The 2016 election of Donald Trump further undermined the role of democracy promotion in U.S. foreign policy. His approach to foreign relations was openly transactional. Governments could win American friendship based on their responsiveness to American interests rather than the virtuousness of their households. It suggested a bracing return to a world ordered by sovereign states and national interest, with far less attention to the democratic and human rights of other countries' citizens.

There was an ameliorative element to the Trumpian retrenchment, particularly to the degree it meant greater American circumspection about military intervention. But without the application of good conscience, this approach can violate norms most Americans have come to expect of their government. The pendulum swung dangerously close to the worst Cold War norms for ignoring atrocities by our friends. Would-be authoritarians were prominent in President Trump's Twitter fandom.

Even as President Trump moved to discard democratic criteria as a means of ordering our foreign relations, the U.S. foreign policy establishment continued to observe the old principles. American embassies still prepared an annual report on human rights, mandated by Congress since the 1970s, requiring that we assess every country's performance against democratic and human rights indicators. The wheels of State still naturally turned toward commenting on the validity of foreign elections. Congress continued to fund USAID democracy and governance programs.[3] The Republican base pushed to protect religious freedom overseas, a campaign that could not easily be separated from advocacy for broader human rights. Nonetheless, the U.S. commitment to promoting democratic norms was weak when I returned to Pakistan in 2018.

Pakistan's Democratic Consolidation

As I arrived back in Islamabad, I consulted with my new team and our colleagues across the mission to assess the vote and its consequences. Setting aside the State Department's hollowed-out commitment to democracy promotion in 2018, we had a pragmatic interest in discerning whether elites and the population would perceive the election as legitimate or whether protests and political challenges might lead to instability. We would also recommend policy, ideally in coordination with like-minded democratic allies, over what, if anything, we should do if the election were fraudulent given our other substantial interests in Pakistan.

A clear-eyed assessment of the July 25, 2018, election required a fair knowledge of the country's tortured governance history, and in particular the role of the military. The Pakistan Army had been a perennial force in the country's politics since the 1950s. Military men had ruled the country directly for three long stretches, the last one ending in 2008. Over the years the army had cut short the terms of elected governments, and it hovered always as a final arbiter in the political realm. Sometimes the interventions were direct, as when chief of army staff Gen. Pervez Musharraf grabbed the reins of power from Prime Minister Nawaz Sharif in 1999; sometimes they were slightly obscured, as when the head of state (the president) was instructed by men in uniform to dismiss the head of government (a prime minister). The latter scenario had been Benazir Bhutto's fate in both 1990 and 1996.

This book will not venture a definitive answer as to why Pakistanis have tolerated the army's large and rarely ambiguous role in politics. The most convincing explanation is that Pakistanis accepted from the outset of nationhood the strategic doctrine that Pakistan was vulnerable to a larger and hostile neighbor, India, and that resources—money, material resources, and, finally, political power—could be justly claimed by the army to defend the country. Certainly there were Pakistanis who objected to the army's intrusions but ultimately not enough of them working together and ready to risk enough in opposition. As it accreted resources from a poor country and a disproportionate share of foreign assistance, the army became a large and effective institution, far superior to the civilian state, political parties, or large industries.

Even during periods of putative civilian rule, the military was never far from power. Under the Pakistan People's Party (PPP)–led government from 2008 to 2013, the military called the shots on all aspects of security policy and the key elements of Pakistan's foreign policy.[4] Some of the civilian government's most difficult moments involved no-win efforts to square American demands with the security policies of army GHQ.

The military's heavy hand during that PPP government surprised not a single Pakistani, but it disappointed many. The reestablishment of civilian government in 2008 had been dramatic. A "lawyers' movement" had taken to the streets in the spring of 2007, provoked by President Musharraf's state of emergency and sacking of judges, including Pakistan's chief justice. The black-suited marchers braved police batons and gradually undercut Musharraf's remaining support.[5]

From the outside it seemed a high point for Pakistani civil society, a nonviolent, nonpartisan mass rally for democratic norms. This was Pakistan, however. There were grounds to suspect the intelligence service was hovering somewhere behind the lawyers, perhaps the hidden hand of the then–director general of Inter-Services Intelligence (ISI), Gen. Ashfaz Pervez Kayani.[6] By this account, Kayani was manifesting the sentiments of senior army officers, weary of Musharraf's overlong stay atop the political and military system. In short order, Musharraf retired from the military and clung to his residual civilian powers. Kayani became the chief of army staff, the most powerful man in the powerful military.

Even before he lost his military billet, Musharraf had been casting about to bolster his tottering government. Once hailed in the United States as a stabilizer of Pakistan and an ally in Afghanistan, Musharraf had shed much of his international appeal as Pakistan's support to the Taliban resistance in Afghanistan became more apparent. Within Pakistan, the economy and citizen security were both in decline. Musharraf had been in discussions with Benazir Bhutto about the prospect of her returning from exile to Pakistan to rejoin the political process, a goal pressed energetically by Washington. Musharraf's intention was to broaden the government and win support to stay on through a new five-year term as president.

In choosing to work with Benazir but not the similarly exiled political leader Nawaz Sharif, Musharraf was resurrecting one of the military's oldest tricks: playing the country's civilian politicians against one another. This pattern had been established in the country's first decade. It was perfected in the 1990s, with the military playing off the country's two leading parties, Bhutto's PPP and Sharif's Pakistan Muslim League—Nawaz (PML-N). The party out of power in the 1990s could always be induced to raise corruption charges against its rival and endorse military-orchestrated moves to weaken the government. Complicating matters, the corruption charges often had merit.

Cognizant of these mistakes, Bhutto and Sharif, in late 2006 in London, signed a Charter for Democracy. The document included an array of commitments to enhance civilian control, including in national security and foreign policy. Most significantly, the two leaders pledged: "We will respect the electoral mandate of representative governments that accept the due role of the opposition and declare that neither shall undermine each other through extra constitutional ways. We shall not join a military regime or any military sponsored government. No party shall solicit the support of military to come into power or dislodge a democratic government."[7]

Although the PPP and the PML-N collaborated in Parliament to enact some of the ideas encompassed in the document following the civilian restoration in 2008, the solidarity against military encroachment would not endure. With its undiminished authority over its soldiers, its popular support, its penetrating economic interests, and its rumored possession of compromising dossiers on the leading politicians, the Pakistan Army was not going away as a political force.

The dynastic nature of the PPP and the PML-N also rendered them less effective as advocates for civilian control. Unlike Western parliamentary parties, which typically sack a leader once he or she loses an election, the Bhuttos and Sharifs remained firmly in control of their political parties through good times and bad. Neither party could rise above the misdeeds of past leaders because the leaders were never past, except in death.

Bhutto came home to Pakistan in 2007 to inspired crowds, but there were also threats. The country was fighting brutal ethno-Islamist militants and suffering frequent terrorist bombings in the cities. Bhutto, like Musharraf, was among their targets, and terrorists killed her and scores of civilians with a bomb following a campaign rally in Rawalpindi on December 27, 2007. Authorities delayed the vote by only a few weeks.

The PPP surged to a plurality of 40 percent of the seats in the national election, significantly more than Musharraf's party, which was in second place. The PPP formed a governing alliance. Months later, with support from Sharif's PML-N, the civilian parties pressed for Musharraf's resignation from the presidency, threatening him with impeachment. After nearly a decade in power, the general was out.

The newly seated national and provincial representatives convened to select Asif Ali Zardari, Benazir's widower, as president. He was a most unlikely face for Pakistan's return to democracy. Calling him "Mr. Ten Percent" for the widely held belief that he had taken that much from government contracts during his wife's two turns as prime minister, many Pakistanis viewed him as among the most corrupt.

Despite the probable corruption at the top, the PPP was then and is now the only significant national party with a secular bent. It maintains a good standing internationally through a group of broad-minded and well-educated second-tier leaders with no other party to join, and it has remained politically relevant even in decline because of a secure electoral base in rural Sindh Province. I valued conversations with the urbane intellectuals in the party, great public servants gathered under a sadly tattered flag. Zardari, charged with multiple cases of corruption by 2017, remains a force in the party, even while the public face has shifted to the more appealing Bilawal Bhutto, Benazir and Zardari's son.

A relatively free and fair election in 2013 resulted in Pakistan's first-ever civilian transition at the end of a full government term, in this instance from the PPP to a PML-N government under Nawaz Sharif. Once a beneficiary of military favor and then a frequent thorn in the military's side, Sharif became prime minister for a third time. And for the third time, he would not complete his term in office.

The clashes came early. Imran Khan's Pakistan Tehreek-e-Insaf (Movement for Justice, or PTI) had achieved its best election result yet in 2013—second in votes and third in parliamentary seats—but less than its partisans had expected. A year later Khan took his followers to the streets, denying the PML-N government's legitimacy. By early 2014 the PTI established a large sit-in, or *dharna,* in front of Parliament, alleging the PML-N had won by fraud.[8] I came to know one of the deep-pocketed entrepreneurs who said he helped fund the protests. I have no reason to doubt his contributions, but many Pakistanis were certain the intelligence services also lent a hand.[9]

The PPP, critically, would not follow Khan's lead in rejecting the election, instead voicing support for the PML-N's mandate to govern. That part of the Charter for Democracy held. Nonetheless, the 2014 protests weakened Sharif.

By 2016 the military seemed to have decided that Nawaz had to go. Despite the PML-N's apparent success at attracting major Chinese investment under the China-Pakistan Economic Corridor (CPEC), economic growth remained tepid, the mediocre performance viewed by GHQ as a national security threat. The military blamed the civilian leaders, ignoring the military's huge demands on the budget and its distorting presence in the economy.[10]

The military wanted change, but it was reluctant to rule directly. A return to military dictatorship would have repelled foreign investment and risked Western sanctions. And the military's record in government was spotty. Ruling directly meant taking the blame. Indirect rule was safer—if the civilians remembered their place. Nawaz Sharif had forgotten his.

Dawn Leaks and Panama Papers

Two events in particular spurred Nawaz's political collapse. The first occurred when journalist Cyril Almeida, reporting in the leading daily *Dawn*, revealed the civilian leaders had criticized the military in a closed meeting. The civilian leaders had questioned the military for intervening to release detained anti-India militants, thereby risking Pakistan's international reputation.

The leaks infuriated the army leadership. The prime minister was convoked to Rawalpindi for a discussion of security policy, a symbolic demonstration of the army's power. Nawaz and his lieutenants paid obeisance, firing a few scapegoats and encouraging measures to censure (and censor) both *Dawn* and Almeida.[11] Nawaz stepped back from open war with the military, but he was wounded.

The second blow unfurled more slowly, but it proved fatal to his prime ministership. In April 2016 a German newspaper and the International Consortium of Investigative Journalists published leaked documents, primarily from a Panamanian law firm, suggesting tax avoidance schemes and unaccountable assets for politicians from around the world. Among those exposed were the Sharifs—Nawaz's children in particular—with large bank accounts and expensive properties overseas. These assets suggested illicit gains, though the family clumsily argued otherwise.[12]

The Supreme Court sealed Nawaz's fate on July 28, 2017, barring him from politics based on the evidence of corruption. The PML-N remained in charge of the government, but official leadership passed to secondary figures. The civilian government was hobbled for the remainder of its term. Whether the military played a role in the court's decision is a matter of conjecture.

Useful Extremists

If Rawalpindi played a role in Nawaz Sharif's downfall, this was not the full extent of the military's political interference before the July 2018 election. The most unscrupulous play was its apparent sponsorship of a radical, murderous street movement, the entire justification for which was to demand the death penalty for those accused (in most cases, even if it was merely a rumor) of committing blasphemy against Islam. The security establishment had given support to conservative Islamic parties in the past, including Jamaat-i-Islami (JI), but its decision to support the Tehreek-e-Labaik Pakistan (TLP) in 2017–18 was more reckless. Its apparent goal was not to see the TLP gain power but to weaken the PML-N and thereby improve the election prospects of Imran Khan's PTI, which by 2017 was thought to be the army's new hope for better (or more tractable) civilian government.

The TLP coalesced in 2016 to make a martyr of an assassin. In 2011 the killer had gunned down Salman Taseer, the governor of the Punjab, proclaiming the murder a justifiable response to Taseer's public advocacy for a Christian woman falsely accused of blasphemy (described more fully in chapter 14). The assassin became a hero to many in Pakistan, and, when the government executed him in 2016, he became their martyr.

The TLP called its followers to the streets in 2017 to reject a small change to the country's oath of office proposed by the PML-N.[13] The protests blocked major intersections in the capital and other cities, and the PML-N looked weak and powerless in response—and no wonder, as the country's military refused to intervene and was even shown to be providing food, money, and water to the protesters.[14] After weeks, the army brokered a compromise in which the law minister resigned.

The deep state of military and intelligence operators found more uses for the TLP. Pakistan's courts allowed the movement to run as a political party in the 2018 elections, despite legitimate arguments that its violent actions in 2017 contravened democratic norms. The newly formed "party" took the fifth-highest vote total nationwide. Its vote was dispersed evenly rather than concentrated in one region, which meant that it won no seats in Parliament. Analysts argued, though, that the TLP pulled votes away from the PML-N in Punjab races for both national and provincial assemblies, allowing the PTI to pick up numerous seats where it did not win an outright majority.[15] If tolerance for the TLP was in fact part of an intelligence operation, it was effective; it also left the country with a strengthened extremist movement capable of mischief and mayhem.

The Elections Brief

Pakistan's military establishment had done much to weaken the PML-N before 2018. As the election neared, it turned also to the more familiar tools of electoral manipulation, most of which were apparent to the media and other Pakistani observers, and ultimately to diplomats watching the events unfold.

The military allegedly pressured the media to aim its critical coverage at the PML-N and PPP. It pressured "electables"—powerful local politicians—to switch parties, likely using both inducements and threats.[16] On Election Day, thousands of soldiers deployed to protect the voting, raising concerns their presence alone might have swayed outcomes. (It was also a reasonable response to a series of attacks on the election process by the terrorist group ISIS-Khorasan.) Soldiers took full control of the counting in some competitive districts, raising further suspicions. To complete the picture, computers at the Electoral Commission went dark for hours after the votes started coming in.

In the end, Khan's PTI won the most seats in Parliament but did not secure a majority. As my team watched the postelection political landscape take shape that first week of August, small parties came over to the PTI, ensuring Khan's election as prime minister.

In Punjab, Pakistan's largest and most important province, the PML-N placed first but fell short of a majority. There too, independents began to fall in line, and the PTI took control of the provincial government. The loss of Punjab was a sharp blow to the PML-N. The PTI gained control of the budget and patronage prizes that came with provincial government, unseating the PML-N on its home turf. Nationwide, Imran Khan's party won control of three of four provinces: Punjab, Khyber-Pakhtunkhwa (KP), and, through local allies, Baluchistan. Only Sindh remained in opposition hands, under the PPP.

International observers and a Pakistani nongovernmental organization, the Free and Fair Election Network (FAFEN), gave mixed marks to the vote. FAFEN acknowledged complaints about the presence of military personnel at polling stations but credited them with performing impartially in most instances. Despite concerns generated by the temporary shutdown of the tabulation system, FAFEN asserted "significant improvements in the quality of critical electoral processes in the election cycle that inspired greater public confidence."[17]

A 120-person European Union observation mission said it had witnessed no poll rigging on Election Day but criticized the many ways Khan's PTI had been assisted, including pressure on candidates to switch parties and pressure on the media. It concluded that there was a "lack of equality of opportunity."[18]

This was the puzzle our embassy faced. Boiled down, Khan's victory was built on equal parts chicanery and genuine support. The legitimate element in Khan's victory was impossible to ignore. His popularity outpaced that of any other individual politician. He was a national hero—a longtime international cricket star and captain of Pakistan's World Cup champion team. Pakistanis, even his political enemies, tended to credit the belief he was not personally corrupt and gave him plaudits for raising sums to build and staff a cancer hospital in Lahore, in memory of his mother.

Khan might have been a once-in-a-generation political figure who owed no allegiance to class, ethnicity, or political party. His supporters knew that the PTI had its wealthy patrons and recycled Musharraf-era politicians, but they persisted in an expectation that Khan was uniquely capable of shunting aside greedy interests for the good of the country.

Khan's base of genuine support meant we could not dismiss his victory outright. The voting irregularities, moreover, were problematic but not damning. It is almost certain that actual Pakistani voters gave Khan's party most of the votes credited to it on July 25.

On July 27 the American embassy hosted "like-minded" diplomats from the European Union, Canada, Australia, and Japan. Discussion touched on our manifold concerns about the process, but it was an inconclusive meeting—neither we nor the other missions had instructions from our capitals on how to engage the presumptive new government, or whether to press for some redress for the unfair electoral climate.

Washington issued a reserved statement on July 27, saying, "The United States takes note of yesterday's election results in Pakistan. The United States commends the courage of the Pakistani people, including many women, who turned out to vote and showed resolve to determine their country's future."[19] The statement amplified criticisms of the elections process. It concluded: "As Pakistan's elected leaders form a new government, the United States will look for opportunities to work with them to advance our goals of security, stability, and prosperity for South Asia." It was neither a congratulations nor a challenge.

I have undertaken this book in part to describe America and Pakistan's search for a new relationship at the end of the 2010s, one that could move bilateral ties out of the long quagmire of distrust and bitterness over Afghanistan, anti-India militancy, and the various sanctions and reproaches leveled by the West over nuclear weapons and human rights. One of the long-standing patterns had been Washington's tolerance of military-led or -influenced governments. In 2018 one conceivable departure from the past could have been a more foursquare Western rejection of antidemocratic manipulations in Pakistan. We might have gone *all in* to press for an unblemished election. It was an idea with no legs.

We had near-term goals that required support from the security establishment, particularly President Trump's top goal of negotiating an exit from Afghanistan. Had we challenged the military's Imran Khan project, it would not have changed the government, but it could have ended hopes for progress on Afghanistan.

Even putting aside Afghanistan, however, a full-court press for democracy would have been problematic. Popular will and commitment are essential to the success of any campaign for democratic redress; the impetus cannot come from abroad. In the wake of the 2018 election, that commitment was not there. There was no evidence the Pakistani people were spoiling for a fight, ready to reject the results. There were no large protests. The PML-N conceded the election on July 27. The PTI, moreover, was genuinely popular, and any move to delegitimatize Khan's election would have provoked a counterprotest of considerable strength.

Our history in Pakistan also suggested humility. From Pakistan's founding, the United States had provided crucial assistance to the Pakistan Army, quickly building it up as an anticommunist ally but also giving it strength and financial resources out of alignment with the weak political parties and civilian bureaucracy. When military governments came on the scene, America continued its support. The justifications changed, from anti-Soviet in the 1960s and 1980s to antiterrorist in the 2000s, but the result was the same. We have been at the front of the line for a half century trying to work with the Pakistan Army. We were not going to erase all that history with a principled standoff in 2018.

Also instructive, the United States had tried a full-court press for democracy once in recent memory, a well-resourced pressure campaign that generated mostly backlash from the Pakistan military. The vehicle was the 2009 Kerry-Lugar bill, legislation to provide a major infusion of assistance to a then-beleaguered Pakistan. The need for the assistance was real, at a time when the Pakistan Taliban was seizing territory and launching terror attacks, one even inside the army's headquarters in Rawalpindi. To make the aid more beneficial to democracy, though, the U.S. Congress and the Obama administration determined to attach

PREPARING THE PITCH

a ropework of conditions—biannual confirmations that Pakistan's civilian government was in control of the military, proof that Pakistan had ceased support to militant groups like the anti-India Lashkar-e-Taiba, and even post-facto reckoning for the illicit aspects of Pakistan's nuclear weapons program.

Not surprisingly, the Pakistan military rallied Pakistani sentiment against this American intrusion. The controversies weakened the Zardari government as it struggled to balance U.S. conditions and the army's objections. The perceptive Pakistani journalist Zahid Hussain describes the initiative as an "extreme miscalculation" by the United States, one that "widened the distrust between the civilian and military leadership, that threatened to derail the fledgling democratic process in the country."[20]

Kerry-Lugar's inconclusive results occurred at a time when the United States was providing substantial flows of aid to Pakistan and when civilian government was freshly restored. It was a period of renewed Pakistani enthusiasm for democracy and a point of maximum U.S. influence. By 2018, as we considered our response to the flawed election, the already much-reduced flow of U.S. economic and military assistance had been frozen. Our leverage was limited, and China was the preeminent source of foreign direct investment and military supply. China was not going to support a challenge over the election's integrity, and a bold American-European demand to rerun the election would have failed spectacularly.

Instead, in July and early August 2018, we pressed Washington on the importance of making a courtesy call on the presumptive prime minister, arguing that his team would view too much delay on our part as a slight, one that would handicap our initial efforts to work with the new government. We saw a few foreign missions make courtesy calls on Khan, including the UK. We were fine with not going first, but we needed to engage.

There were plenty of anti-Pakistan stalwarts in Washington, angry at the Pakistan Army's long-running support for the Afghan Taliban and other militants. There was, it was evident, a temptation to put a stick in the eye of Rawalpindi by further amplifying our doubts about the vote. President Trump had led the charge against Pakistani "lies and deceit," in January 2018, with a tweet excoriating Pakistan for its support to militants and calling for an immediate halt to U.S. military and economic aid to the country. That tweet was manifestly *not* about electoral integrity, however, and by the halfway point in the Trump presidency it was obvious that Washington was not going to make a stand solely for democratic principles.

The forces for engagement rallied, and, with Washington's approval, our deputy chief of mission, as chargé d'affaires, paid a call on the presumptive prime minister–elect at his private home on a hill above the capital. It was August 8, 2018, and I accompanied my boss. It was a timely move, and one that helped ensure our access to the new government as a half-dozen high-profile issues quickly demanded attention.

Khan was cordial in the meeting, going out of his way to thank the United States for its support to police reform in Khyber-Pakhtunkhwa Province during the preceding PTI-led administration there. He outlined his party's commitment to addressing Pakistan's lagging development indicators in health, nutrition, education, and income. If Khan was not a critical thinker on economic and development policy, he proved an eloquent advocate for a government program with the right priorities.

A few weeks later, Secretary of State Pompeo paid a visit to Pakistan, with the newly appointed special representative for Afghanistan reconciliation, Zalmay Khalilzad, at his side. It was the beginning of a gradual improvement in U.S.-Pakistan ties and the start of an intense negotiation process with the Afghan Taliban, the government of Afghanistan, and key regional states to end the war. Pakistan, at least on the surface, was on board.[21]

The question of Khan's legitimacy would percolate in Pakistan, however, fueled by lingering economic stagnation. His anticorruption campaign seemed mostly focused on opposition PML-N and PPP politicians and businessmen, never on the military, and the effort showed no signs of recovering the billions of dollars Khan said would be reclaimed for Pakistan. Khan wasted early months asking friendly countries for donations to overcome Pakistan's crushing debt and balance of payments crises, but soon enough had to request another rescue package from the International Monetary Fund. After years of organizing and agitating in the streets, governing proved difficult for the PTI.

In 2018 and 2019, amid the difficulties of structural adjustment and economic stagnation, Khan's critics grew in voice. One common, derisive epithet hurled at him, increasingly by Bilawal Bhutto and the PPP, was to call Khan the "selected" prime minister. The slight was a reference to the military's role in helping him to power in the form of a cricketing metaphor.

In the sport, national "selectors" pick the players to represent the country in international competitions. Imran as a player had always been a meritorious pick, although he did have relatives on the selection boards in his early playing years. On more than one occasion, as his stature grew, he would publicly call out the selectors to shape a team to his liking. Whether Khan the prime minister was elected on democratic merit or selected by Rawalpindi—or parts of both—was an interesting question. Unfortunately, in Pakistan, the gray answers to that question were embedded in a long history of guided and constrained democracy.

A Governance Postscript: Holding on to the Epaulets

Just a year after the elections, Imran Khan possessed the brief authority to steer the direction of Pakistan's military. As prime minister he had the authority to select the successor to chief of army staff Qamar Javed Bajwa, or, as many guessed, to grant the general an extension rather than retirement.

Within the Pakistan Army there were institutional pressures in favor of a retirement on schedule. Most significant were the prospects of senior three-star generals nearing retirement themselves; Bajwa's extension would end their bid for the top job and a fourth star. More generally, retirement on schedule was good for the institution, sustaining morale by making the army bigger than the man and opening opportunities in the lower ranks.

For Pakistan, where the army has undue political power, civilians place some hope against tyranny in the idea of the military's internal discipline. The chiefs of army staff might be the most powerful politicians in the country, but they come with an expiration date. The powerful army corps commanders changed steadily and exerted collective control over the chief.

The perception of the army's collective resistance to long-term individual rule persists despite a history replete with exceptions. The first three Pakistani commanders-in-chief of the army (equivalent to the role of chief of army staff today) took extensions, with the first, Ayub Khan, becoming a longtime ruler of the country. Among the chiefs of army staff (COAS), four of ten took extensions after three years; two of them, Zia-ul-Haq and Musharraf, also took over the government. The army, it turns out, does generate individuals too powerful to be checked. By law, nonetheless, Pakistan's civilian leader has the authority to pick the army chief.

In 2016, when Prime Minister Sharif selected Bajwa, he passed over more senior candidates, much as he had three years earlier with the selection of Gen. Raheel Sharif. The army accepted both selections. Once the prime minister makes the choice, however, any political leverage dissipates. General Sharif cordoned off the country's security policy from civilian prying; under Bajwa, Nawaz found himself in the military's crosshairs almost immediately.

In 2019 Imran Khan had such a moment of fleeting leverage—with Bajwa and with his possible successors. There were no real crises that summer, nothing that mandated continuity in the person of army chief. I presumed that most of the contending generals felt the same—that there was no national security need for Bajwa to stay in place. At best, I thought, Khan would grant Bajwa a one-year extension, a dollop of gratitude for helping him to power.

Pakistanis asked me about an extension. Many seemed convinced the U.S. government had either influence or secret insight. I can say with some certainty, at least in 2019, that the U.S. government had no interest in advocating for a particular outcome. In the end, Khan gave Bajwa three more years, another full term.

The justification was the "regional security situation," understood as India's August 5, 2019, revocation of Kashmir's special autonomous status under the Indian constitution. The impending Indian crackdown on dissent, the logic went, might spark Kashmiri violence. India would blame Pakistan, and another Pakistan-India conflict might ensue. Pakistan needed a steady hand atop the army in such parlous times.

As descriptions of national emergencies went, this was weak. Pakistanis naturally asked about the *real* reason for the extension.

One popular idea was that Bajwa held compromising information on Khan. The problem with attributing an extension to blackmail is that the secret dossier on Khan would need to have been the exclusive property of Bajwa and his then-trusted director general of ISI, Faiz Hameed, not the broader military-intelligence state. It was possible, but not a probable reason for Bajwa's extension.

More plausible is that Khan felt bound to Bajwa and Hameed as the architects of his 2018 electoral victory and for sustaining his government against challenges. A new COAS, even one selected personally by Khan, might not be as committed to his political survival. A different COAS might even find it useful to jettison Khan if his popularity slipped. Khan might have thought Bajwa the more likely to protect him. (If this was the assumption, Bajwa's apparent turn against Khan in 2022 proved it was in error.)

As the November start of Bajwa's extension approached, Pakistan's chief justice threw the country into modest political turmoil by rejecting the government's process and the grounds for the decision. Justice Asif Saeed Khosa, himself fast approaching an age-mandatory retirement, ruled that the PTI government's case for an extension was poorly reasoned and without legal merit. He dismissed the government's resort to the "regional security situation," writing: "The said words are quite vague and if at all there is any regional security threat then it is the gallant armed forces of the country as an institution which are to meet the said threat and an individual's role in that regard may be minimal. If the said reason is held to be correct and valid then every person serving in the armed forces would claim re-appointment/extension in his service on the basis of the said reason."[22] Khosa was a justice of some backbone, and it is plausible that he was motivated by real concern about the country's institutions and rule of law. Many speculated about hidden hands, however, including opposition from other senior generals. Within days, Khosa offered a workable short-term fix. He ruled that Bajwa could be extended for six months, pending action by the National Assembly to regularize the issues around mandatory retirements and extensions.

If there were in fact conspirators working to frustrate Bajwa's extension, they did not appear to have much of a game plan. By January, the two major opposition parties had agreed to vote with the government in the National Assembly, formalizing Bajwa's extension for the full three years. As almost always was the case, Pakistan's leading civilian politicians had failed to coalesce against the military's accretion of power, a pattern that had held since the 1950s.

2 ON CRICKET, PAKISTAN'S NATIONAL PASTIME

Field hockey is Pakistan's official national sport, but it has long since been eclipsed by cricket as the repository of pride, fan enthusiasm, and youth participation. In Pakistan, cricket occupies the space shared in the United States by football, basketball, and baseball. Field hockey was once prominent, and in its early years Pakistan took three Olympic golds in the sport (and shared two more as colonial India). But field hockey is rarely on Pakistani television today. Sports on horseback, Polo and Buzkashi, hold their discrete fanbases. International soccer draws attention and is making inroads among youth. None of these other sporting entertainments approaches the place of cricket in Pakistan's national psyche.

This chapter offers an outsider's take on cricket's meaning in Pakistan and then describes some of the key rules and terminology. Cricket fans can skim that part, but I offer it as a primer to the newly initiated. I am writing as a fan new to the sport. I hope my recent enthusiasm will overcome gaps in experience. I grew up playing baseball, which is proximate to the sport, and I am convinced my love of that American game helped me relate to Pakistan.

The origins of cricket in Pakistan are easy enough to explain. Britain seeded the sport throughout much of its global empire. In the United States, an early leaver of the empire, it persisted until the Civil War, when baseball shoved it aside.

For fifty years or more, three white teams in the empire—England, Australia, and South Africa—dominated the sport. It was slower to popularity in New Zealand, the other prominent "settler colony" of the second empire. Ireland was long resistant to the empire, and cricket grew there more slowly, finally gaining momentum decades after its independence.

Even if dominated by white colonials, the sport gradually gained support in many of the indigenous-majority countries of the empire. This was true in the West Indies, where Afro-Caribbean and South Asian descendants comprised significant numbers in the top tier of the sport by the early twentieth century. It was true in South Africa as well, where cricket gained popularity among the Black African middle class and South Asian immigrants. And it was true in South Asia, where the sport began with a modest but committed local base. Cricket was not a sport of the masses in colonial India, but it grew, patronized by Anglophile princes, built up in elite colleges, and, to a point, encouraged and dispersed by the colonial authorities.

In 1926 the Imperial Cricket Conference (the ICC, later the International Cricket Council) admitted colonial India as a "test"-playing team, following closely the admission of the West Indies and New Zealand. Before its post–World War II independence, India played all its test cricket (the dominant long form of the sport) against England, either in the British Isles or at home, with no matches played against the other four members. Travel then was by ship, so it was perhaps not surprising that the national teams did not frequent the other extremities of the empire. On India's national team, the best players from different faith communities played together, and many of the top players on the first teams of independent Pakistan and India knew each other from prepartition days.

Two great histories of Pakistani cricket appeared in the mid-2010s, and both trace the development of the sport through its dramatic ascent to both triumphs and defeats. Osman Samiuddin's *The Unquiet Ones: A History of Pakistan Cricket* and Peter Oborne's *Wounded Tiger: A History of Cricket in Pakistan* draw out important insights on the place of the sport in the young nation's psyche and the complex ways that it interacted with political and social developments.[1] I am indebted to these comprehensive and sympathetic works, great reads for anyone interested in the deeper story.

Oborne suggests that there were differences in how the sport developed among the societies that would emerge from colonial India. "Indian cricket before partition," he writes, "repudiated everything that the Congress Party and Indian independence movement was all about. It was collaborationist, divisive, celebrated the British Empire, and used cricket as a method of ingratiation with the ruling elite."[2] Conversely, he argues, among Muslims in areas that became the future West Pakistan, cricket "defined itself in opposition" to England. "In its formative years," moreover, "it was almost exclusively a middle-class sport."[3]

Samiuddin traces the indigenous development of the game in what would become Pakistan. Early clubs in Lahore and a rivalry between Government College and Islamia College created the most prolific nursery for Pakistan's pre-independence talent.[4] Many of the all-India teams featured a disproportionate number of Muslim players, the community a source of much of India's pace bowling talent. Cricket grew as well in Karachi, Rawalpindi, and the former princely state of Bahawalpur, patronized there by the ruling family.

With independence and partition of the subcontinent into India and Pakistan, some future Pakistani players then in their prime had to choose whether to play internationally as India or wait and hope that Pakistan could gain international test status. Unlike the partition of government resources in 1947, when the equipment and supplies of British India's government were to be split roughly 80 (India)–20 (Pakistan), in nongovernment endeavors like industry and sport there were no guarantees. India inherited most of the industry. It took all the cricket bureaucracy. It was home to every one of the subcontinent's certified test pitches, and it alone inherited ICC membership. From its base in Mumbai (Bombay), the Board of Control of Cricket in India pressed Muslim players, even those now living in independent Pakistan, to continue playing internationally as "India." Most chose not to, although India has always had Muslim citizens on its national team.

In the confusion of partition, questions of citizenship and the totality of separation were not as clear as they seem in retrospect.[5] This added to the burden of this choice, but Pakistan attracted enough talent and able administrators to push forward. Its march to international cricket legitimacy was astonishingly rapid. India had a head start, but the loss of most of its fast bowlers, who happened to be Muslim, created a weakness characteristic of the team for years.[6]

In late 1948, with the wreckage of partition still all around, Pakistan prevailed on the West Indies to add a visit to Pakistan to its first-ever India tour. Pakistan managed a draw (a tie, not an uncommon outcome) in the unofficial test match in Lahore, gaining some early credibility. The breakthrough for Pakistan, though, was 1951, when Pakistan won one of five matches against the visiting English, the Marylebone Cricket Club (MCC), in Karachi. The ICC invited Pakistan to join as an independent member in 1952.

The Founders

In the annals of Pakistan's first decade of international cricket, a period of important successes for the new country, four names stand out. The story of each one reveals something about the country's evolution.

Abdul Hafeez (A. H.) Kardar was Pakistan's first captain and later an impactful (and controversial) president of the Pakistan Cricket Board. At independence he was one of the country's few cricketers to have played test cricket for colonial India but still young enough to play competitively. Oxford educated and polished in the ways of the West, he was in many respects perfectly suited to guide a team of young and inexperienced players in their first international forays. He also became a fine captain, directing the team to seminal wins and draws.

Kardar was, according to his own writings, less a democrat than a nationalist. He led the team under early nondemocratic regimes and was close to the populist and autocrat Zulfikar Ali Bhutto in the 1970s. Kardar did institute a lasting tradition of Pakistan promoting young and promising players, sometimes over established players who were passing their prime. Samiuddin describes this as the "one policy that so many admire and are envious of in Pakistan's cricket."[7] Kardar, like Imran Khan decades later, underscored his emphasis on meritocratic selections by dismissing one of his cousins from the team.

An anticolonialist Anglophile, Kardar personified the curious relationship of many elite Pakistanis—and many cricketers—to England. Of his nationalist bona fides there could be no doubt, and he maintained a global anticolonialist commitment throughout his life, applying a firm brake against any Pakistani coexistence, in cricket, with apartheid South Africa. But cricket itself, the yardstick that Pakistan came to adopt in sports, was the most British of global sports. In describing the explosion of popularity of cricket in Pakistan following a momentous home series against England in 1978, Imran Khan evoked a still potent colonial legacy: "Cricket had always been a glamorous game, [thanks to] Fazal, even

Kardar. So it always had that glamour but it was also the only sport we competed in at an international level with others . . . for instance it was a frontline sport in England, Australia, South Africa. So it was the only sport where you competed at that level. Hockey was not a global sport with the same appeal, for example, it wasn't a main sport in England. And this is still the colonial hang-up in our country, so [we had] to compete in that."[8]

Not surprisingly, the English connections have declined in Pakistan since the days of Kardar and even of Imran the player, as the last generation that lived under Britain's rule has aged into its senior years. Still, cricket remains a bond between Britain and its former colony, even in rivalry and antagonism.

Kardar would return to Pakistani cricket as president of the Pakistan Cricket Board from 1972 to 1977. He was a close follower of PPP leader Zulfikar Ali Bhutto, and the prime minister would take an occasional interest in the management of Pakistani cricket. Kardar strengthened the administration of Pakistani cricket while leading the PCB, and he pressed the International Cricket Council for greater representativeness in the game's power structure.

In the end, the PCB replaced Kardar following a meandering series of pay disputes with the increasingly prominent players of the mid-1970s. The old "skipper" found it difficult to come to terms with the pay demands of players in an emerging new age of commercialized cricket. Despite the rough exit, Kardar's legacy was secure—the great teams of Pakistan's golden era were just emerging at the end of his watch.

Among the sport's other fathers was Alvin Robert Cornelius, a Christian who stayed with Pakistan at partition and rose to become a chief justice of the Supreme Court, serving in that position from 1960 to 1968. Cornelius was an early vice president of the Pakistan Cricket Board and played a profound role in setting its administration on a solid footing. He recruited Kardar to the captaincy. Cornelius also played a role in founding the annual "Eaglets" tours of Britain in the 1950s. These were tours by young talents, enabling them to gain international experience and benefit from British coaching.

Cornelius, unfortunately, harkens to a time when Pakistan founder Mohammad Ali Jinnah's vision of a Muslim-majority state that was still home to vibrant minority communities was more possible than today. A

Christian could not be chief justice in modern Pakistan, a country where violent street movements and terrorism have risen to defend conservative Muslim prerogatives. Cornelius thrived in an early Pakistan that even had an Ahmadi Muslim as its first foreign minister, even more unthinkable today. As described later in this book, in 2018 Prime Minister Khan rescinded his appointment of a prominent Ahmadi economist to a national council in the wake of bigoted street protests.

A third figure from Pakistan's early cricket was its first great and glamorous fast bowler, Fazal Mahmood. With good looks, well-coiffed hair, and a dapper fashion sense, Mahmood also bowled with exceptional success through the 1950s.

In Pakistan's first tour as a test nation, to India in 1952, Fazal was instrumental in Pakistan's first and only win, at Lucknow. There he took a remarkable 12 wickets over two "innings," leaving India short of Pakistan's total runs before Pakistan could even come to bat a second time. Indian fans reacted angrily to the lopsided loss, though India prevailed 2–1 in the series.

Two years later Fazal was instrumental as Pakistan achieved a stunning victory over England in a test match at the Oval in London. He again took 12 wickets over two innings. It was the first time a visiting country had won a test against England in its debut tour, and the win at the Oval led to a tied series (1–1, with two draws).

Mahmood's exceptional performances against rival India, just three years removed from the two countries' inaugural war, and against England, just six years removed from independence, elevated the game of cricket in Pakistan's national psyche. It also established pride of place in Pakistani cricket for fast bowlers. As Samiuddin writes, Mahmood "in those first years imparted on Pakistan the one truth that still holds: your batsmen may be jokers and your fielders clowns, and your captain may be anyone and everyone, but your fast bowlers are diamonds and forever responsible for glory."[9]

Even in its lean cricket years, from 1960 to 1975 and again in the past decade, Pakistan has been known for spotting and developing fast bowling talent. Samiuddin describes a strikingly meritocratic national network of talent spotters able to identify up-and-coming fast bowlers even at the rural village level.

If Pakistani bowling has been a calling card, anemic batting has often been its Achilles heel. The greatest early exception to this rule was Hanif Mohammad, a standout performer in Pakistan's first international matches.

The Mohammad family would be a prolific source of Pakistani cricketers. Three of Hanif's brothers played test cricket for Pakistan, and at least one of the four would play in 100 of the country's first 101 test matches over a span of twenty-seven years.[10] The family was also representative of the millions of Muslims who left their homes in postpartition India to join Pakistan. The family moved with few resources and a terminally ill father to Karachi to build a new life. They left the state of Gujarat, where cricket had long been part of the family's sporting life.

Hanif was a schoolboy wonder, graduating to test cricket at an early age. At seventeen, he scored a team-high 51 in the first innings of his—and his country's—first international test match, in Delhi. Through many matches Hanif played a crucial role in stabilizing Pakistan's innings, able to occupy the crease (the batter's box in baseball) with defensive proficiency, beating off hostile bowling that bounded unpredictably on poorly prepared pitches. This skill is as critical in test cricket as is the ability to score runs, which Hanif also did on most occasions.

Hanif and his brothers would come to represent a more workaday, middle-class element in Pakistani cricket compared to the old Punjabi society of Lahore that produced Kardar and Mahmood. They represented Karachi, an up-from-the bootstraps commercial city that attracted a mix of Pakistanis from all ethnic and linguistic groups and many of the Urdu-speaking immigrants from the Indian side of partition. One sportswriter described Hanif's popularity even in cricket-aggrieved East Pakistan (now Bangladesh), where he scored back-to-back centuries in a test against England in 1962.[11] After retirement, Hanif jointly founded and edited the *Cricketer Pakistan*, a glossy English-language standard in the 1970s that proved influential as Pakistan moved toward its real golden age of cricket.

Why Cricket?

That Pakistan played competitive international cricket in the 1950s, the early years of a vulnerable new state, did much to plant the sport in the hearts of Pakistanis. I suspect another part of cricket's appeal rests on the attention that it naturally centers on individual players, easily made heroes or chokers. Batsmen in test cricket may be the center of attention for hours, and the best bowlers return to the action throughout the match. While it is true the biggest global soccer stars can shine as brightly as any cricketer, most of the action in soccer rests on the team's movement and play—crisply passing, building pressure, locking down on defense. Cricket, conversely, is played on a discernably individual level—bowler running up, batsman swinging, the keeper lunging for a nicked delivery. In cricket today, we see these individual efforts in constant high-definition close-up, under the lights.[12]

In a societal landscape that often values conformity to the needs of religion, community, or family, cricket is a safe space for a narrative of individualism. The players are still striving on behalf of a team, but within that construct operating very much as agents of their own destiny. In many other sectors in Pakistan—business and government most particularly— merit alone is often not enough; patronage and class are critical. In cricket, Pakistanis can see a rare glimmering of equality of opportunity.

Why cricket has blossomed equally in the different societies of South Asia—in India, Afghanistan, Sri Lanka, and Bangladesh—is a larger question I do not have the background to approach. Some of it may be this geographic connection. Cricket is important to Pakistan in some measure because it is important to India, so that competing well against the Indian teams becomes a regular measure of national prowess. So too the comparison to England. There is nothing quite like beating the former colonialist.

Why not soccer, the global game? This is harder to say. It may be simply because most play that game in short pants, a dress completely foreign to Pakistan. Or it may be more particular—soccer was never big in colonial India, never became a sport handed down from parent to child. South Asia may catch up along with the global wave. But it takes time to develop a national identity in a new sport, and cricket is what Pakistanis have been quite good at, among the best in the world. If I were a Pakistani child today, I imagine I would dream of superstardom in cricket.

The Rules of Cricket, Long and Short

Cricket in the traditional test format is an acquired taste. In the standard test match, both sides send up to eleven batsmen to the crease (the batter's box), two times through the order, and the batsmen can linger indefinitely if they can protect their wicket (the stumps and bails stacked behind them) and avoid being caught out. There is a time limit to the contest, but it is measured in days. Worse, for modern sensibilities, those days of play often result in a draw.

Batters can be cautious, knocking aside the tougher deliveries and standing pat in the crease, running for a score only when certain of success. Each journey through the lineup constitutes an "innings." In my first exposure to test cricket, as a diplomat watching South African television in Botswana, I reveled in the fact that I could doze off for a nap and awake to see the same batsmen at work. If baseball seems slow to contemporary American sports fans, inured to jump cuts and highlights, test cricket would be a snail's pace. The format has its merits and its satisfying rhythms, but it does not move quickly.

The long-run format of test cricket made open world championships impossible. When a match requires three days to complete, a multi-team tournament would have required months. Test competitions were two-team affairs, storied contests like the "ashes" between England and Australia.

Enter "limited-overs" cricket in the early 1970s, and the stage was prepared for a wider, inclusive competition. In this format, each team received and delivered 50 or 60 "overs," each over comprised of six (or sometimes eight) deliveries (pitches in baseball). With a limited number of deliveries to strike, a batting strategy of defensively deflecting balls to the field but not running is less effective. Limited-overs cricket both shortened matches and changed the strategy.

The one-hundred-overs contests are still long for team sports, running four to eight hours, but the innovation made a multiple-team contest feasible. In 1972 women's cricket led the way with a World Cup competition. It was a proof of concept, and that same year the ICC announced plans to host its first global competition for men, in 1975.

For the first three Cricket World Cups, in 1975, 1979, and 1983, England hosted. England—or later England and Wales—offered a compact geographic space with good infrastructure for the competition. More important, England had resident diasporas of most of the major cricketing powers, meaning good ticket sales.

The Rules of Cricket

Pakistanis and Americans tend to get on well, at a personal level, once outside the bounds of antagonistic national policies. There may be many reasons for this, or it may be imagined, but I like to think one wellspring of mutual understanding is the cultural affinity created by national pastimes featuring bat and ball.

Baseball and cricket are closely related, coming out of British and Irish traditions. Baseball in its early forms was around in America before the American Civil War. It was not a direct descendant of cricket, emerging more from a game called rounders. Cricket was bigger in America before the Civil War, but with the spread of Union armies, with only limited time for recreation, the faster game of baseball won out. In cricket, a good batsman can remain at bat for long stretches, hardly a morale boost for the other soldiers waiting for the chance to swing. By comparison, baseball speeds through a lineup. It may be that Americans were already too impatient for a sport like cricket, even in the 1860s.

The following chapters will recount at least a dozen Pakistani cricket contests with rival national teams. I will try to avoid the jargon, some of which I still struggle to follow despite several years as a fan. I can get lost in a *Wisden* match description, wondering if I speak the same language. But the fundamentals are easy.

Most briefly, cricket is played in the round, so that a ball hit in any direction, even behind the batsman, is in play. (In this sense, at least, nothing is "foul.") The field is circular or oval, with a 22-yard rectangular "pitch" in the center where the bowling and running take place. The bowler delivers the ball, and the batsman uses the bat to prevent the ball from knocking over the blocks of the wicket. The batsman also seeks to score runs for the team by hitting the ball far enough away on the ground (or to the field's boundary) so that the batsman and a partner can run the length of the pitch, in opposite directions, before the fielders can get the ball in and knock over the same wickets.

Bowlers deliver the ball with a straight, overhead windmill arm; their elbows can only bend to a slight degree. Bowlers do not generate quite as much speed as a baseball pitcher torquing an elbow and wrist, but with a sprint before releasing the ball, a fast bowler can get to speeds over 90 mph That is remarkably fast in a sport that still allows you to aim the ball at the batter! The bowler purposefully bounces the ball off the ground as it approaches the batsman; the alternative, a "full toss" with no bounce, is considered easy to hit.

Also similar to but a little different from baseball is that there is something much like a "strike zone"—the vertical "stumps" and horizontal "bails," which the bowler aims to strike and the batsman to defend. If the bowler can knock down one of the blocks, the batsman is "bowled"; in cricket it takes only one such strike to make an out.

Subjective calls by the umpire come into play in cricket as in baseball. For example the batsman is called out if a leg rather than the bat or batting glove stops a ball from hitting the wicket (a "leg before wicket," or "lbw"), a call that requires the umpire to judge that the delivery would have continued to the stumps if not blocked. Some of the great match controversies over the years have been generated by umpires' calls or non-calls of lbw. Today at most high-end cricket competitions, quick video replays with computer-generated projected paths of the ball can easily determine if it would have gone on to hit the stumps and where it deflected off the batsman—bat or body. The computer replay, "DRS," is determinative, unlike in baseball, where umpires are still the final arbiters of strikes and balls. My impression is that this invention has eliminated a great deal of the complaining that had been a hallmark of this "gentleman's" game.

DIMENSIONS OF THE GAME

The pitch and creases—Cricket fields are irregular in size and shape (circular or oval), with curved boundaries, but at the center lies the rectangular "pitch" with regulated dimensions, 22 yards between the cricket stumps at either end and 305 centimeters in width. (Hand it to the English for the mash-up of empire and metric measurements.) The ends of the pitch are marked by a perpendicular line, the "bowling crease," behind which the bowler must release the ball. Slightly closer together (about

18 yards apart) are the "popping" creases, which runners must reach to be safe from dismissal.

The wicket, bails, and stumps—A "wicket" consists of three vertical stumps (28 inches high) with two horizontal "bails" resting on top. Bails today are fitted with electronic sensors that light up when disturbed, but a bail must fall to the ground for a dismissal by bowling. Fielders "remove the bails" by striking them with the ball in hand, aiming to do so before the batsman can run across the popping crease. Taking or conceding a wicket refers to the dismissal of a batsman.

Boundary—Heavy rope or low canvas sheeting demarcates the edges of the cricket field. A fielder may not touch the rope or the ground beyond when making a catch. Batsmen aim to get a ball across the boundary, either on the fly for six runs or bouncing for four.

A cricket bat is also noticeably different from a baseball bat. It has angled surfaces and can be wielded in a variety of directions. A skilled batsman may swing away for power much like a baseball swing. More often, it is a matter of quick wrist action and footwork, repositioning the bat to deflect the ball to a gap in the field or simply to the ground to prevent it from hitting the wicket. Everything is in play, meaning the defending fielders must patrol a 360-degree oval, a more complex task than defending the 90-degree span of a baseball field. In "limited-overs" cricket in the 2000s, there are also rules to limit how many fielders can patrol the deep parts of the field at different points in the match. These periods, called "power plays," may allow for more aggressive batting and more scoring.

As in baseball, a batted ball caught in the air by a fielder means the batter is out (or "dismissed"). Except for the wicket keeper, who plays like a baseball catcher, the cricket fielders play the game without a glove.

In cricket, the running is famously different from baseball, with the receiving batsman and a partner running from one end of the rectangular pitch to the other, bats in hand, heavy protective pads on their legs, sometimes looking less than gazelle-like. Going for two or more runs means stopping and turning in the opposite direction, a less fluid motion than arcing extra-base sprints on a baseball diamond. In running, communication is vital, as the batsman and the partner must decide together when to run, when to go for two, and when to retreat to the popping crease. They cannot end up at the same end of the pitch, something that has happened infamously in big match moments.

If the running results in a single, the batsmen change positions, and the running partner becomes the striker. This can be important in a close match if a proficient batsman is partnering with a poor hitter. (Bowlers must be in the batting lineup, and some are much better bowlers than batsmen.) If circumstances are desperate, the runners may push for two runs to keep the better batsman in the crease.

In addition to running the crease one, two, or even three times before the fielding team gets the ball back in, teams may also score by hitting the ball to the boundary. If it gets there on the bounce, before a fielder can intercept it, it counts for four runs; if it reaches the boundary on the fly, it goes for six, cricket's version of the home run.

There are hundreds of finer distinctions between baseball and cricket, but these are the fundamentals. Also different is how the game plays out.

In the ODI format, one side bats through its order, stopping only when it has given up ten wickets (outs) or when it has used up its allotted 300 balls. Rather than dividing play into the alternating innings of baseball, where batting and pitching sides switch after three outs, in cricket one side takes all its swings and scores all its runs before the other has a turn. The second team "chases" the run total put up by the first. Because the surface of the pitch may dry and crack as the day wears on, with implications for bowlers or batters, the choice to bat first or second is important, with a coin flip determining who chooses.

The sport offers a satisfying mix of teamwork and individual effort. A batsman's "century" (100 runs or more) becomes a noted individual achievement. A bowler taking several wickets in a match, or simply forcing a low run rate, can be decisive. Taking a wicket is akin to notching a baseball "strikeout" but is more, as each side gets only ten such outs per match, not twenty-seven as in baseball. Taking the wicket of a great batsman means that he or she is done batting for the match.

The mounting tension of a close run chase in cricket is both dramatic and extended—each ball brings joy or heartache to the committed fan. A match can turn on the results of a single six-ball over, a shoestring catch, a brilliantly spun ball, or a wild misplay in the field. Or it can build incrementally, over hours, toward a decision on the final swing of the bat. This would prove the case in the 2019 World Cup final, described in chapter 13.

At the World Cup level, finally, we take this majestic and often exciting game and mix in the flavors of national pride and identity. The South Asian center of gravity in modern cricket brings Bollywood—colors, chants, costumes, and song. Huge quantities of collective wagers, most formally illegal, open the door to allegations of bribes, match fixing, and other forms of illicit play. And South Asia's conflicted history ensures that, at least for Pakistan, three or four of the nine matches will carry implications for national pride and even regional peace.

3 CHINA AND AMERICA IN PAKISTAN

Pakistan's two most important geostrategic partners do not play high-level cricket and have never come close to qualifying for a World Cup competition. Both are mostly secular powers, suspicious of the place of Islam in Pakistan's government. One, the United States, enjoys legacy ties with Pakistan, from the Cold War and the war on terror, and connections through language and proximity to the British Commonwealth. The other, China, benefits from geographic proximity, a shared rivalry with India, and the rapidly growing clout of its expansive economy, foreign investment, accessible weapons, and rising military power.

Pakistan's two partners have become intense rivals. Through circumstance and skill, Pakistan has not yet had to commit to an exclusive relationship with either. The People's Republic of China (hereafter China or PRC) has long since surpassed America as Pakistan's top suitor, but the Pakistan Army and its leading politicians would like to keep America around.

The last decade witnessed the incremental disengagement of the United States in Pakistan and a corresponding expansion of China's role, but into the early 2020s there were manifold signs that Pakistan would sustain strategic relationships with both countries. If aspects of Pakistan's grand strategy have been damaging to U.S.-Pakistan ties, particularly its commitment to militant proxies, Pakistan's lingering cultural, tactical, and personal connections to the West are allowing the relationship to find a modest foundation as the region realigns after the U.S. departure from Afghanistan. These sturdy strands emanate from a historically brief but complex history.

Cold War Years

That Pakistan benefited from extended periods of alliance with both Beijing and Washington is an accident of the Cold War and geography.

The United States and Pakistan became allies at Pakistan's inception, as Washington found Pakistan to be the more cooperative of British India's two successor states. Where Nehru's India was inclined to nonalignment between the Soviet- and U.S.-led blocs, Pakistan was reliably anticommunist. From the early 1950s, the United States moved swiftly to bolster Pakistan and its army. Along with the Shah's Iran, Pakistan was to serve as a bulwark against Soviet expansion toward the Indian Ocean.[1]

Pakistan's anticommunism did not prevent it from developing an early appreciation for communist China, a potentially useful ally against India. China could not provide significant material aid until years later, but the two countries established friendly relations.

Pakistan and China both had disputed borders with India, and both fought for them. They avoided such conflict between themselves. In 1963 Pakistan ceded to China a slice of high mountain terrain, the Trans Karakoram. India also claimed the ceded territory, but Pakistan then possessed it and saw fit to give it away. The gesture opened the way for construction of a strategic overland link between China and Pakistan. It also meant that China and Pakistan each has a side of K2, the world's second highest peak.

Eventually the United States and China also found each other, building on their mutual concern over the Soviet Union's growing military power. Pakistan famously played a role in this entente, facilitating Henry Kissinger's secret travel to China and paving the way for Nixon's historic opening.

The America-China strategic alignment was to be short-lived, barely two decades long, tarnished by the Tiananmen Square massacre in 1989 and then losing its raison d'être with the collapse of the Soviet Union a year later. Still, as Beijing and Washington moved through the stages of decoupling into strategic rivalry by the early 2000s, Pakistan found room to maneuver between them.

American Complaints, China's Beguiling Call

Pakistanis identify the 1990s as the decade in which China began to supplant the United States as a strategic partner. Up to 1989 U.S. administrations largely gave a pass to Pakistan over its semi-secret effort to develop a nuclear weapon. The Soviet defeat in Afghanistan that year made Pakistan less necessary to the United States, however, and Washington became more critical. Congress sanctioned Pakistan for its program (though by that point Pakistan might already have been "nuclear capable").[2] The United States restricted military sales to Pakistan, including withholding twenty-eight F-16 aircraft that Pakistan had already purchased.

This American about-face left Pakistan vulnerable. It continued to face a much larger Indian army, and the West was now limiting its access to conventional armaments. China's military hardware was still two steps behind American technology, but the terms were good, and it was available.

On May 11, 1998, India exploded a nuclear device, its first acknowledged test since its breakthrough to atomic bomb status in 1974. Although Pakistan hesitated, receiving calls from Washington and other quarters urging restraint, it went forward to demonstrate its capability and barged into the nuclear club. It exploded five devices simultaneously under a mountain in Baluchistan.

Western powers put new sanctions on both Pakistan and India following the tests, but the sting was sharper for Pakistan, which was still dependent on Western conventional military hardware and needful of spare parts.[3] India, conversely, had long relied on Soviet weaponry, giving it a degree of immunity to the sanctions. For Pakistan, China's weapons filled an existential requirement, and China became the indispensable ally—the only one standing. The American freeze proved short-lived, but Pakistan lost trust in Washington.

With 9/11 and the United States' occupation of Afghanistan in 2001, Pakistan was again a critical ally to Washington. Pakistan controlled the only viable ground and air access to land-locked Afghanistan. Threatened and cajoled, Pakistan agreed to help. Washington, in return, quickly set aside the sanctions, and for a decade Pakistan got U.S. military hardware again, including a package of more advanced F-16 aircraft. The sales included five hundred AMRAAM air-to-air missiles, a bit of hardware that would loom large in the February 2019 dogfight between Pakistani and Indian jets above Kashmir. Although justified by the Bush administration as counterinsurgency tools to use against terrorist groups linked to al-Qaida, the advanced aircraft and armaments were easily pointed at India.

After 9/11, terrorism was both glue and wedge in the U.S.-Pakistan relationship, at times an impetus to cooperation, more often a source of

PREPARING THE PITCH

sharp distrust. The convergence was over al-Qaida, which both countries opposed, and then over the Pakistan Taliban, the TTP, which the United States helped Pakistan fight. Western militaries trained and cooperated with Pakistan in counterinsurgency campaigns, Pakistan allowed (deniably) the use of drones above its skies, and U.S. law enforcement and intelligence support played a critical role in early successes at wrapping up clandestine al-Qaida networks in Pakistan. No longer quite allies, even if both capitals occasionally used the term, the United States and Pakistan managed an effective, mutually beneficial relationship for most of the century's first decade.

By 2009, at the start of the first Obama administration, the winter romance between Pakistan and America was fading. In American eyes, Pakistan's tolerance of and covert support to the Afghan Taliban and the lethal Haqqani Network in Afghanistan weighed most heavily, but Pakistan was also tarnished by its links to the group that launched a devastating terror attack in Mumbai, India, in 2008. For its part, Pakistan began to complain more loudly about the U.S. occupation of Afghanistan, which it portrayed as at best a recipe for disorder, violence, and refugees and at worst a magnet for global terrorist recruitment and Indian subterfuge.

Each country came to blame the other for the torment of its killed and wounded soldiers. In Pakistan, the suffering turned into tens of thousands of Pakistanis lost to violence in the insurgencies and terrorism that followed America's intervention.

By mid-2011 the relationship was spiraling. The United States went it alone to kill Osama bin Laden in Pakistan in May of that year, humiliating the Pakistan military. America's surge of troops into Afghanistan had produced no strategic gains, and it was clear the war was a stalemate. Washington blamed Pakistan for the Taliban's persistence. Moreover, the Obama administration had ramped up coercive tactics with Pakistan—conditions placed on proffered U.S. assistance and a flood of intelligence operatives entering Pakistan—pressure that Pakistan's military was bound to resist.[4]

Finally, Pakistan felt less need for American counterinsurgency support as it gradually found its footing against the Pakistan Taliban. In the coming decade, Pakistan would conclude that Chinese arms were good enough and its own skills sufficient to contain anti-Pakistan militants.

China has been comparatively soft-spoken on Pakistan's role in fostering other militant groups, whether Pakistan's support to anti-Indian groups or its tolerance of the Taliban and Haqqani Network in Afghanistan. Beijing's demands on terrorism were narrower, only that Pakistan act energetically against Chinese Muslim Uyghur militants and dissidents it calls "ETIM" (the East Turkestan Islamic Movement). Pakistan has been willing. More recently, Beijing has demanded more robust Pakistani action to protect its workers and investments from rising lethal attacks by Baloch terrorists on projects associated with the China-Pakistan Economic Corridor (CPEC).

For Pakistan, vigilance against Chinese Muslims was a small price. If the deal was distasteful to Pakistanis who might otherwise find common cause with China's oppressed Muslim population, army GHQ saw it as cheaper than the proofs required for Washington's love and affection. With the Uyghur box "checked," China responded with weapons and investments, with no conditions for human rights, democratic practices, or nonproliferation.

Though terrorism and nuclear proliferation were the main drivers of U.S.-Pakistan troubles over the last forty years, American concerns over Pakistani governance and human rights proved a persistent earworm, setting both capitals on edge. The United States would intermittently intercede to scold Pakistan on the rights of women and religious minorities, on the imbalance between excessive military and weak education and health spending, or over the army's inveterate intrusions into politics.

America's vocal moralism was naturally problematic for Pakistan's top generals, but it proved surprisingly off-putting to Pakistan's champions of democracy. Civilian politicians and public intellectuals claimed hypocrisy, inconsistency, and a whiff of neocolonialism in the U.S. lectures. The United States, after all, had tolerated military governments since Pakistan's early years.[5] For decades, up to and through my Washington briefings before going to Pakistan for the first time in 2010, Washington experts portrayed the Pakistan Army as the only force for order in the country, the one institution preventing the emergence of a nuclear-armed Islamic theocracy.

U.S. moralist diplomacy in the 1990s and 2000s followed a set pattern, equal parts irritating and accommodating to Pakistan's leaders. The

United States would annoy the generals with conditions and interference and then disappoint the democrats, returning like a guilty lover to the doorstep of army headquarters. China, by contrast, was more transparent. It delivered few lectures on governance and asked only for a stable climate for business. It has paid no price for its "amoral" approach, as Pakistan's civilian leaders rarely criticize China.

The Overwrought Drama in U.S.-Pakistan Ties

My first Pakistan tour, beginning in August 2010, witnessed one of our most concentrated efforts to shore up the U.S.-Pakistan relationship. It would be mostly unsuccessful. It was, on its face, a long shot, and a series of challenging events ensured its failure.

As the new deputy political counselor, I got to know the country with an exceptional political counselor, one who would invest years of his career into dealing with the country. The U.S. presence then was large and crammed into old and inadequate buildings. Our military arm, the Office of the Defense Representative–Pakistan (ODRP), led by a vice admiral, was large, as was our U.S. Agency for International Development mission, moving up to $1.5 billion a year in development assistance into Pakistan, not always carefully enough. We were beginning to channel that assistance through the government of Pakistan rather than U.S. contractors, a massive experiment in aid delivery destined to founder against weaknesses in Pakistani governance.[6]

Despite the big cooperative programs—military hardware and training, development aid, and law enforcement assistance against drugs and terrorism—the bilateral relationship was overdramatic and fraught. Afghanistan had poisoned things, and there was more activity than the relationship could absorb.

What progress we might have made through our generosity up to 2010, including a large humanitarian response to a 2008 earthquake and to the Indus River floods in the fall of 2010, was erased completely by three events in 2011. The first was an act of overzealous self-defense by an American contractor operating out of our Consulate in Lahore. Claiming that two young men were threatening him on the busy streets, he reached for his gun and shot them dead. He then tried and failed to force his way through traffic and crowds back to the Consulate. Two American security officers sent from the Consulate to bring him back could not reach him, in their haste killing a motorcyclist in traffic. The United States quickly flew the security officers out of the country. Pakistan police arrested Ray Davis, the contractor.

With three dead at the hands of Americans, Pakistani public opinion took a sharper than normal anti-U.S. turn. For the public, Davis's guilt was indisputable. The United States, however, was determined that he never come to trial. Foreign diplomats accredited to capitals have immunity for both personal and official actions (at the discretion of their government), and we chose to demand it. Pakistan disputed Davis's accreditation, with some justification, though in the end the legal ground for immunity was plausible.

In Steve Coll's account of the incident, the Davis case led to sharp exchanges between the CIA, which might have hired him, and the ISI. Coll also maintains the case led to internal disputes among the country team over tactics.[7] I can say only that it occupied considerable attention and effort across various agencies.

In all this, Pakistan's military leadership faced both dilemma and opportunity. The opportunity was to press the United States to curtail the scores of spies and special operators Pakistan suspected were coming into the country on diplomatic visas.[8] The risks were real as well, however, as neither the army nor the civilian government was ready for a deep rupture with the United States. The army and the civilian government wanted a solution, but both wanted the other to capitulate, to take the hit with the Pakistani public.

President Zardari seemed close to crafting a deal for Davis's release at one point in late February, but his foreign minister—Shah Mahmood Qureshi, the same man who returned to the job under Imran Khan's government—refused to sign off, resigning instead. The crisis went on for weeks.

The administration at this point dispatched Senator John Kerry, chair of the Senate Foreign Relations Committee, to Pakistan to resolve the problem. I served as his in-country "control officer," managing his schedule and briefings. The future secretary of state was well familiar with Pakistan and an experienced international negotiator.

The visit propelled negotiations toward the obvious solution, the payment of "blood money" to the families of the two shooting victims. But there was one hiccup along the way, when Senator Kerry called on the just-resigned foreign minister at his home. Kerry knew Qureshi and thought the visit could be helpful. Qureshi welcomed Kerry but then called an immediate press conference to restate his rejection of U.S. demands.

After the Qureshi speed bump, Senator Kerry called on President Zardari, who greeted our delegation with a warmth that could have frozen vodka. One of his ministers pantomimed military epaulets as he shrugged at the civilian government's inability to resolve the crisis. The gesture is familiar to all Pakistani politicians, a way to suggest the military's role without saying it out loud, for fear of eavesdropping. Zardari asked Kerry why he had called on the former foreign minister, saying, "I had that under control." Nonetheless, Zardari knew he needed a solution and kept talking.

Later that night we took Kerry to see chief of army staff General Kayani, at Rawalpindi General Headquarters. This was a familiar stop to senior U.S. diplomats sent to resolve bilateral crises. Kerry and Kayani conversed until two in the morning and apparently agreed that the CIA and Pakistan's Inter-Services Intelligence (ISI) needed to mend fences. It was a view at best reluctantly accepted by CIA headquarters.

Within a couple of weeks, the payments were made, and Pakistan allowed Davis to leave. The day after Davis's release, U.S. drone strikes killed twenty-six people at what the U.S. government said was a gathering between Taliban and local elders in northwest Pakistan.[9] To some, it seemed like a blunt repudiation of fence mending.

The second incident of 2011 was Abbottabad, the *Zero Dark Thirty* killing of Osama bin Laden. As described in more detail in chapter 11, Pakistanis of all stripes were resentful that America had exposed Pakistan as bin Laden's refuge. Few questioned America's prerogative to go after bin Laden, but almost none thought it right to go after him in Pakistan without collaborating with Pakistani authorities.

The final 2011 blow to U.S.-Pakistan relations came late in the year. In this event, commonly referred to as the "Salala Incident," NATO forces used heavy airpower (a U.S. C-130 gunship, F-15s, and Apache helicopters based in Afghanistan) to take out two Pakistan military posts on a ridgeline near the Afghan border (definitively on the Pakistan side of the line). The official U.S. Central Command investigation sustained NATO and Afghan allegations that Pakistani troops had fired on them first as they pursued escaping Taliban, but the report also pointed to failures in calibrating the response and coordinating border operations in advance with Pakistan.[10] The NATO strikes killed twenty-eight Pakistani soldiers and sparked a new round of popular outrage. In response, Islamabad shut down NATO's supply lines to Afghanistan for months.

The United States was slow and peevish in its apology for the incident. Pakistan, many American hardliners seemed to believe, deserved the blow due to its continuing duplicity on Afghanistan and specifically for allowing its border posts to serve as shields to retreating Taliban. The Salala Incident lingered for years as a source of mistrust.

China Becomes Pakistan's Indispensable Partner

China-Pakistan relations are a story without much drama. Both countries have suffered great bouts of domestic tumult, but their bilateral relations have been steady. Their ties advanced year-on-year, whatever authoritarian, military, democratic, or revolutionary governments ruled in either capital. China's turn to a stable authoritarian-capitalist dispensation after Tiananmen Square—particularly its steadily rising power and wealth—deepened its appeal to Pakistan. By 2010 China was Pakistan's indispensable ally.

One foundation for the relationship was military hardware, particularly as the West became an unreliable provider. The two countries jointly produce Pakistan's mainline fighter bomber, the JF-17, a serviceable and affordable mainstay of Pakistan's future air force. The JF-17 is among several systems Pakistan sells abroad, as arms and ammunition have emerged as one of the country's few growing export sectors.[11] China sells Pakistan tanks and submarines and many of the high-tech tools of Pakistan's nascent surveillance state. As important, the arms and training signal a robust security relationship, a reality India must consider in dealings with rival Pakistan.

Beginning in the 2010s economic investment became another important bond. CPEC, first announced in 2013, encompassed a variety of state-led Chinese investments in Pakistani infrastructure—power, roads, transit, ports. Much of the work was funded by loans, but Pakistan, at least under the PML-N government of Nawaz Sharif, was happy to take on the future burden. No other lender could match the scale. No other lender would run the risks of Pakistan. Tens of billions of dollars in projects took shape. (I met a few Pakistanis who got rich on the projects and others who complained of being frozen out of the work.)

CPEC was the most ambitious element in China's Belt and Road Initiative (BRI), the massive Chinese investment in trade and political connectivity across Asia, reaching to Africa and Europe as well. The "roads" of BRI, a bit counterintuitively, are the sea lanes through the East China Sea and the Indian Ocean, branching out to East Africa, the Persian Gulf, and the Suez Canal. China has built the "maritime road" around port construction, new facilities at which its goods and middlemen will enjoy preferences. Prominent among the Indian Ocean projects are Hambantota in Sri Lanka, Gwadar in Pakistan, and Djibouti.

Pakistan is an offshoot of the "belt" as well, in this case the interconnected land arteries being upgraded to promote Chinese trade across central Asia and beyond, the "new Silk Road." The belts extend into Pakistan's economic heartland, the Punjab, connecting its large market with western China.

Encompassing both "belt" and "road" has been China's major investment in highways leading from China to the port of Gwadar in Pakistan's far southwest. The roads stretch over high mountains and then across the expanse of Pakistan's largest and least populated province, Baluchistan. It is a project that defies economic sense. Gwadar may one day prove a useful consolidation point for Chinese shipping to the Middle East and Europe, but it holds little promise in terms of Pakistan's internal market. Located in the desert of Pakistan's far southwest, it is disconnected from the country's economy. Traders prefer Karachi, much closer to Pakistan's main markets.

More important, the connections from Gwadar to China are treacherous. Winter weather often closes the Karakorum Highway. Baloch separatists have repeatedly attacked Chinese workers and equipment, motivated by the perception that the Gwadar development has quashed local economic concerns and attracted non-Baloch Pakistanis to jobs in their homeland.

Because the economics of Gwadar seem so parlous, analysts have been quick to suggest the project is a strategic rather than commercial investment. Gwadar sits next to Iran and close to the mouth of the Persian Gulf. It could someday be a useful Chinese naval base if Pakistan were ever to allow such a thing.

Above all, Gwadar and CPEC are symbolic, testaments to the importance China places on Pakistan and its desire to enmesh the two countries going forward. China signals its commitment diplomatically as well. Able to threaten a veto on the UN Security Council (even if reluctant to use it alone), China has long protected Pakistan from more punitive international sanctions over terrorism or aggression toward India.

To 2018: A Diminished American Presence

By the time of my second tour in Pakistan, the country's relations with both China and the United States had achieved a steady state. Ties with the United States remained strained, suspicious, and often hostile, but there was also much less bilateral activity to spark potential crises. China was the ascendent ally, critical to Pakistan in several areas, but there was more caution after the unmet promises of the first CPEC. Pakistan, benefiting from the dueling attentions of these rivals, worked consistently to avoid taking sides in the emerging great power rivalry.

The United States remained an impactful power in Pakistan, commanding influence through its military presence in Afghanistan and its legacy influence over the institutions and alliances of the West. The United States still shaped how the West responded to Islamist militancy in South Asia, and it commanded major roles in the international financial institutions vital to Pakistan.

At the same time, the U.S. government had a smaller presence in Pakistan. Long gone were the days of heavy American military advising, provisioning, and intelligence collaboration under Presidents Bush and Musharraf. The United States had scaled back its diplomatic presence, in part under Pakistan's pressure, just as its massive new diplomatic compound opened. Pakistan's spymasters were not yet satisfied, continuing to limit diplomatic visas, but they had already shrunk the U.S. presence.

The impetus to reduce the American presence came as much from Washington as from Rawalpindi. In the later Obama years, the United States steadily reduced assistance and military engagement. Then, in January 2018, President Trump announced via Twitter a halt in U.S. assistance to Pakistan due to its "lies and deceit" on Afghanistan. The administration halted development assistance, although the "pipeline" of old money already appropriated by Congress would take some years to spend down. Entirely suspended by Trump's order were hundreds of millions in Coalition Support Funds, direct payments to Pakistan for its support of U.S. supply routes to Afghanistan and for counterinsurgency operations. The administration slashed military assistance to near zero.

If America's profile in Pakistan was much reduced, there was still potential for the old patterns of diplomatic offense to roil relations. On the eve of my 2018 arrival, the embassy and Pakistani authorities concluded a drawn-out negotiation over the departure of an embassy military attaché, an army colonel, who had killed a Pakistani motorcyclist in a traffic accident. The standoff over his exit frayed relations for weeks. Pakistan allowed the colonel to fly out in mid-May, but a tit-for-tat round of travel restrictions on diplomats in both capitals continued. Things were not as bad as in 2011, but not that different either.

After Ambassador Hale's departure in August 2018, Washington quickly dispatched a veteran diplomat, Paul Jones, to take his place, but as a chargé d'affaires without ambassadorial confirmation. Jones had been an accredited, confirmed ambassador to both Poland and Malaysia, and we in the embassy responded enthusiastically to his tireless engagement. Nonetheless, the Trump administration's decision to forgo Pakistan's formal *agrément* to Jones as ambassador rankled, perceived as a symbolic downgrading in the relationship. Over time, Jones's seniority and manifestly good intentions won out, and he became an effective interlocutor with Pakistan.

Simultaneous to the extended nadir in America's influence in Islamabad, U.S. travel restrictions and cumbersome vetting of Muslim travelers began to limit the flow of Pakistanis to America. More began to travel to China. It signaled the loss of one of our longest-running areas of competitive advantage in this great power competition: the appeal of a professional or educational visit to the United States, including through the government-funded International Visitors Leadership Program.

The State Department's Pakistan visitor program remained the department's largest single bilateral program through my tenure in 2019. In my view it accrued significant dividends in shaping the views of the small elite who influence public opinion and state policy in Pakistan. By 2018, however, most Pakistani influencers—politicians, military officers, journalists, academics, and think-tank mavens—had also traveled to China, at Beijing's expense. Businesspeople regularly traveled there. If New York and Washington still stood above Shanghai as prestige destinations for Pakistanis, the difference was no longer great.

While the embassy's public affairs and consular sections could usually work through the new regulations to get visas for the Pakistanis participating in the official visitor programs, Pakistanis studying or doing business in America on their own dime confronted uncertain prospects. Pakistanis had their studies interrupted; others did not bother to begin. Europe, the Persian Gulf, China, and Australia became the beneficiaries of Pakistani tuitions and talent that had once been destined for Indiana or Texas.

Also damaging to American influence was the emergence of China as a destination for Pakistani military officers sent abroad for training. The U.S. International Military Education and Training (IMET) program, designed to provide professional training to foreign officers at United States military command schools, has over the years been a great tool of residual connection to the Pakistan military. For little cost, young Pakistani officers—often future service leaders—gained a more nuanced understanding of the United States. Some of the officers established enduring professional ties to American counterparts.

Pakistani participation in IMET was in decline before 2018, in part because the Pakistan Army was concerned about exposing too many officers to American influences. President Trump's aid cutoff then halted it entirely in early 2018. In the embassy we worked assiduously to restore the program (a proverbial drop in the bucket in terms of cost, at only one or two million dollars a year). The State Department and our military colleagues argued that IMET not be characterized as simple military assistance but instead as an investment in our influence.

Skeptics responded that some IMET graduates had gone on to pursue anti-American policies once in leadership. This was missing the point. Pakistan state policies toward the United States are determined by a collective—corps commanders, retired senior officers, the inertia of deep-state activities—not by individuals inclined or hostile toward the United States. We do not pursue IMET to turn individuals against their institutions. Instead, IMET builds relationships, access, and professional respect across services. IMET helps us get in the door. The meetings that follow have sometimes gained us time or even gradual calibrations to objectionable policies.[12]

Pakistan's top generals complained to us about this cut: connection to the British and American militaries was "in the DNA" of the Pakistan Army, one leader emphasized to us repeatedly. Pakistan wanted its officers to study at the Army War College in Carlisle, Pennsylvania, or at other command and technical schools. China was Pakistan's biggest friend, we would hear, but their ties to America should endure. By December 2019 policymakers in Washington had agreed to resume the program.

Pakistan and China Have Their Own Problems

As China's influence in Pakistan has crested, that relationship too has generated tensions. Both sides have complaints, and both sides are fearful that the other's demands will be too great.

China has no bigger geopolitical ally than Pakistan, in part because it has few true allies. In Pakistan, China finds its most cooperative partner against Muslim militancy (or dissent), its commercial foothold on the Arabian Sea, and a useful and costly distraction for its rival India. The Pakistan military's long-standing ties to the Sunni Persian Gulf monarchies is a vital diplomatic connection for China to its most important petroleum suppliers. Whatever frustrations China might express with Pakistan, it is unlikely to back away from Sino-Pakistan ties, already "deeper than the ocean and higher than the Himalayas" in popular hyperbole.

China has geopolitical reasons to calibrate its embrace of Pakistan, nonetheless, including its own interests in India. When not engaged in brutal, high-altitude military brawls against each other, the two countries, representing almost 35 percent of the world's population, must coexist.

They share a long if inhospitable border. Chinese businesses want access to the huge Indian consumer market.

By calibrating its relationship with Pakistan and other South Asian countries, China also hopes to discourage India from overcommitting to security ties with the United States. These various interests—and weariness with Pakistan-linked extremism—help explain China's willingness to sign on to a 2017 declaration at a BRICS Summit (Brazil, Russia, India, China, and South Africa) condemning Pakistan-backed terrorist group Lashkar-e-Taiba (LT) by name.

Although China benefits strategically from the way Pakistan-sponsored Muslim militancy frustrates India, Beijing is not a great fan of ethnoreligious militancy. During my tenure, the eloquent PRC ambassador in Islamabad, Yao Jing, shared with Pakistani audiences and with Ambassador Jones his concerns that continued violence in the region limited Pakistan's economic prospects and endangered the major Chinese investments going into the country. He spoke to us frankly about security concerns in Baluchistan and about the failure of Pakistan to provide an economic model to make sense of the Gwadar port expansion.

When confronted with proposed terrorist designations of Pakistani militant proxies in international bodies, China has shied from the role of Pakistan's lone defender. In June 2018 China acceded to Pakistan's placement on the "grey list" of the Financial Action Task Force (FATF), an international anti-money-laundering organization. The FATF grey list is a warning that a country lacks sufficient guards against money-laundering and that terrorists or criminals are exploiting the gaps. Pakistan was faulted in part for failing to stop fundraising by the Fatah-e-Insaniat Foundation, the "charitable" front organization for LT, the largest of the Kashmir-focused militant-terrorist groups.

The grey list designation deterred commercial banks and other creditors from doing business with Pakistan. It also portended Pakistan's potential inclusion in the more punitive FATF "blacklist" if weaknesses persisted. China was likely to block any move to "blacklist" Pakistan, but it let the grey listing remain. China protects Pakistan on these issues, but only to a point.

China's readiness to let Pakistan suffer some consequences for its support to terrorist proxies was attention-getting in Islamabad. When coupled with Western sanctions, the PRC's implicit scolding spurred Pakistan toward modest progress to improve its banking regulations and demonstrate public vigilance against these violent groups.

In May 2019 China compromised on a FATF terrorist listing of Masood Azar, leader of Jaish-e-Mohammad (JeM). JeM was tied to the deadly 2019 Valentine's Day attack on Indian police forces in Pulwama, Kashmir. The United States spearheaded a concerted diplomatic push for his listing. Responsive to Pakistan to a point, China worked to moderate the wording, but it conceded Azar's designation.

The most significant constraint on China's support for Pakistan is economic. Even amid its military rise and strategic quest for influence and allies in the Indian Ocean, China maintains a focus on economics and business—on its bottom line. If Beijing cares not at all for democratic niceties, it can demonstrate impatience for meandering economic governance. Burdened by its military economy and by unmet development needs, Pakistan continues to underperform. It is one sin China does not easily abide.

Pakistan too is less bullish today on the promise of China's economic beneficence. It is not immune to the damage caused by China's aggressive global trade practices, policies that have driven deindustrialization in the developing world as much as in the West. Even as Pakistan struggled with its balance-of-payments crisis, its trade with China remained wildly out of balance, with imports from China exceeding exports to China by a margin of seven to one. (Conversely, Pakistan runs a slight trade surplus with the United States.)[13]

There was even more imbalance in finance. Pakistan bought the high-profile CPEC projects with loans from China, adding to an emerging repayments burden. Many of the projects relied heavily on Chinese capital goods, materials, and labor, meaning much of the loaned capital went immediately back across the border to Chinese enterprises. There has been little in the way of multiplier benefits to local contractors and workers. The opacity of CPEC projects, moreover, has consistently raised suspicions about kickbacks and other malfeasance.

With CPEC one of many contributing factors, Pakistan in 2018 became hostage to a balance-of-payments crisis. Pakistan's new prime minister, Imran Khan, inheriting a sluggish economy and an untenable position for the Pakistan rupee, railed against the prospect of having to approach the International Monetary Fund (IMF) for a bailout. He had also questioned the benefits of the bulky CPEC projects launched under the government of Nawaz Sharif. He could do little to unwind these projects in the face of the Pakistan military's commitment to China, but the PTI's open skepticism on CPEC created waves.

Khan sought another way to press for China's help, seeking out concessional sovereign loans and grants. He traveled to China, Saudi Arabia, and the United Arab Emirates but came back with pittances. In the embassy we reported to Washington on Khan's risky use of his political honeymoon on a quixotic effort to raise concessionary loans from Pakistan's friends. Political opponents described Khan's efforts as a "begging bowl" tour.

China, however committed to Pakistan, was not inclined to selfless generosity, or to throwing good money after bad. It wanted to see fiscal reform in Pakistan, all the better if the IMF imposed the conditions and took the blame. By mid-2019 Pakistan turned to the IMF for a new loan package, one that would bring with it intrusive conditions and policy benchmarks.

Questions about CPEC persisted. Soon after the PTI government was in place, Khan's commerce minister went so far as to suggest a yearlong freeze and review of the projects, later clarifying that he had been taken out of context.[14] Both China and the Pakistan military were caught off guard by the PTI's essay against CPEC, with Beijing rejecting any renegotiation and Pakistan Army chief Bajwa flying to China to mend fences.[15] When Khan traveled to Beijing a short time later, his reception at the airport by only a deputy mayor of Beijing was much commented on in Islamabad as a signal of Chinese ire.

Pakistan's brief complaint about CPEC, however, was part of a significant international trend. The BRI's aggressive terms had generated pushback from many partners. China came under discomfiting criticism that it was conducting "debt trap diplomacy." The suggested playbook involved inducing governments of developing countries—including through corrupting enticements—to take out unpayable loans for Chinese-built vanity projects (palaces, underutilized highways and railways). Once the unpayable loans came due, the Chinese companies (themselves deeply enmeshed in the ruling Chinese Communist Party) would demand concessions—sometimes sovereign rights and management concessions at major ports. Indictable cases had occurred among the "pearls" of the Indian Ocean periphery—Djibouti, Sri Lanka, Maldives—and many wondered whether Pakistan might be walking into the same trap.

China denied these suggestions of nefarious intent, but the high-profile failures had tarnished BRI.[16] In the PRC's uniquely cautious and orchestrated way, the government began to acknowledge errors in BRI implementation and promised reforms.[17]

China agreed to recast CPEC. In response to critiques from the PTI and others, China and Pakistan announced that the second phase, "CPEC 2.0," would focus less on infrastructure and more on industrialization, agriculture, and socioeconomic development.[18] Translated, the desired output in Pakistan was jobs.

In addition to reorientation, for Pakistan there would be a retreat. Facing a fiscal crunch and a long-term balance-of-payments crisis, Pakistan erased matching support for CPEC projects from its budget, and China began a slower introduction of new projects.[19] Behind the recalibration also was a recognition that Pakistan's need for an IMF rescue precluded the assumption of new nonconcessionary debt to China. Washington was already vigilant against its IMF shares going to service bad PRC loans.[20]

Beyond the surprising notes of commercial, diplomatic, and financial discord in the officially harmonious China-Pakistan relationship, there was also, at the personal level for Pakistanis, the challenging task of dealing with Chinese traders and workers. Chinese businesspeople in Pakistan have a reputation for playing hardball, whether in a market or bidding on contracts. Special restaurants catering to the Chinese could sell beer and pork, contravening Islamic norms. By 2018 individual complaints of Chinese business practices had grown to the point where Parliament announced a review.[21]

Other tales were darker: of Chinese traffickers inducing Pakistanis into sham marriages and prostitution across the border, rampaging Chinese workers fighting with Pakistani police. The government seemingly buried investigations to protect the positive official narrative of China-Pakistan relations.[22]

As China's profile rose, then, so too did concerns and criticisms. There was also some public criticism of China's heavy repression of the Muslim

Uyghur population in western China, though Washington's insistence that the embassy amplify these criticisms probably did little to advance the grassroots critique.

China has remained unrepentant on the oppression of Uyghur Muslims in its western Xinjiang province. Its economic and financial weight across Asia means that few countries will press the issue. But there has been a cost to China as the stories have spread on their own. Muslim audiences have come to view China as not much different from other great powers.

Despite the occasional nod to making corrections, Beijing pressed its narrative of CPEC benefits. In Pakistan, the propaganda role fell to the Chinese Embassy's second in command, Zhao Lijian. In contrast to the amiable ambassador, the pugilistic Zhao, a longtime veteran of the Chinese-Pakistan relationship, was an active, provocative presence on social media. He was a constant champion of CPEC.[23] He was not above suggesting the United States supported Baloch separatists against Pakistan, among other nefarious conspiracies.

Whatever the troubles and unmet expectations in China-Pakistan ties, however, China remains Pakistan's military lifeline. The consistency of their security relationship is vital to Pakistan's sense of geopolitical safety. It also has contributed to the steady erosion of democratic institutions in the country. It has protected Pakistan from the full costs of its support for militancy. With reason, India sees China's support to Pakistan as providing a security umbrella that enables Pakistan's sponsorship of militants.[24]

Simultaneously, China's security technology is quite likely building the infrastructure for more effective repression in Pakistan, all under the guise of public safety. In sum, it is impossible to dismiss academic Daniel Markey's conclusion that "China is not yet contributing to Pakistan's political or economic reform in ways that are likely to produce long-term stability. To the contrary, the Sino-Pakistani relationship is reinforcing unhealthy political and economic patterns and worsening domestic strains."[25]

Not Letting Go: Pakistan's Residual Interest in American Ties

For Pakistan, the increasingly encompassing U.S.-China competition poses a dilemma. If forced to choose between its two patrons, it has no choice but to go with China. China is its surest source of weapons, investment, and diplomatic support. Pakistan, however, hopes that it does not come down to a choice.

Army GHQ wants to avoid an overdependence on China for arms, training, and finance, fearful that China's demands could rise. It also hopes to mitigate America's strategic embrace of India by maintaining dialogue and addressing some of the American demands.

Pakistani strategic thinkers anticipate a cautious reciprocation from Washington. They presume that the United States has a residual interest in Pakistan's military strength and societal coherence—a failed Pakistan, after all, would destabilize the region and threaten "loose nukes." They presume that Washington values Pakistan's stabilizing military support to the Sunni monarchies of the Persian Gulf, and they anticipate the United States will continue to seek Pakistan's help with a Taliban-controlled Afghanistan.

For Pakistan, the technology, schools, investments, markets, and financial linkages of the West remain critical to economic prosperity and identity. Pakistanis sustain cultural affinity to the West, in literature and arts and higher education, and keep a foot in the world of the British Commonwealth, including through cricket.

As I discuss in the closing chapter of this book, I expect mutually beneficial engagement between Pakistan and the United States to endure, not with all the bells of 2002 or sirens of 2011, but at some ebb of collaboration. It seems less likely today that the United States will choose to disengage, and Pakistan's troubles with Taliban-controlled Afghanistan are likely to accelerate its reevaluation of Islamist militancy as a tool of statecraft. Diplomatic work is required for a better outcome, but there are capable women and men in both capitals taking up the challenge.

Cricket in America

One potential avenue of American connection with Pakistan (and India) seems as far off in 2022 as it was in 1948: cricket. Despite the steady growth of recreational cricket in the United States, primarily among South Asian diaspora families, it has not caught the broader public's eye.

In 1958, at the start of Pakistan's only exhibition cricket tour in the United States, Pakistan's "playboy" ambassador to the United Nations, Prince Aly Khan, suggested to *New York Times* writer Gay Talese that he saw "no reason why cricket should not become popular in this country."[26] A *Times* writer covering the match on Randall's Island apparently saw a reason, commenting on the length and slow pace of the match and "the lack of compulsory action when the ball is hit" (ignoring the equivalent lethargy of the foul ball in baseball).[27]

The tongue-in-cheek treatment of the matches aside, the tour, sponsored by the Eisenhower administration's People-to-People Initiative, harked back to the positive first decade of Pakistan-U.S. relations. Talese covered the team's visit with New York mayor Robert Wagner and described the Pakistan side as "manned by gentlemen."[28] The treatment of team captain Kardar in an appearance on the American game show *To Tell the Truth* was for the most part respectful.[29] In all, the Pakistanis were treated as curious if distant British cousins.

In Pakistan, American sponsorship of the tour was welcomed with "great enthusiasm," according to a U.S. Embassy cable. News of the matches was carried in all the papers, and a post-tour panel discussion at the United States Information Agency drew a large crowd. Kardar and other members of the team "paid glowing tribute to the American people and spoke warmly of their reception."[30] This was old-school American public diplomacy; from the perspective of sixty years it seems both quaint and successful.

In 2015 two international cricket greats brought a team of mostly retired global all-stars to a series of matches in the United States. This time the crowds were larger, filling the lower decks of baseball stadiums with appreciative fans from the British Commonwealth's American diasporas. Pakistani great Shoaib Akhtar played on a team captained by legendary Indian Sachin Tendulkar.

Unfortunately, the high spirits around the 2015 tour had little lasting effect on the growth of a top-tier game in the United States. If the slow growth of soccer is a model, it may take some time. Moreover, money troubles and governing board controversies have derailed efforts by the ICC to organize and compete for the lucrative American market.[31]

PREPARING THE PITCH

The 2024 T20 World Cup, to be hosted in the United States and West Indies, may yet make an impression, but with the soccer World Cup following in North America just two years later, cricket may once again be swept aside for alternative sports. One comfort, however, at least from a strategic perspective: cricket seems to be going equally poorly in China.[32]

Part 2

PAKISTAN AND THE CRICKETING WORLD

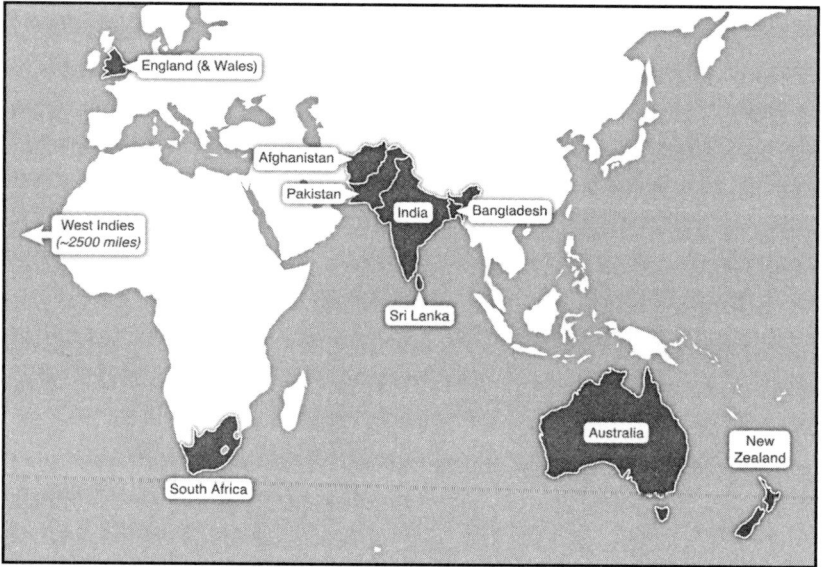

Map 1. 2019 Cricket World Cup qualifying national teams.

4   DECOLONIZING A SPORT

Pakistan vs. West Indies
First Match of Group Play for Both

Little of cricket got through to an American boy growing up in Kansas in the 1970s, but two sets of images found their way. One was the indelible, leonine grace of Pakistan's star and future prime minister, Imran Khan, whether photographed on the cricket field or outside a nightclub. The second was West Indian cricket, those dominant teams of the late 1970s and 1980s, taking it to the English in London, their diaspora fans energizing the staid cricket grounds.

The drama of West Indian cricket seems at once ancient history and as topical as ever today. The West Indies were one of the first nonwhite teams in any sport to assert equality on the international stage and then to dominate their sport. They were as respectful of cricket traditions as any national team, more than most, and their fans across the scattered islands were known for their knowledge of the game. But they learned to play aggressively and without apology. In the second half of the 1970s, the West Indies turned to a feared fast-bowling attack that left opposing batsmen injured and bruised.[1] Although white bowlers for Australia, England, and South Africa had used aggressive bowling to dominate the sport for years, it was another thing entirely for Black bowlers to do so. But they persisted.

For the West Indies teams, made up of cricketers from the English-speaking Caribbean, questions of race, colonialism, nationalism, politics, freedom, and income inequality were bound up with cricket from early on. Although begun by white settlers and administrators throughout the islands, cricket by the turn of the twentieth century had taken hold among the Afro-Caribbean majority, the descendants of the enslaved people kidnapped from Africa to sustain lucrative sugar and spice plantations.

Cricket took hold as well among the region's second largest population of exploited workers, the descendants of indentured workers brought by the English and Dutch from South Asia.

From early on, the small numbers of colonials scattered across the islands meant that British sportsmen needed locals to play the game. (Twenty-two players are required for a regulation contest.) Moreover, it was the norm that few of the gentleman amateurs wanted to bowl much, preferring batting to the taxing athleticism required to toss good pace balls and spinners. In the West Indies, this meant a reliance on local athletes of color to bowl, a dependency that extended to the West Indies' international test teams. As C. L. R. James remarks, this was the "traditional order" until after World War II, "a line of white batsmen and a line of Black bowlers."[2] Given the much larger Black and Indo-Caribbean populations playing cricket, it was a certainty that not all the white batsmen selected for the early teams were the best available players.

One of the pleasures of making a brief foray into West Indian cricket is the necessity it creates to read James. I had read his book on the Haitian revolutionary Toussaint L'Ouverture, *The Black Jacobins*, decades before in graduate school. Now I approached his idiosyncratic and beautifully written *Beyond a Boundary* for my work writing this manuscript, mostly for the simple pleasure of reading. The book is a successful amalgam of memoir (the author's early life in colonial Trinidad, his love of cricket, his long residency in Britain), an analysis of some of the great early West Indian cricket stars, a political treatise on the cultural power of sport, and an exploration of the many points at which cricket intersected with James's causes of racial equality and independence for the West Indies. It is much more: an exploration of art and ethics and, surprisingly from a Marxist intellectual, a stodgy complaint about changes in cricket.

I will describe one argument in his history that I found relevant to British legacies in South Asia: his description of the many ways race played out in Trinidadian and West Indian cricket and how it intersected with anticolonialism for the first half of the twentieth century. The sharpest racial divide was certainly between white people and all comers. Slavery had been abolished in British colonial possessions in 1834, and, in some respects, the societies of the islands made greater progress in advancing the political and economic rights of Black people than did the American

South after the Civil War (albeit, not much of a yardstick). Still, there remained a sharp hierarchy of power on the islands, with white people exercising most of the power in government posts, sugar mills, and secondary schools.

It was, nonetheless, a hierarchy, not a fixed bifurcation. James describes the complex landscape in Trinidad, with the island's main sports clubs delineated by race, caste, and religion.[3] James dispassionately explains one dynamic: for a West Indian, a sign of success was to socialize with "people lighter in complexion than himself." He provides a snapshot of the strictures falling away for West Indians living abroad. For example, in England, James's host, the great cricketer Leary Constantine, would be approached for support by lighter skinned Trinidadians, "who at home would never have asked him to dinner."[4]

For James, nonwhite families' careful delineation of their place in society based on different shades of skin color is an explicable result of marginal economic prospects under a minority-ruled colonial regime. With only a small white English population on the islands, colonial rulers fostered differentiation and co-optation of some local groups into the lower rungs of the governing system to maintain power. It was a method also used across British India.

Cricket originally reinforced this system with segregated teams and the tradition of white captaincy and then, beginning in the 1950s, it became a force for change. West Indians of all hues came to cheer a steady stream of outstanding, mostly Black players: Leary Constantine in the 1930s, George Headley after him, the great Barbadian "three Ws" in the 1950s (Clyde Walcott, Everton Weekes, and Frank Worrell), and their prolific countryman Gary Sobers. All were outstanding players and recognized as such in England; several would be knighted.

In the immediate post–World War II years, the majority-Black West Indian teams would be a focal point of agitation for independence (for most of the cricketing islands, that meant independence from Britain) and for questions about whether the tiny islands would adhere to a single political confederation or become independent, small states. British touring teams in the 1950s were met with hostile crowds as the cause of independence gained steam, although James suggests the hostility was directed more against the biased power structure of the islands than against the touring Englishmen.[5] It was not until 1960 that West Indies cricket appointed its first regular Black captain (Frank Worrell), and that only after a sharp public campaign calling for merit-based selection.

The West Indies cricket team today includes players from ten independent countries and five overseas territories (three British, one Dutch, and the U.S. Virgin Islands, marking America's small slice of international test cricket). Jamaica and Trinidad are the biggest, most populous islands, and Guyana the lone continental entity. Barbados was the source of many of the early cricket legends and site of its most famous pitch, the Kensington Oval.

All told, the West Indies' contributing countries today have a total population of 6 million. By contrast, India draws the best players from a population of 1.3 billion and Pakistan from a pool of over 200 million. West Indian selectors and coaches also face unique challenges in assessing young players emerging in the schools and clubs of the dispersed islands, and then in coalescing the players into internationally competitive teams.

Given these handicaps, it is remarkable that for almost twenty years, the "Windies" were often the greatest team on Earth. The West Indies was dominant in long form test cricket in the late 1970s and throughout the 1980s, but they also ruled in the one-day format: they took the first two cricket World Cups, in 1975 and 1979, and were runner-up in the third, a surprise loss to what had been a middling India side.

With largely Black and South Asian–heritage rosters, the West Indies of the 1960s and 1970s became symbols of anticolonialism and Black nationalism. Reggae and calypso bands sang their praises; the West Indian communities of Britain revered them. They also brought change to the game, with their powerful batting and with aggressive fast bowling.

To a degree, Pakistan and the West Indies found some common ground over the years as challengers to the pale powers of England and Australia. The West Indies became a force in the sport earlier than Pakistan, but as Pakistan emerged as a contender in the 1980s, test series against the West Indies were valuable measures of progress.

The West Indies were also the first test-playing team to visit Pakistan, just a year after Pakistan's independence, when they added a Pakistan stop to a tour of India. Encouraged by the Indian captain to view the

Pakistanis as "a schoolboys' team," the West Indies were surprised by good bowling and respectable batting in the only two-innings match of their tour, hosted in Lahore. The match ended in a draw, for Pakistan a moral victory as it launched its campaign for international test status.[6]

By the time Pakistan first toured the West Indies, in 1958, a new wave of talented players graced the pitches of the Caribbean. The islands were in constant agitation against London's control, but the cricketing team was solid and formidable. The first match produced an epic stand by Pakistani batsman Hanif Mohammad in the second innings. Struck repeatedly on his thighs by fast balls bouncing unpredictably on the unprepared pitch, Hanif nonetheless protected his wicket for almost one thousand minutes, scoring 337 runs over parts of three days and earning the team an improbable and epic draw after it had been down by 473 runs.[7] The West Indies won the next three matches, with Pakistan salvaging pride with a win in the final match in Trinidad.

Pakistan won a three-match test series on the West Indies' return tour of Pakistan later that year, but then the teams would not meet again until 1975. From that point on, the teams were well balanced, with the West Indies winning more often in the late 1970s, the two teams breaking even in the 1980s, and Pakistan winning more often in the 1990s and 2000s.

The gradually shifting results by the late 1980s reflected Pakistan's rise in world cricket and the West Indies' decline. West Indies teams since the mid-1980s have been less consistently great. Economic struggles and the rise of soccer among the islands contributed. The squad coming into the tournament in 2019 barely made the top ten, but it secured a test series victory against a strong English team before the tournament. The squad was a bit of a mystery. It was a mystery Pakistan would not solve.

PEAKING TOO EARLY?

Two years before the opening match of the 2019 World Cup, Pakistan had been the surprise winners of the ICC's Champions Tournament, then the sport's second most important open tournament. Pakistan looked like legitimate contenders for the 2019 World Cup. Their batting was sometimes anemic but with flashes of respectability. The bowling was outstanding. Fast bowler Hasan Ali, with 13 wickets taken across the five matches of the Champions Tournament, was "Player of the Series." The redeemed Mohammad Amir, convicted of spot-fixing years earlier, had withstood the pressure of great batsmen and hostile fans to become a star.

After the Champions Trophy, however, Pakistan began to stumble. It lost ODI series against New Zealand (0–5), Australia (0–5), and England (0–4). It lost matches against India and Bangladesh and a series against South Africa (2–3). Wins against lightweights Zimbabwe, Hong Kong, and Afghanistan could not disguise the slide. Pakistan's biggest and growing weakness was its batting, particularly for power.

Going into the World Cup, Pakistan ranked sixth in the world, good but not great. The team showed no swagger.

THE DEBACLE

Short ball bowling in cricket is a high-risk, high-reward strategy that most teams use only sparingly. The crux is that the bowler bounces the ball closer to his point of delivery, meaning it will drift higher by the time it reaches the batsman, often head high. Opposing batsmen frequently crush these deliveries to the boundary. Steady batsmen can tee off. The unsteady, however, fear for their teeth.

When mixed in with regular, lower deliveries (bounced much closer to the batsman), the occasional short ball can produce an awkward swing and a ball launched straight up, an easy catch. The West Indies indulged the technique against Pakistan, going to the trick repeatedly. Pakistani batsmen responded with some sixes early on, but in the middle of their order surrendered quick wickets. The bottom part of their lineup looked nervous, backing up deep toward the stumps and taking defensive swipes at the deliveries. In a blink, Pakistan had collapsed, bowled out with an anemic, humiliating 105 runs in its World Cup opening.

For the Windies' batsmen, the 105-run target did not justify breaking a sweat. Muhammad Amir would give Pakistani fans something to cheer with three wickets taken, but no one doubted the outcome. Chris Gayle, a thirty-nine-year-old West Indies star on his way to retirement, stole the show with 50 runs, including three "sixes" and six "fours." In short order, the West Indies passed the Pakistani run total, using only 13½ overs to do it. The West Indies had an amazing 218 deliveries still on the table when they won the match, the most ever in a World Cup tournament.

In Pakistan, the result was jarring. The team had looked unfit, lethargic, and weak. It was a start that would shade Pakistani perceptions of the tournament, even after some inspiring Pakistani wins. It was the loss that should not have happened. Pakistan rounded into better form as the tournament progressed, and the West Indies rapidly faded. After looking like world beaters against Pakistan, the West Indies side would go on to an abysmal tournament, winning two and losing six. They finished ninth of the ten teams, ahead only of Afghanistan.

The poor Pakistan performance reflects a standard lesson from cricket, one equally applicable to diplomacy: a batsman should not swing with a particular shot in mind regardless of the delivery but must be flexible and adapt to the reality of what is offered. Pakistani batsmen failed to do this against West Indies. Both Pakistan and the United States, arguably, did something similar in Afghanistan, doggedly pursuing an idealized outcome that proved impossible to achieve in the face of Afghan realities. Both paid a price, though the cost for America has mostly been expended. Pakistan's heavy price from militant rule in Afghanistan is probably just beginning to come due.

MATCH RESULT

Pakistan 105 runs (21.4 overs)
West Indies 108 runs/3 wickets (13.4 overs)
West Indies wins by seven wickets.

5 BRITAIN'S IMPERIAL LEGACY IN PAKISTAN

June 3, 2019, Trent Bridge, Nottingham
Pakistan (0-1), 0 points, vs. England (1-0), 2 points

Even two decades into the twenty-first century, an American diplomat serving in Pakistan needed to know something of British colonial rule and its legacies. British rule disappeared a long lifetime ago, but British India's customs, injustices, successes, and absurdities have been passed forward through Pakistani generations, still remembered today by those who were children in the final years of the Raj. The economic legacies of Britain's extractive rule are more pernicious. Bangladesh, India, and Pakistan struggled as developing economies for decades after independence. It would be a challenge to identify an economic malady among the successor states that did *not* have an antecedent in colonial India.

The nature of Britain's departure produced additional challenges. Partition of India into two new independent countries, India and Pakistan, and the bloodshed and dislocation that accompanied these events from 1946 through 1948, sundered local economies and broke cultural and political ties among elites. The quick descent to open warfare between the inheritor states laid the foundation for the persistent pathologies in their relationship. Partition is at once history and current injury.

In addition to the problems between them, Pakistan and India both inherited the challenge of empire, of ruling disparate and resistant peoples across vast lands. Cleaving the subcontinent by its two leading confession groups had been just one of innumerable possibilities for India's post-colonial dispensation, but it was the one used. Untested was the idea of creating new states around ethnic nationalisms. Both Pakistan and India inherited aggrieved would-be nations. India fought off the centrifugal forces of ethnicity and nationalism with an appeal to democracy and socialism (though Hindu nationalism was never far beneath the surface). In Pakistan, Islam was to be the glue.

As described in more detail in chapter 12, the glue was not enough to keep West and East Pakistan together. A combination of Bengali separatism, Punjabi chauvinism, and the natural incongruities of such a geographically divided state split Pakistan in 1971, leading to the emergence of independent Bangladesh from the former East Pakistan. Pakistan today continues to mismanage two additional potent nationalisms, Balochi and Pashtun, but it has maintained the territorial integrity of the former West Pakistan for seventy years and likely will continue to do so.

American diplomats did not come quickly to an understanding of ethnonationalism or the legacies of empire. The United States occupied much of her history building a continental empire. With the brutal diminishment of its own Native peoples and with the requisite assimilation of immigrant newcomers, it was a country where nationalisms went to die. Italian neighborhoods, Irish bars, Cape Verdean music, and little Saigons could all thrive in the American fabric, but once they arrived in the United States, immigrants abandoned the idea of ethnic self-rule.

The United States eventually captured an empire of sorts, the long-restive islands still attached to Spain in 1898, but the lessons of Cuban and Filipino resistance to American rule were absorbed as anticolonialism rather than nationalism. Even as a global leader in the Cold War, America did not have to concern itself greatly with the force of nationalism. Africa's wave of decolonizing leaders kept a purposeful lid on ethnic separatism, pledging to each other to respect colonial borders, and conflict in Latin America was about other things. Europe, where nationalisms would eventually reemerge, was locked down during the Cold War by two antagonistic alliance systems. There were exceptions, including allied Pakistan's loss of Bengali-nationalist East Pakistan, but it was only with the end of the Cold War that American diplomats began to confront the power of ethnic, cultural, and linguistic nationalism.

Over time, American diplomats, intelligence officers, and military attachés made themselves expert on specific regions and peoples, informing policy. But for Americans raised on a liberal American Creed, as were most diplomats and spies raised in the 1950s through 1980s, an understanding of nationalism did not come with our civic DNA.

In Pakistan, American diplomats, keen to promote democratic norms and human rights, have at times been surprised by the power of nationalisms. Of even greater moment has been coming to terms with the Pakistan Army's fear of nationalism, of movements that might threaten the cohesion of the country. Pakistan's raison d'être is Muslim identity; its bedrock is that Islam is sufficient glue for the country. Its leaders view challenges to that ideology as existential.

Empire's Heirs: The Pakistan Military and Its Western Frontiers

For imperial Britain, modern Pakistan's northern and western reaches were not the valuable part of the South Asian Empire. The rugged land and tribes that dominated the terrain made colonial extraction difficult. The jewel of the crown ran between the Indus and the mouths of the Brahmaputra, the populated heartland that produced staples like cotton and rice, valuable spices, tropical produce, and tax revenue to turn the wheels of empire. By contrast, the British valued the remote northwestern frontier mostly as a buffer, a shield against whatever threats might emerge from the endless marches of central Asia. Britain was an active force on the border, but it governed indirectly, elevating tribal leaders to exert control and punishing whole tribes for slights. The Pashtuns were at the heart of this diplomacy, the Baloch a distant second.

Balochistan was less strategic than the Pashtun lands astride the border with Afghanistan, and the British did not incorporate it into the Raj until the 1880s. Balochistan is Pakistan's largest province by land area, but much of it is sparsely populated and poorly watered, rugged desert and mountains and rocky coastline. Except at its northeastern stretch, where high passes connect Kandahar in Afghanistan with the southern Indus valley, the province does not offer an aggressor a logical approach to Pakistan's valuable parts. Situated east–west between the Indus and Iran, and north–south between Afghanistan and the Arabian Sea, Balochistan became a Cold War strategic preoccupation briefly—in the 1980s, when opinion writers warned that the Soviets might advance from recently occupied Afghanistan through Pakistan's restive Balochistan to the Indian

Ocean, gaining thereby a "warm water port" on the edge of the oil-rich Persian Gulf. This concern has reemerged in this era of great power competition, as the United States eyes warily the Chinese interest in the Baloch port of Gwadar.

The Pashtun areas were more important to Britain. Demarcated by today's Khyber-Pakhtunkhwa (KP) province and northern areas of Balochistan Province, the Pashtun lands came under the authority of the British East India Company after its defeat of the Sikh Empire. The Sikh states had been a powerful buffer state between central Asia and British East India. When British India dissolved the Sikh state, Britain inherited the strategic concerns of the Pashtun-dominated frontier with Afghanistan. The Pashtun belt on the southern and eastern flanks of the Hindu Kush mountains looms close to the upper Indus valley and to the Punjabi heartland further east. (See map.) The Khyber Pass marks the easiest crossing to and from Afghanistan, a route for invasion in either direction—west toward Kabul or east toward Punjab and the plains of India. Pakistan's capital, Islamabad, and its military headquarters, Rawalpindi, are within a short drive.

For British colonial India, the northwest frontier was for decades the only threatened border, until Imperial Japan threatened from the east during World War II. Tsarist Russia had steadily incorporated central Asia, leaving only Afghanistan independent. It was dominated by Pashtuns, cousins of the Pashtuns of the Raj. Pashtuns became a focus of political and military machinations within the "Great Game," the century-long cold and hot contest between British and Russian proxies.

With independence, Pakistan incorporated both Balochistan and the Pashtun tribal areas. The Pashtuns came willingly enough, although their discontent would later grow. Balochistan had mixed sentiments. Baloch elites had harbored a preference for autonomy within a whole, undivided India rather than subservience to Punjabi leaders in a new Pakistan. One of its four princely states held out for a brief time against accession to Pakistan.

Pashtuns and Baloch had different relationships with both colonial India and modern Pakistan. Pashtuns were valued as good soldiers, lumped into a racially tinged nomenclature as a "martial" caste by the British and to this day recruited in strong numbers by the Pakistan Army, second only to Punjabis. They were also watched with suspicion, the Pakistan military always mindful of their ties to Afghanistan. Afghanistan's Durrani Empire had once stretched far beyond today's border into what is today Pakistan, encompassing Pakistani-Pashtun forbears. At Pakistan's independence, Afghanistan agitated against Pakistan's inheritance of Pashtun lands, wishing to press its borders eastward. The legacy of Afghan ties and claims to the Pashtun homeland is still on the mind of the Pakistan Army.

Balochistan was less central to Britain's or Pakistan's core strategies, its people playing little role in business or the military or national governance. But if the Baloch were of little import to Pakistan, their vast province was. It offered strategic depth, minerals and hydrocarbons, and a toehold near the Persian Gulf. From the start, Pakistan's rulers had every intention of holding the province.

Baloch and Pashtuns have consistently agitated for greater autonomy from the central state, for political rights or a greater share of resources; some, particularly among the Baloch, rebelled for separation. Baloch uprisings and insurgencies have spanned decades, fueled by Pakistan Army abuses and the exploitation of local resources, with pauses for political settlements that would eventually fray.

In 2018 one movement among the Pashtuns took on a special weight. It was a morally unassailable campaign that the military establishment found threatening, a grassroots movement that burst onto the scene to complain about military—and militant—abuses of the Pashtun people. The Pashtun Tahafuz (Rights) Movement, the PTM, built through social media and sustained in mass rallies and protests, has shown staying power since then.

Founded by a young leader, Manzoor Pashteen, the PTM emerged over several years, channeling broad-based Pashtun rage that so many sons and husbands had been killed or "disappeared" by either insurgents or the military. Forty years of conflict spilling in from Afghanistan had transformed their communities and destroyed families. Millions of refugees from Afghanistan scattered in Pashtun lands attracted conservative Islamist teachers and fighting. Insurgencies, terrorists, bandits, and the military's counterinsurgency campaigns disrupted livelihoods and increased insecurity among vulnerable populations, particularly women and youth.[1] The PTM called out both sides of the conflict.

The Pashtun complaints were familiar, not that different from what they had lodged against the British a century before. Security forces, British or Pakistani, held villages responsible for insurgents or criminals because it was too difficult to track down individuals. Sometimes with justification, sometimes without, authorities blamed the village for hiding the man. If the village gave up the man, however, militants or gangs just as quickly targeted the village for reprisal. It was a no-win for the civilians in the middle.

This mode of governing was formalized through the British Frontier Crimes Regulations, which elevated tribal agents to positions of authority and denied individuals due process or recourse to formal courts. The Frontier Crimes Regulations were bequeathed to Pakistan and used to govern the Federally Administered Tribal Areas (FATA), the remote Pashtun border districts that were not incorporated as regular parts of Pakistan, specifically into the Khyber-Pakhtunkhwa (KP) Province, until 2018. Today the region's leading anti-Pakistan insurgency, the Pakistan Taliban, makes reversing that incorporation its top political objective. Other tribal leaders seek a return to the social and legal structure that sustained their patriarchal roles.

In addition to criticizing the military and the Pakistan Taliban, secular or moderate Muslim Pashtuns who coalesced into the PTM had also directed complaints at the United States, most specifically for the intense drone campaign of the Bush and Obama years. The missile strikes were concentrated in North and South Waziristan, within the FATA. Even though carefully vetted and presumably launched only against particularly dangerous terrorist leaders, the strikes sometimes killed women, children, and men guilty only of proximity to the suspected terrorist. Over the years, almost one thousand Pakistani civilians not confirmed as bona fide targets lost their lives to apparent U.S. missile strikes.[2]

There are diverse views about whether drone strikes generated significant local grievance. One careful study by scholar Aqil Shah suggested many Pashtuns recognized the value of the campaign in disrupting terrorist groups. He suggests it had a deterrent effect, discouraging new recruits. In this argument, the destructive interventions of the Pakistan Army provoked much greater resentment.[3]

The seemingly minor event that ultimately sparked the PTM was the January 2018 assassination of a Pashtun shopkeeper in Karachi, far from the Pashtun heartland. The young man, clearly not a militant, was emblematic of the millions of Pashtuns displaced from their homes and villages. In Pakistan's non-Pashtun cities, like Karachi, they faced harassment from local networks wary of interlopers and from the police.

In the case of the Karachi victim, Nageebullah Mehsud, police said he died in a street battle against terrorists. The charge of terrorist affiliation was patently false, and pressure mounted for an investigation. The resulting report acknowledged police killed Mehsud as part of a "fake encounter" with terrorists.[4] This was just the type of extrajudicial killing too familiar to Pashtun families. This incident, perpetrated by a rogue senior policeman—just one of many outrages attributed to the man—had nothing to do with counterterrorism.

In response, the PTM organized a march to Islamabad. Major political parties briefly lent support to the protest, and then-candidate Imran Khan, descended from a prominent Pashtun family, expressed sympathy. Soon, however, the army waved off the political parties and news media, signaling that the PTM was out of bounds. The army viewed the movement with suspicion because it demanded accountability from all the Pashtuns' tormenters—militants *and* security forces.

The PTM has pressed the government to release hundreds detained without trial. They asked for answers about those taken long ago and presumed dead.[5] Their most notable rallying cry was directly provocative to the military establishment: "This terrorism," they shouted in Urdu, "behind it is the uniform."[6] The PTM challenge was reminiscent of past "leftist" and "secular" movements among the Pashtuns, long considered threatening by the state and long vulnerable to violent attacks from both Islamic militants and the army's proxies.[7]

The PTM persisted and even seemed to grow through 2018, its large rallies not covered by the press but widely known, videos of crowds and speeches propelled through social media and encrypted applications. Assailants attacked PTM rallies. Sometimes the attackers seemed to be the Afghan Taliban, enjoying refuge in Pakistan and some debt to the

Pakistan Army.[8] Marchers and leaders proved undaunted in the face of the attacks, responding with a stoic refrain: "We're dying anyway."[9]

The PTM carefully avoided any suggestion of separatism or even demands for autonomy. It sought only the protections due to citizens. This stance vexed the intelligence operatives charged with squelching the movement; claims the group was disloyal rang hollow. The PTM also demurred on forming a political party, avoiding direct competition with other civilian politicians. Two of its leading advocates were elected to Parliament in July 2018, but as independents.

As the military pressured the rest of Pakistan against engaging with the PTM, foreign journalists and foreign embassies became prominent among those still able to talk to its advocates. Reporting officers in our embassy or consulates sustained some contact. Our goal was neither to encourage nor discourage, but to understand the activities of a significant human rights movement in a critical part of the country. Our annual human rights report, moreover, required us to describe rights denied: for the Pashtuns these included assembly, speech, due process, and human security.

By early 2019 our contacts with the PTM activists provoked a leading Pakistani general into the only intemperate encounter I witnessed from him, a long jeremiad delivered to Ambassador Jones against alleged American support to Pashtun separatism. The charge was without foundation, and, to his credit, Ambassador Jones responded forcefully and moved to end the meeting. The military's point made, the general relented, and the business of the meeting resumed.

The outburst represents a reality that the Pakistan military has suffered as well in dealing with the security challenges of the northwest frontier. Four soldiers had died in a roadside blast just prior to that meeting.[10] There were Pashtun militants attacking the Pakistan military. Unfortunately, the persecution of the PTM amounted to blaming the victim. Authorities detained and charged the two PTM-affiliated National Assembly members more than once. The government charged one of the MPs for provoking violence at a May 2019 rally where the military was almost certainly at fault for the escalation. Security forces shot and killed thirteen protestors at the event.[11]

As noted, there is a violent rival to the PTM in Pashtun lands—the confederation of militant tribal groups fighting under the banner of the Tehrik-e-Taliban Pakistan, the TTP. I discuss this militant insurgency in detail in the following chapter. Suffice it to note here that its goals often transcend the concerns of the ethnic Pashtuns in the remote tribal regions of the former FATA to encompass pan-Islamist ideology. It is a far different movement than the PTM, though both complain about the Pakistan military.

If Pashtun nationalism is a real force in Pakistan, in both its peaceful and its violent manifestations, it rarely runs toward the idea of separatism. In Balochistan, by contrast, Pakistan government policies have fertilized sustained local interest in Baloch independence, at least among a restive minority.

For the Baloch, who had been incorporated late into colonial India and then with a large degree of autonomy, incorporation into Pakistan meant subjugation to Pakistan's Punjabi and Sindhi leadership. Over the years since, exploitation of the province's minerals and hydrocarbons by the national government and non-Baloch companies led to further grievances, as did a series of political steps by the national government, including harsh security policies under Zulfikar Ali Bhutto in the 1970s. President Musharraf applied provocative restrictions more recently.

There have been decentralized Baloch insurgencies in most of the past seven decades, fights that have ebbed and flowed against crackdowns and compromises from the national government. Even with substantial military deployments, the vast size of the province makes counterinsurgency a challenge. Additionally, there are populations of Baloch across the borders in Iran and Afghanistan, facilitating flows of weapons and money into Pakistan to sustain insurgencies. Non-Baloch have also joined the fighting in the province, exacerbating a sense of disorder there.[12]

Given the geographic challenges in Balochistan, Pakistan's establishment has preferred cooptation of elites to heavy military deployments. When it has turned to coercive counterinsurgency, the campaigns have been counterproductive, with forced disappearances and unaccountable military excesses spurring fresh rebellion among the population. The most recent and longest lasting insurgency began in earnest in 2006 following the death of a prominent Bugti tribal leader during a military operation.

The conflict began over disputed mineral rights, a continuing source of unrest.[13] Throughout periods of unrest, families and tribes among the Baloch have been divided over the prospect of taking up arms.[14]

Balochistan is more remote than Khyber-Pakhtunkhwa and so typically a less compelling concern to the army, but the province's strategic value is increasing. The expansive territory far from India has always allowed Pakistan space to train pilots and test nuclear weapons, and its gas fields are a critical source of energy independence. In recent decades, China's interest in the Baloch port of Gwadar has served as a critical foundation to Pakistan's most important foreign partnership. The China-Pakistan Economic Corridor (CPEC) is centered on Balochistan, with a major highway constructed through remote tracts of the province to connect Gwadar with western China.

As government policies generated dissent and distrust in Balochistan, CPEC itself became a target of both political agitation and terrorist attack. Over the past decade, militants have killed dozens of workers, including Chinese, at remote CPEC projects.[15] Local politicians have complained of the dilution of the Baloch language as émigrés from other parts of the country descend for CPEC contracts. Balochis protest the unequal distribution of work and income under CPEC and the displacement of Baloch from traditional homes.

By 2018 the latest round of Baloch rebellion was winding down, contained by political and economic concessions, the killing of some insurgent leaders, and extensive fencing and border monitoring on both the Pakistan-Iran and Pakistan-Afghanistan frontiers. But the most violent of Baloch separatists then became more audacious. In November 2018 the Balochistan Liberation Army (BLA) struck the Chinese Consulate in Karachi, killing two Pakistani police and two private citizens. Six months later, the BLA attacked Gwadar's high-end hotel, the Pearl Continental, known as a home to Chinese visitors. The attackers killed four hotel employees and a soldier, and the Pakistan military was embarrassed when it took several hours to quell the attack.

As the terrorist attacks increased, the Pakistan military made consistent claims of foreign ties to the insurgents. It alleged complicity by both the Afghan National Defense and Security Forces (ANDSF) of the former Kabul government and the Indian spy agency RAW, formally the

Research and Analysis Wing. That Baloch insurgents found refuge in Afghanistan fueled the allegations, as have occasional pro-Baloch comments from Indian leadership.[16] In early 2022, as Baloch attacks spiked again, Pakistan continued to blame India even though there were no more Indian diplomats in Afghanistan after the Taliban takeover—and no more ANDSF for them to allegedly work through.

Pakistan's establishment had also long viewed America as sympathetic to the Baloch cause, even if the primary basis for this suspicion was simply that a few members of Congress or Baloch expatriates had used American media to call out abuses by the Pakistan government. Because of this suspicion, our meetings with Baloch in Islamabad were rare and challenging. Pakistan's police and spy services made meetings difficult, intimidating Baloch contacts.

More broadly, Pakistani authorities generally have made Balochistan off-limits to American diplomats and Western journalists. Up to 2011 the United States maintained various platforms in the province—drone platforms for counterterrorism and helicopters for counternarcotics. In 2011 I was able to visit Quetta for meetings with local leaders. By 2018 the air wing was gone, and our diplomats could not obtain "no objection certificates" from the Foreign Ministry to visit any part of the province.

Visiting Gwadar was difficult even in 2011 and was impossible during my second tour. Rather than standing open to various sources of foreign investment and commerce, Pakistan's highest profile development project, the port of Gwadar, remains cloaked in secrecy. Pakistan can hardly blame Western critics, then, if they postulate the secrecy has something to do with Chinese projects and intentions.

Restive Pashtuns and Baloch today represent the largest challenges to Pakistan's cohesion, but the country takes in millions more who do not fluently speak the national language (Urdu) and who maintain some sort of grievances against the state. From the army's perspective, Pakistan can lose no more territory without endangering cohesion. It can endure no more ethnic challenge without undermining the founding ethos of Pakistan—that Islam is sufficient glue. Not surprisingly, the Pakistan Army reacts overzealously to these threats, continuing the story of abuse and provoking further rebellion. It is not too different from chapters of British rule.

Cricket, Royals, and British Influence in Pakistan

The American Embassy and British High Commission in Islamabad are often close partners, and I was not the first American diplomat there to seek out smart, connected British colleagues to help me interpret Pakistan. Although the UK does not wield the geopolitical weight in Pakistan of either China or the United States, it does have legitimate interests and influence. Its sway in Pakistan's capital has always been stronger than that of its mission in New Delhi.

With the British in Pakistan, our roles and views were close, beginning with our shared interest in the safety and success of our coalition soldiers then still fighting next door in Afghanistan. Pakistan's de facto status as patron and refuge for the Taliban meant it exercised heavy sway over that conflict, and both we and the British were pressing Pakistan to pressure its Taliban tenants. We also shared interests in seeing Pakistan and India avoid war, ensuring that Pakistan's nuclear materials did not leak from government control, and advocating for the rights of civil society.

In Islamabad, my counterpart as British political counselor was as sharp as they come, always a bit more aware than I expected of American policies and activities. His accomplished wife was a fellow member with me on the International School's Board, a legacy American interest despite the absence of American children in our diplomatic mission since the early 2000s.

In addition to the simple skills and charms of its diplomats, British influence in Pakistan rests on a gamut of shared history and current interests. Some of this arises from the soft power of long familiarity and still strong connections, in some ways magnetic, both repelling and attracting. A 2019 visit by Prince William and Duchess Kate, for example, came off better in Pakistan than some of their visits to other parts of the Commonwealth.

London as a tableau for famous Pakistanis, not just cricketers, is an enduring component of Britain's "soft power" as well. For Pakistan's elite English learners, the top-notch private schools in Pakistan often pointed the way to British universities. For those with the means to travel, London for decades was among the first destinations, even if the ease, prices, and great air connections of the UAE and Qatar have made them bigger draws today. Talented Pakistanis have made a place in English literature, British television, and London-based music.

In Pakistan's first decades, an elite with deep ties to British traditions led the country. Many of its leading military officers, industrial magnates, and politicians had attended one of the famed missionary schools. The schools no longer aimed at converts, ensuring their continued place in the country, but they did offer English-standard curriculum, inculcating aspects of British culture.

This was also true among the military officers, for whom British norms of social interaction, rank, structure, and even drink (scotch and gin) held sway. Pakistan's first two postindependence military commanders were British generals, charged with minding the institution until Pakistani generals could gain sufficient rank for the job. Pakistani officers would for decades train at Sandhurst and other British military academies, as they would in the United States. These affinities have declined but are not extinguished.

Another legacy source of British influence was Pakistan's sometimes awkward but enduring place as a Cold War ally of the United States and the United Kingdom. Whereas India after partition followed its anticolonialist, nonaligned nationalism to the far side of the Cold War, dependent on military hardware from the Soviet Union and critical of capitalism for its first fifty years, Pakistan pursued alliance with the West as both necessary and beneficial.

Pakistan needed Britain's support from the start. Under the terms of partition, Pakistan was to receive a predetermined amount of the British Indian Army's weapons and ammunition, a disproportionate amount of which was stuck in what became rival India. As the two new countries fell immediately into conflict, India naturally shorted Pakistan on the distribution of guns and ammo.[17] Pakistan would call on London to resupply its British-outfitted military. Within a few years, the United States had taken on the role of Pakistan's major military patron, providing large packages of weapons, ammunition, training, and construction, but Britain was always present as the emeritus partner in the Western alliance system.

Another major source of British influence in Pakistan—and Pakistani influence in the UK—is the large Pakistani diaspora there. This community of over 1.5 million is a source of remittances to families in Pakistan and a dynamic cultural and political tie to Britain. Although British Pakistanis run the gamut, from wealthy to struggling, most are better off in the UK than in the lives they left behind. Kashmiris make up a significant part of the community, many families dating their immigration to the time of partition. The Pakistan-heritage community is the UK's second largest Asian diaspora, accounting for quite a few critical votes in any election. During my time in Pakistan, both the mayor of London (from the Labour Party) and the home secretary (a Conservative) were Pakistani-Britons.

Pakistani-Brits embody positive and negative experiences with the UK for their Pakistani families back home: they were subject to intense racism in the 1970s, and when three of the four suicide bombers of "7/7"—the 2005 attacks on the London underground and buses—were confirmed as the sons of Pakistani immigrants, the community suffered the profiling and hostility familiar to Muslims elsewhere in the West. At the same time, the UK was still "home" to this community, a place of better education, health care, job opportunities, and greater gender equality. Few have moved back to Pakistan, though many of the ethnic Kashmiris have built large status houses in the Muzaffarabad environs.

The United States gains some leverage as well by being a major home to immigrant Pakistanis, many of whom have become successful as businesspeople or medical professionals. Still, the Pakistani American diaspora is not deeply invested in Pakistani politics. While Pakistani Americans might sustain ties of family and obligation to individuals back in the home country, these ties are less dynamic than ties between the British diaspora and Pakistan.

Also different from the British diaspora, the Pakistani community does not exercise much political weight in the United States, where it is far less influential than the assertive Indian American community. Still, Imran Khan's PTI, just like the other major parties, had designated fundraisers to seek donations from the large communities in the UK and the United States (as well as from what is now the larger center of the Pakistani diaspora and finance, the Persian Gulf). These ties came under scrutiny later, when the PTI was out of power in 2022. Among all these levers of influence and channels of information, one in particular stands out for

Britain's insights into Pakistani politics: the use of London as a refuge for Pakistani politicians on the outs back home.

London: A Safe Haven for Pakistani Politics

British colleagues could always tell us something about Pakistani politics from what was happening in London. Pakistan's two main parties from the days before Imran Khan's PTI—the PPP and the PML-N—as well as an influential smaller party, the MQM, all had active offices in London. Most significant during my tenure was the PML-N of Nawaz Sharif, three-time prime minister. When I arrived back in Pakistan, he had just returned from semi-exile in London to face charges of corruption. He would remain in jail through my departure, released only briefly to attend the funeral of his wife, who died in London without him, battling cancer.

The Pakistan People's Party too had historic ties to London. Benazir Bhutto studied at Oxford and developed lifelong ties to influential British politicians and writers. There, she even had a friendship with Imran Khan. Britain was her refuge after her release from house arrest in the early 1980s and her exile after her first unfinished term as prime minister. The Bhutto-Zardari family would accumulate their own expansive foreign assets in England, just as had the Sharif family.

Most controversial of all the London expatriates was Altaf Hussein. His political party, the MQM, based in the Urdu-speaking population of Karachi (immigrants from the India side of partition, settled in the late 1940s), was a unique amalgam of political movement and criminal syndicate.

During my first tour, I interacted a great deal with his deputies. The party was a crucial swing vote and was part of the PPP-led government. Its members offered an antiextremist, secular ideology and portrayed themselves as pro-American. There was some truth in this. The other truth was a dangerous syndicate of extortion and criminal enterprise. Hussein maintained his influence through murderous enforcers, extending even into London, and through a charisma that he channeled home through videos full of fervent exhortations. My main MQM contact in 2011 always seemed to be looking behind him for someone approaching with a knife.

By 2016, with the MQM's hold diminished and British legal cases against him mounting, Hussein overreached, calling on his supporters to take to the streets in Karachi to fight all comers. It was more than the army could tolerate. The military intervened forcefully, arresting, detaining, and killing. The MQM splintered into factions, and, in the 2018 national election, took only a handful of seats. Now distanced from Altaf, the smaller MQM nonetheless was a courted coalition partner. Imran Khan's PTI, which failed to win an absolute majority in Parliament in the 2018 elections, accepted its support.

Finally, in London, as in Washington, there was the new wave of expatriate Pakistanis thronging to the PTI. Throughout his time in office, Khan seemed more popular among expatriate communities than he was at home. The reasons were understandable. He was glamorous, photogenic, and not personally corrupt. Pakistan's most famous man, he had rubbed shoulders with royals, movie stars, and global political leaders. It was a public face Pakistanis living abroad could be proud of, an antidote to the bad name Pakistan had acquired in the West as a hotbed of extremism and corruption.

Cricket: A Valued Inheritance, Fiercely Contested

England is the inventor of the game Pakistanis love. For half a century, it was the top destination for a national match. England's "county cricket" leagues were for decades the best option for Pakistani cricketers looking to hone their skills and earn a wage.

Pakistan's most famous cricketer, Imran Khan, and his equally successful contemporary, Javed Miandad, would each spend most of two decades in British county cricket. The two were the cornerstones of Pakistan's golden age of cricket and had deep ties to England.

Given England's pride of place in the cricketing world, it is a given that serious Pakistani fans of a certain age will have mental connections to England—with its cricket fields, stars, and sports writers. The Oval, Lord's, Edgbaston, Trent Bridge—Pakistan has played them all, in triumph and disappointment. This legacy of cricket is a bond between the two countries.

Against the idealized imaginings of lush English cricket pitches, Pakistanis also have recollections of many rough patches in the cricketing relationship. The dustups were usually on the pitch, but the most infamous incident was the wildly ill-considered decision by a touring English "second eleven" to briefly kidnap a Pakistani umpire in Peshawar in 1956. In Peter Oborne's careful study of the incident, what is most apparent is a deeply colonial mindset among the English players about what treatment of a foreign official might be appropriate.[18]

The English would complain for decades that Pakistani players did not sufficiently adhere to the rules of cricket on the pitch, that they pressured umpires and pleaded too vehemently for calls they wanted. The mind boggles, though, at the likely reaction in Britain had a visiting Pakistani team kidnapped an English umpire from his hotel. England's cricketing establishment apologized for the Peshawar incident, but it left a mark.

A Pakistani fan of a certain age can recount various injustices meted out by the English. With Australia visiting only rarely, New Zealand a poor team until more recently, India often an impossibility due to tensions and wars, South Africa ruled out due to apartheid, and the West Indies too far away, a disproportionate number of Pakistan's international tests from the 1950s through the 1970s were against England. This has meant a lot of match history. Pakistan has taken a sizable number of these contests over the years, but every tour brought disputes.

There were also oddly politicized trips by British cricketers to Pakistan, encouraged by the Foreign Office, to show support for the Pakistan government (usually a military one). One such tour was in 1969, when the government encouraged the touring Marylebone Cricket Club (MCC) to follow through with a tour even as prodemocracy protests were breaking out across Pakistan against the military government of Ayub Khan. Even more dramatically, the Foreign Office pressed the MCC to go to Dhaka midtour just as East Pakistan was sliding into public disorder, the population agitating for autonomy or outright independence from the western half of Pakistan.[19]

Issues of race and class go far back in the British colonial spread of cricket. Segregation was the norm in British cricket grounds. While the colonials encouraged local teams as necessary competition, they treated the local players differently in the clubhouse.

This colonial baggage, mixed with the fierce disputes on the pitch, suggests cricket might be a wedge in British-Pakistan ties, and it has created actual diplomatic disputes. But intense sporting rivalry binds as much as it divides. Greatness requires a formidable opponent, and the victory is sweeter if the opponent is disliked. Even with its blemishes, then, Pakistan and England's matches link the two peoples.

In recent years, some of the edginess has fallen away. Most important, the huge population of Pakistan-heritage immigrants to England means that "away" matches there feel like home contests to Pakistani players. This was particularly striking in an era when security concerns meant that Pakistan rarely played in front of a crowd in Pakistan. The divided British stands sometimes led to scuffles between white Britons and British Pakistanis, but at the 2019 World Cup the fans were positive, even celebratory.

An Urgent Need to Bat Better

After Pakistan's dismal opening against the West Indies, its 2019 World Cup campaign threatened collapse. England had scored a convincing first match win and were tournament favorites. They were a team that rarely lost at home and now hosted a demoralized Pakistan—loser of eleven straight matches going into the tournament.

Pakistan, however, was playing to home fans. Buoyed by a crowd evenly divided between England and Pakistan partisans, the Pakistanis rallied as if a team of yesteryear to salvage honor and competitive pride. Batting first, Pakistan more than tripled its dismal output of the first match, scoring a massive 348 runs. England undermined its effort with sloppy fielding, but up and down the lineup Pakistan was energized and skilled at bat.

The landslide of runs gave Pakistan's bowlers a secure cushion. Still, centuries by two England batsmen, Joe Root and Jos Butler, threatened a dramatic chase. Pakistan's bowlers would prove just steady enough, with Mohammad Amir taking two wickets, including that of Butler. Wahab Riaz, a bowler called out for criticism by his manager before the match, took another pair of late wickets to effectively end the match.

The great match and Pakistan's win offered a range of lessons: fielding matters, as it undermined England; the team matters, as Pakistan succeeded with contributions across its lineup. Its first five batsmen all scored over 35. It was the sort of complete performance Pakistan would fail to deliver for the next several matches.

With a 14-run win, Pakistan enjoyed a brief multiteam tie atop the tables. English fans reacquainted themselves with fears of another World Cup collapse. As can happen in cricket, rain would come to dampen Pakistan's brief momentum.

MATCH RRESULT
Pakistan 348/8
England 334/9
Pakistan wins by 14 runs.

6 THE CHALLENGES OF INSURGENCIES AND TERRORISM

June 7, 2019, Bristol County Ground
Pakistan (1-1), 2 points, vs. Sri Lanka (1-1), 2 points

One unfortunate aspect of the Cricket World Cup is the rain-induced draw. A tournament staged in England will inevitably run into some rain; like baseball, cricket cannot be competitive in much more than a drizzle. In this tournament, a rain-out meant a draw rather than a rescheduling. Pakistan versus Sri Lanka, which should have been a competitive match, was a victim of rain. Both teams lost a chance at two points in the standings with a win, avoided the damage of zero points for a loss, and came away with a single point each.

With all other results unchanged, the extra point of a win would have ensured Pakistan's place in the semifinals. Pakistan's rival for a final semifinal spot, New Zealand, probably benefited most from rain, gaining a draw against India early in the tournament when India was at its best.

In diplomacy and cricket, a force majeure can intercede to undermine an anticipated win; effective country plans account for the prospect of an unanticipated reverse. In Pakistan, the U.S. Embassy seemed to encounter such events more often than statistics would dictate—an unfortunate comment from Washington, a diplomat's traffic accident, or a terrorist attack that changed the tenor of bilateral conversations. They were as inevitable as the rain in England but unpredictable in their timing. For Pakistan and Sri Lanka in the 1990s and 2000s, public safety and cricket suffered from a deluge of tragic shocks.

Pakistan and Sri Lanka: Friends with Histories of Violence

For both Pakistanis and Sri Lankans, their countries' place in international cricket is a point of pride. It was a loss for both, then, that terrorism prevented them from hosting matches for long stretches.

The most dramatic year in Sri Lankan cricket, encapsulating moments of grievance, perseverance, and triumph, was 1996. Before those events could occur, Sri Lanka first had to fight its way to test status, a process that took decades longer than in Pakistan.

The country's colonial cricketing history was not unlike that of India and Pakistan, with the game's seeds broadcast by British plantation owners, administrators, and soldiers in the 1800s. There was, as elsewhere, the steady push-pull of inclusion and colonial division, the native population occupying an inferior position in the sport, often divided by ethnicity, but also coached and encouraged.[1] It was the sport of Anglophiles and remained that way for some time, and it found greatest traction among the Sinhalese majority, developing more slowly among the Tamil and urban Muslim communities.

Perhaps because it had enjoyed some level of self-government as Ceylon, Sri Lanka did not have as much need for a sport to bolster its project of nationhood after independence. Sri Lankan cricket also did not have the early success of Pakistan.

By the late 1960s, however, cricket was becoming more popular, and the government began to invest. The country's private sector saw opportunity for profit in a bigger sport, particularly as it tied into the growing mass audience of India. The sport had foreign help; both Pakistan and India offered tours and coaching to develop Sri Lankan cricket, motivated in part by their rivalry for influence.

In 1981 the ICC admitted Sri Lanka to test status. Up to the 1996 World Cup, it was still considered a weak side, known for creative batsmen but iffy bowling. One exception in the 1990s was a spin bowler named Muttiah Muralitharan. Muralitharan was a Tamil, rare in the country's cricket; he also had an unorthodox motion that attracted criticism and challenge from those who lost wickets to him. In 1995 an Australian umpire called a "no-ball" on Muralitharan (for "chucking" the ball—or throwing it as in baseball with more torque in the elbow). As Stephen Wagg notes, Sri Lanka's anger at the call was stoked by the steady racist taunts from fans and "sledging" (trash talk) from Australia's players.[2] The anti-immigrant opposition leader John Howard, later prime minister, was a vocal Muralitharan critic.

Sri Lanka's grievance against Australia took a deeper turn a year later when Australia (and the West Indies) refused to play their World Cup matches in Sri Lanka's capital, Colombo, citing concerns about safety. Sri Lanka was a cohost for the first time, partnering for the second South Asia–hosted competition with India and Pakistan. Australia's and the West Indies' decisions stung, in part because they had merit.

At the time, the separatist LTTE, or Tamil Tigers, violent insurgents and terrorists, were on the rise. The group had detonated a bomb at the Sri Lankan National Bank in Colombo just eighteen days before the inaugural match, killing ninety-one and injuring well over one thousand. Security was a reasonable concern.

In a bit of karma, Sri Lanka surprisingly advanced to the tournament final, where it faced Australia. As in 1987 neither India nor Pakistan made the final of a World Cup they were hosting, so Sri Lanka ably assumed the role of "home" favorite in the match played in Lahore, Pakistan. The lightly regarded Sri Lankans made good on their opportunity, defeating the Australians by seven wickets, with four overs to spare. Though he took only one wicket, Muralitharan was the most economical of the Sri Lankan bowlers, surrendering just 31 runs in ten overs (60 balls).

Sri Lanka's World Cup win was an unanticipated underdog surprise, and the country has continued to see cricket prosper. In 1996, however, Sri Lanka had more than a decade of civil war still in front of it.

Pakistan was a friend to governments in Colombo throughout the years of Sri Lanka's internal conflict, a slightly counterintuitive Muslim backer of Buddhist-oriented Sri Lankan governments. Pakistan provided arms and training. There had been, up to 1971, a grand strategic rationale for Pakistan's ties to the country: it was a critical transshipment and refueling bridge between Pakistan's western and eastern halves. The island nation was critical to Pakistan, particularly during periods of Pakistan-India conflict, when India closed its airspace to Pakistani flights. This was most apparent, for the final time, in the 1971 conflict when the Pakistan Army desperately sought to hang on against East Pakistan's Bengali separatists and then against the Indian Army. It sent reinforcements and supplies to the east through Sri Lanka.[3]

Pakistan partnered with Colombo as Sri Lanka faced decades of insurgency from violent Tamil separatists, who gathered financial and material support from the Tamil heartland in southern India. In the 1980s the mostly Hindu Tamil separatists received training, supplies, and support from the Indian intelligence service RAW and from the leading political parties of India's Tamil Nadu state. In 1987 India airdropped supplies to the besieged Tamil rebels in Jaffna.[4] Pakistan found it natural to support the Sri Lankan government against these India-linked rebels.

If India occasionally stoked the conflict, it was not responsible for its root causes. At independence, Sri Lanka inherited communal divisions between the majority Sinhalese, primarily Buddhist, and the minority Tamils, primarily Hindu but also Muslim. The British transplanted many of Sri Lanka's Tamils from mainland India to the island to work Ceylon's large plantations, though much of the community had lived and worked in Sri Lanka for generations.

As Ceylon became independent Sri Lanka in 1948, the Sinhalese refused citizenship to Tamils born in India. Government repression against the Tamils became the norm. Tensions simmered until civil war broke out in 1983, and the war lasted a quarter century, featuring atrocities by the military and rebels alike. The Tigers emerged as one of the world's most violent insurgencies, pioneering the use of male and female suicide bombers.[5]

India for a time played both sides, encouraging mediation, dealing with the government in Colombo, but also allowing private support to flow across the Palk Strait to the Tamils. As the LTTE's extreme violence began to erode support in India, New Delhi changed its approach and sent in troops to support a negotiated but doomed peace agreement.[6]

India abandoned the peacekeeping role in 1990. Indian prime minister Rajiv Gandhi was assassinated a year later by an LTTE-linked Tamil, sapping most of the remaining sympathy in India for the Tigers. India would come around to fully supporting the government.

In 2009 the Sri Lankan military completed a final rout of the LTTE, sweeping them from longtime refuges on the northern and eastern sides of the island. It was a brutal campaign, with press blackouts only partially veiling the civilian casualties inflicted by the military. Though international human rights advocates were critical of the army's techniques, the government persisted. Sri Lanka emerged into a new future of political intrigue, questionable governance, electoral shenanigans, and still-simmering ethnic tension, but at least without the steady warfare and urban explosions.

Sri Lanka has consistently sustained positive ties with Pakistan, but it has mostly toggled between tilts toward China and toward India since the end of its war. China invested heavily in the port of Hambantota, gaining the privileges of lead investors, including sovereign protections for Chinese businesspeople. This investment has further bound Pakistan and Sri Lanka as part of China's Indian Ocean "string of pearls." It also created controversy in Sri Lanka as a potential debt trap. In recent years, Sri Lanka has leaned back toward India for investment and financial relief.

Pakistan's Mosaic of Militancy

In 2009, just as the Sri Lankan government defeated LTTE, Pakistan began its own long winter in international cricket, unable to host international competitions due to a plague of extremist violence, most of it homegrown. The catalytic event that year occurred in Lahore in March, when gunmen opened fire on the bus convoy carrying the Sri Lankan national team to a test match against Pakistan. The terrorists killed six policeman and two bystanders, and five members of the Sri Lankan team were injured. For Pakistan, this was the cusp of a wave of terrorism and insurgency that would deeply imprint on global consciousness—and cost tens of thousands of Pakistani lives.

The militant groups plaguing Pakistan can be categorized based on religious or nationalist inspirations, on their relationship to the Pakistan state, or on their targets.[7] Three of these clusters of violent actors are known to even the most casual observers, though the ties among them and the nuance in their composition, goals, and tactics might be less familiar.

The first group are internationally focused Islamist terrorists grounded in Salafist schools of Sunni Islam. These include al-Qaida and its come-later rival for jihadi leadership, the Islamic State of Iraq and the Levant/al-Sham (ISIL/ISIS). Although the authorship is still in question, al-Qaida may have played a role in the massive truck bombing of the Marriott Hotel in Islamabad in 2008, a blast that left 54 people dead (including three Americans), and over 250 wounded.[8]

No incident better epitomized Pakistan's twenty-first-century reputation as a dangerous place than the Marriott bombing. Official American visitors had been using the hotel heavily before the attack, and the bombers evidently hoped to cause foreign casualties. Despite al-Qaida's significant presence in the wilds of Pakistan in the 2000s, the group's attacks tended to align with the group's international focus rather than with targets representing Pakistan. An earlier al-Qaida attack in 2008 had hit the Danish Embassy in retaliation for the private publication in Denmark of cartoons negatively depicting Islam's prophet.[9]

Of the same flavor as al-Qaida is the branch of ISIS operating in Afghanistan and Pakistan, "ISIS-Khorasan" (ISIS-K or ISKP), which emerged around 2014. As with the core ISIS in the Middle East, ISIS-K shared a genealogy with al-Qaida but situated itself as a more committed and consistent carrier of armed and murderous jihad, against a broader range of targets. It gained early adherents and commanders from disaffected members of other militant groups operating in Afghanistan, including from the Taliban. It also offered better pay.

In Afghanistan, ISIS-K advanced a more violent and more apocalyptic program than could be tolerated by the nationalistic Afghan Taliban (longtime associates of al-Qaida). Unlike al-Qaida, which had pledged fealty to Mullah Omar and the Taliban, ISIS-K sought to supplant the Taliban. Consequently, the Taliban and ISIS-K fought for terrain and the allegiance of local leaders even as both targeted the Afghan government and allied forces in the country.

The ISIS fight became a distraction for the Taliban, to the point that the U.S.-backed Kabul government at times seemed to welcome ISIS, sparking conspiratorial charges in Pakistan that America was a quiet supporter of ISIS in Afghanistan. The charge had no merit, but it fit well with certain Pakistani narratives.

By 2018, before the Taliban victory over the Afghan government three years later, the combined pressure of the Taliban, Afghan security forces, and U.S. airstrikes had driven ISIS-K out of the territory it had occupied in eastern Afghanistan. It became a clandestine organization but remained large and potent, capable of sending out suicide attackers frequently. It opportunistically attacked the Kabul airport during the international evacuation, killing over 180, including 13 U.S. service personnel. It persists in attacking Shia targets and the Taliban regime.

In Pakistan, ISIS-K and its spinoff ISIS-Pakistan conducted a series of complex attacks: on lawyers in Quetta (2016, ninety-four dead), police cadets in Quetta (2016, sixty-one dead), Sufi (Sunni) shrines (for example, in 2017 at Sehwan, in Sindh, killing eighty-eight), voting stations (2018 in Quetta, killing thirty-one), and repeatedly against Shia mosques and markets. As with ISIS in other regions, ISIS-K acted on a broad list of targets, including governments, representatives of Western democracies, Shia, and jihadist rivals.

A second cluster of well-known violent actors associated with Pakistan includes the Afghanistan Taliban and the associated Haqqani Network. These fighters enjoyed refuge in Pakistan and support from its spy service, the ISI, while waging guerrilla war against the Afghan government and U.S. and allied forces in Afghanistan.

Pakistan's security planners had any number of reasons for tolerating or supporting these groups. Most determinative was its interest in them as a hedge against perceived pro-India groups in Afghanistan, including the "Northern Alliance" elements in the Karzai and Ghani governments. Unlike the Uzbeks and Tajiks of the north, the Taliban were mostly Pashtun, intimately linked to Pashtuns in Pakistan. Pakistan had history and some leverage with the Taliban, which had already demonstrated its bona fides in limiting India's presence during its rule in the 1990s.

A strong second reason for Pakistan's forbearance was that it rightly feared the cost of pursuing the Taliban in Pakistan, given the group's popularity and deep ties to the restless tribes and families of Pakistan's Pashtun areas. Even the restrained effort it made against the Taliban in the early days of the American Enduring Freedom intervention in Afghanistan led thousands of Pakistani Pashtuns to rebel against Islamabad.

Among the Taliban, the Haqqani family remains a unique entity, with strong and lasting ties to the ISI, al-Qaida, and a host of other militant groups it helped to train and arm since the 1970s. Its leaders today hold key positions in the Taliban regime. Chapter 11, on Afghanistan, offers more detail on the long ordeal of Pakistani tolerance for the Taliban and Haqqanis and the ways that this shaped the U.S.-Pakistan relationship and the Afghan conflict.

The third well-known cluster of militants encompasses the Kashmir-focused jihadists, sponsored by Pakistan's security establishment as asymmetrical weapons against rival India. Indian officials, and many Pakistanis, would define the largest of these groups, Lashkar-e-Taiba (LT), as a fully owned proxy of the Pakistani military, an entity that until 2019 ran its own mosques, ambulances, hospitals, and beneficent organizations in Pakistan. LT was responsible for the multipronged attack by ten gunmen on Mumbai, India, in December 2008, a terror that killed 164 people and paralyzed India's most important city for three days.

Even ten years later, we do not know whether the Mumbai attack was an operation sanctioned by Pakistan's military-intelligence leadership or the collateral consequence of "deep state" operators overstepping their authority, but it is evident that the attack received substantial support from within the government.[10] Then–Pakistan ambassador to the United States Hussain Haqqani wrote that the then–director general of the ISI, Lt. Gen. Ahmad Shujah Pasha, admitted to him privately the involvement of ISI-linked operatives but said Mumbai was not an "authorized ISI operation."[11] The attack challenged the worldview of rational Pakistanis long committed to militancy on behalf of Kashmir's liberation. It was another level of violence, repugnant to most. Some responded with denial, including the popular view in Pakistan that Mumbai was a "false flag" operation, orchestrated by India.

Less familiar in the West than the previous three clusters of terrorists are the amalgam of militias and tribal leaders that have sharply challenged the Pakistan state and nation: Tehrik-e-Taliban Pakistan (TTP), the "Pakistan Taliban." The TTP is a coalition of groups and clans that sometimes follows centralized leadership. It is focused on Pashtun ethnoreligious grievances against the Pakistan military and is linked by kinship to the Afghan Taliban. Unlike the nonviolent PTM, described in the previous chapter, which is comprised mostly of Pashtuns from settled cities and towns, the TTP's base is in the rugged highlands bordering Afghanistan.

The TTP traces its origins to 2002–3, when Pakistan security forces began operations against al-Qaida remnants in the rugged mountains of northwest Pakistan, areas long resistant to the control of British or Pakistani authorities. The United States encouraged the military operations, but they were heavy-handed and provocative to the local communities. By 2007, following a government assault on the militant Red Mosque in central Islamabad, significant elements of Pashtun resistance coalesced into the TTP and swelled in strength in Pakistan's formerly designated Federally Administered Tribal Areas (FATA) and parts of North-West Frontier Province (now Khyber-Pakhtunkhwa), including the idyllic Swat Valley, just over one hundred miles from Islamabad.[12]

The TTP was Pakistan's most costly militant challenge, a group that continues to find refuge in Afghanistan despite Pakistan's demands that the new Taliban regime control or expel them. Pakistan tried bargaining with the group more than once, deals that let the group seize more ground and claim more lives. The horrific and widely viewed violence of the TTP when it occupied Swat changed the dynamic, inspiring the army to intervene with force rather than negotiate.[13]

A fifth strand of violent actors in Pakistan are sectarian terrorists, primarily anti-Shia in orientation. Shia make up 15–20 percent of Pakistan's Muslim population, a large, sometimes beleaguered minority. Most prominent among the anti-Shia terrorist groups was the Afghanistan-based Lashkar-e-Jhangvi (LEJ), responsible for a host of attacks on the Shia community but also likely the 2009 attack on the Sri Lankan cricket team. It is also linked to the murder of *Wall Street Journal* reporter Daniel Pearl in 2002. In recent years, ISIS has intruded into LEJ's anti-Shia space, claiming responsibility for bigger anti-Shia attacks. Pakistan's military flirted with anti-Shia militants up to the 1990s but has turned against them since.[14]

Two other groups demand attention in this snapshot of Pakistan's violent actors. First, the ethnic Baloch insurgency described in the previous chapter, mounting attacks in Balochistan and Karachi. The causes are ethnonationalist, ranging from a desire for separate nationhood to grievances against the Pakistan government, military-run companies, and Chinese investors.

The other strand increasingly active in Pakistan are militants and protesters motivated to protect Islam from alleged insult and heresy. The largest of these groups, Tehreek-e-Labaik Pakistan (TLP), became a major challenge to the government after 2016, although its tactics are those of riotous disobedience rather than indiscriminate terrorist attack (more in chapter 14). Not to miss out, the TLP in 2020 also claimed its place in the anti-Shia world.[15] In recent years, the TTP (although Pashtun and from the Deobandi school of Islamic thought) has encouraged the TLP (largely

Punjabi and Sindhi, and from the Barelvi school), worrying some about a potential joining of two broad strands of extremist thought in Pakistan.

This survey of Pakistan's various Islamist and ethnonationalist tormentors leaves a key question unanswered. Why Pakistan? By most lights, its syncretic Barelvi tradition in Islam is far removed from the stark fundamentalist traditions in the Arab world that seemed to spawn the radical violence of al-Qaida, yet Pakistan has suffered more than most Muslim majority countries from Islamist terrorist violence.

The answer, not surprisingly, is complex and open to a great deal of debate. Among the contributors are a political system that has produced heads of government with limited legitimacy, leading many past rulers to appeal to a more conservative Islam to bolster their fortunes. As important, Pakistan's security establishment has long instrumentalized Islam, using it as a useful foundation through which to support strategically beneficial armed proxies against India or Afghanistan. Arguably, this state-sponsored ideology has leaked back into Pakistan's domestic politics. Since the 1857 "mutiny" against British rule in India, moreover, conservative Deobandi Islam has been invoked to rally resistance to the state, a tradition that continues with anti-government Islamist rebellions in Pakistan today.

A range of additional causes stand out as probable contributors—the Western and Saudi funding for an Islamist-based resistance to the Soviet occupation of Afghanistan in the 1980s, the influence of Saudi-funded Wahabi madrassas in Pakistan, and the limited economic prospects available to so many young men in the country. In short, Islamist violence is a curse with many fathers in Pakistan. Despite the many weaknesses, however, Pakistan appeared to steadily climb back toward safety and order through the late 2010s.

Pakistan's Hard and Incomplete Win

Most of these strands of political violence were present in Pakistan by 2009, when the attack on the Sri Lankan team took place. The Marriott bombing was recent and the attack on Mumbai just months away; the Pakistan Army was liberating the Swat Valley from the Pakistan Taliban, but the group still held towns and districts throughout northwest Pakistan. There were some terrorist bombings in urban areas, including Lahore,

Karachi, and the capital, Islamabad. Benazir Bhutto, then a candidate for prime minister, was murdered in December 2007 by a suicide bomber in Rawalpindi—probably by a variant of the TTP.[16] International cricket had reason to avoid the country.

Pakistan and India were among the planned hosts for the 2011 Cricket World Cup, scheduled to take place eighteen months after the Mumbai attack. This time Bangladesh and Sri Lanka were also hosting. For Pakistan and India, it was to be their third time as hosts. LT and their handlers in the Pakistan deep state may well have aspired to scuttle this sort of positive sports diplomacy. If that was the goal, Mumbai was superfluous; the attack on the Sri Lankan team was sufficient for the ICC to remove Pakistan as a host. That visit would be the last by international cricket for a decade.

By contrast, Sri Lanka reemerged by 2011 as a destination for adventure travelers and spa seekers. It hosted its World Cup cricket matches in 2011—twelve fixtures at three different venues. The matches came off peacefully, the enthusiasm of the crowds infectious in the broadcasts. Pakistan seemed a long way from such an opportunity as I watched the matches from Islamabad that year.

Throughout the 2010s, Pakistan "hosted" its international cricket matches in the United Arab Emirates, where at least the expatriate Pakistani workforce could cheer the team. Even more strikingly, Pakistan's domestic professional league played its matches there, so that teams representing Peshawar, Quetta, and Multan never played in their hometowns. Despite the strained local connection, the matches were a steady diet on Pakistani television, regularly broadcast in shops and coffee houses. The sport retained its popularity.

The second decade of this century was one of clawing back to a state of normalcy for Pakistan. Pakistan had cut disastrous deals with the TTP before 2010, but the group's brutality, including the executions of Pakistan Army prisoners, hardened the Pakistan military to develop a counterinsurgency capability.

Early on, Pakistan received direct support from the U.S. military. U.S. special operators collaborated with the Pakistanis while U.S. drones flown from Pakistani bases but controlled by Americans struck at the TTP and al-Qaida insurgents. America pressed Pakistan in these years, even promising to discourage any possible Indian aggression if Pakistan moved troops from their traditional deployments on the eastern border with India to the northwest to take on the pro-Taliban insurgents.[17]

The militants were brutal. They struck girls' schools, mosques, shrines, and churches with machine guns or suicide belts. Markets in cities like Peshawar and Quetta became dangerous. In some cases, foreign militants were the principal operatives in TTP-claimed attacks—Afghans, Uzbeks, even Uyghurs from China—underscoring the worrisome presence of hundreds of al-Qaida-linked foreign fighters in Pakistan.

The low point is easy to identify: In 2014, even as elements in the new PML-N government, as well as Imran Khan's political movement, the PTI, were encouraging new negotiations with the TTP, the group committed a string of atrocities. They slaughtered at least two dozen captive soldiers, on video, in early 2014; conducted a brazen attack on Jinnah International Airport in Karachi in June, killing 36; and then, in December, attacked an army public school near Peshawar, killing 149 children and teachers. Even before the army school attack, Pakistan's security establishment had gotten more serious about the TTP, launching clearing operations in the TTP stronghold of North Waziristan.[18]

I was serving in Washington at the time of the TTP attacks: deputy director for the State Department's Office of Terrorism Analysis in the Bureau of Intelligence and Research. Although Pakistan often blamed the former Afghan government and India for alleged support to the TTP, there were no direct links between Afghanistan or India and these attacks. Whatever modest foreign support the TTP might have gathered in Afghanistan, the group was still fundamentally Pakistan's creation and challenge. Over the next three years, Pakistan's military succeeded in weakening the group.

Journalist Anatol Levin describes the Peshawar school attack as an inflection point changing the nature of Pakistan's counterinsurgency effort by giving it popular legitimacy.[19] In the early 2000s, the public questioned the army's ventures into FATA. Commentators and politicians argued the costly operations were responsive not to Pakistan's interests but to American demands. The Pakistan Army, moreover, had trained and structured itself to fight India in a conventional war rather than domestic militants through counterinsurgency. It quickly committed most of the familiar mistakes—using too light a footprint to secure territory, committing provocative abuses, and departing too early, thereby jeopardizing the lives of any tribal elders who had collaborated with them.

Until the Peshawar massacre, many questioned the wisdom of persisting in counterinsurgency. During these years, the intensive American drone campaign may have helped stave off disaster, removing TTP leaders and attack plotters and disrupting the group.[20]

After the Peshawar army school massacre, civilian politicians came into line as public support for the TTP evaporated.[21] The Pakistan Army, by this point, had also become better at counterinsurgency. It moved with force into FATA and moved civilians out of the way. It avoided rape and looting, but also indiscriminately eliminated problematic young men. Those insurgents or suspects not killed in action were afforded minimal due process in detention.

The abrogation of some basic rights was embodied in the Twenty-First Amendment to the Pakistan Constitution, a simple directive establishing military trials for terrorism suspects. In the wake of the army school massacre, Pakistan's politicians had supported the measure without objection.

Pakistan's military tribunals were secret and unfair—often "confessions" extracted under torture were the grounds for convictions, and death sentences were common.[22] The extraordinary measure had been given a two-year sunset clause but was extended for two more years in 2017.

In 2019 my embassy political section kept close watch on the politics surrounding another proposed extension of the military tribunals. The department's annual human rights reports had described our concerns about these courts, but we took no position on the proposed extension, in part because no good could come from American advocacy on such an issue.

Terrorism, by this point, had dropped significantly in Pakistan. Unable to muster support in Parliament, the government let the measure lapse. By 2020, however, Pakistan faced unsurprising legal challenges—prisoners were lawyering up and appealing their military court convictions through the regular judicial system.[23]

Another decisive measure taken by the government in its counterinsurgency and counterterrorism push was the construction of fencing along Pakistan's rugged 1600-mile border with Afghanistan. The fencing was expensive and ambitious in remote and sometimes hostile borderlands (see map 2, p. 101). Pashtun families and tribes had lived connected, bestriding the line, for generations, conducting business that was legitimate (herding) or tolerated (smuggling). The entire border remains in official dispute between Pakistan and Afghanistan, moreover, and Afghanistan, even under the Taliban, questions the de facto border in some stretches. To effectively block movement through a valley or across a mountain pass, Pakistan at times strayed into Afghan territory to build the fence, risking a clash between its forces and those of the American-backed Afghan military, later the Taliban.

The fencing project was risky for Pakistan's relations with the Taliban insurgency, which relied on easy access to its Pakistani safe haven. The fence caused some complications but ones that local military and customs officials learned to evade. "Good" Taliban could pass through. For the TTP, which conversely uses Afghanistan as a rear base, the fence was a constraint, making it harder to ferry supplies and fighters back and forth. TTP attacks dropped significantly until 2020, and the fence may have been a factor.[24]

From 2013 to 2019, civilian deaths from terrorism fell sharply in Pakistan, from over 2700 deaths in both 2012 and 2013 to 142 in 2019.[25] There had been horrendous bombings in the run-up to elections in 2018, but, overall, the Pakistan I returned to that year was much safer than it had been during my previous tour, seven years before.

The cost of the long conflict and the price of the military's success has been the highest for the people living in the border regions. Regional conflict expert Simbal Khan describes some of the most severe consequences, including violence against vulnerable populations and massive flows of internally displaced people. The heavy securitization of the border, including fencing, has cut sharply at livelihoods.[26]

All of Pakistan paid a heavy price as well, including the diversion of government resources, military casualties, and forgone growth and development. The army, feeling deeply its sacrifice in these campaigns, seems also to have emerged less tolerant than ever of Pakistan's political parties. The deep state has curtailed press and academic freedoms. If Pakistan in 2018 was safer than before, it was also less free. The price of its success in the war on domestic terror was a state more than ever under the thumb of military direction.

In late 2021, TTP attacks in the borderlands were again on the uptick, a suggestion that the Taliban's win in Afghanistan may not have resolved Pakistan's militant problem. Previously, in 2018, the TTP had returned to the historically dominant Mehsud clan in selecting their fourth leader. Mufti Noor Wali Mehsud has since reunited splintered factions of the group and attempted to rehabilitate its image in Pakistan by focusing primarily on military targets. It has acceded sufficiently to Afghan Taliban demands that it negotiate with the Pakistan government to sustain its safe haven in Afghanistan, all the while continuing strikes on Pakistani targets. Though formally involved in an indefinite ceasefire with Pakistan, its demands in talks far exceed what Pakistan can entertain, suggesting that conflict will continue.[27]

The Taliban, meanwhile, faces competing interests when it comes to the TTP—satisfying its most important bilateral partner, Pakistan, to be sure, but also potentially sustaining a proxy force to leverage Pakistan when needed. More importantly, the Taliban is likely reluctant to risk turning the battle-hardened TTP into domestic enemies in Afghanistan. In short, the price to fully bring the group under control may prove higher than the Taliban regime is prepared to bear.

Though a much safer place in 2022 than a decade before, Pakistan remains at risk from the many strands of militant Islamism it has tolerated or sponsored at different points in its history. Sri Lanka is also much improved from the bloody decades of the 1990s and 2000s, but in 2019 terror returned. On Easter Sunday, ten attackers struck four different sites in Colombo and two more in other cities. Three bombs went off in packed Christian churches, three more in hotels. As bad as LTTE terrorism had been, the Easter 2019 attacks were startling in their coordination and their focus on a specific faith and holiday. The death toll was 269.

The Easter attacks were conducted by a local radical Islamist group, one that drew inspiration from ISIS. The event was a rare and shocking instance of terrorism emerging from Sri Lanka's traditional, small, and prosperous urban Muslim community (distinct from the Tamil Muslims, who suffer much the same prejudice as Hindu Tamils). It was appalling in its carnage, but it did not signal the beginning of a wave.

The ISIS playbook since 2015 has been to exploit, in a one- or two-shot spree, the most susceptible and alienated potential recruits in a particular country. Attacks by individuals or small groups struck France, Germany, Australia, Bangladesh, Thailand, the United States, and others, and then the violence dissipated. Better policing was in part responsible, but the one-and-done incidents suggest that in most countries there is a finite supply of young, malleable men and women willing to kill innocents.

In South Asia, the frightening ISIS-linked attacks in Dhaka, Bangladesh, and Colombo, Sri Lanka, did not inspire new ones. Locally generated attacks in India have been small. Law enforcement and other security efforts deserve the credit, but the truth is al-Qaida and ISIS in South Asia have found few recruits among huge Muslim populations in the region—outside the areas of perpetual conflict along the Afghanistan-Pakistan border and in Kashmir. Whether the Taliban's victory and its links to al-Qaida will change that dynamic is uncertain.

Cricket's Corrupt Blemishes

Apart from each having its own history of national violence menacing the sport, Pakistan and Sri Lanka share similar highs and lows on the pitch. Both countries have won the World Cup tournament once, Pakistan in 1992 and Sri Lanka four years later. Pakistan was runner-up in 1999 and Sri Lanka twice, in 2007 and 2011. Although Sri Lanka arrived on the scene later, both countries have a flair for developing transcendent talent. By the twenty-first century, however, both countries had also come to know the trauma of seeing star players succumb to greed or need, taking money to deliver something less than their best.

Cricket today attracts billions in gambling wagers, much of it in India. Wagers can be small-scale but given the size of India they build to massive sums. Such gambling is officially illegal in India but not aggressively pursued, the norm in most of the cricketing world. Where goes gambling so too unscrupulous bookies and mobsters looking for an edge, offering bribes to players to alter a match.

These temptations for the players from South Asia can be strong, although there have been match-fixing scandals in every major cricketing country. For a young Pakistani or Sri Lankan, life at the apex of the sport

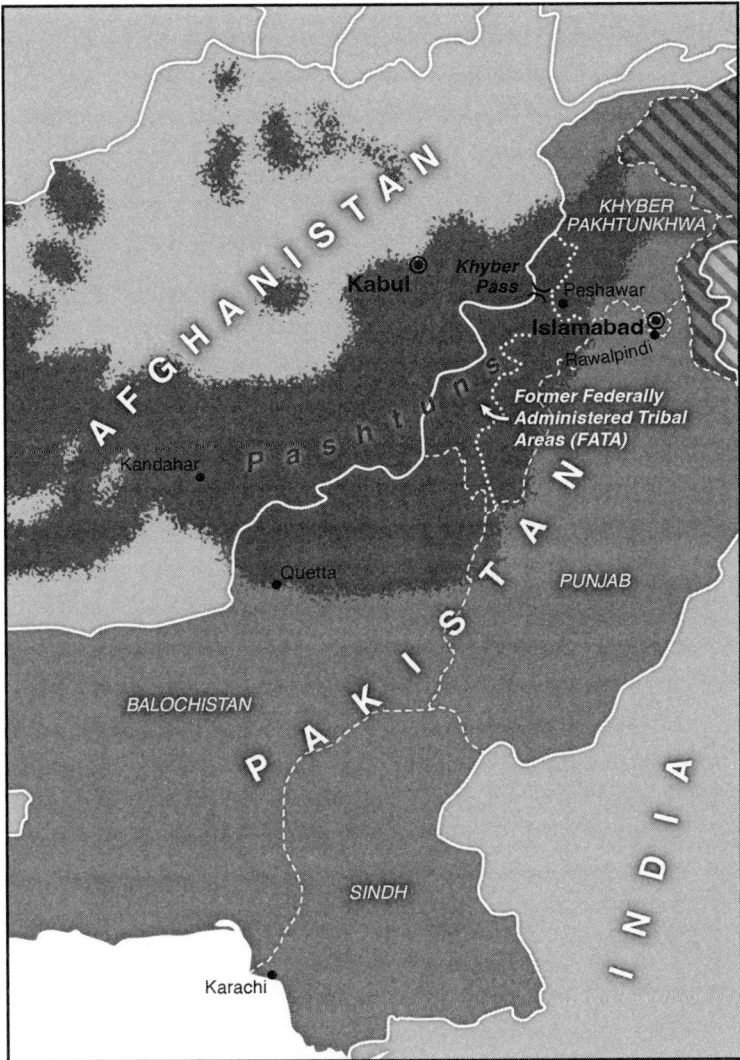

Map 2. Afghanistan-Pakistan border.

may be fleeting, just a few years. National salaries have come up and star players earn good wages, but it is not lifelong employment.

In the stratified societies of South Asia, people experience few opportunities for upward mobility. In Pakistan, former military men or the politically connected sit throughout industry, commerce, and government, limiting the prospects of others. A successful cricket player in either country may feel pressure to exploit his fleeting time at the top; he may be the only member of his family for several generations with the opportunity to make money and change a family's circumstances.[28]

For Pakistan, the most painful incident of alleged match fixing occurred in 1999, when experts gave the strong national team good odds to win the World Cup. Instead, Pakistan went out meekly against Australia in the final in London, scoring an abysmal 132 runs, "all out" after 39 of their 50 allotted overs. Pakistani law enforcement had trailed the team in London through nights of carousing and drinking in the run-up to the final. At the least, several players were in poor shape for the Sunday final.[29] But Pakistanis to this day will tell you there was more involved and can replay deliveries and swings that suggested the fix was in.

The disappointing outcome added luster to the memory of Imran Khan as a player, captain of the victorious 1992 squad. He had been controversial throughout his playing years, criticized for spending too much time with attractive women or chasing a high salary in Australia, but he led Pakistan to a championship.

Khan too was accused of cheating, but only, to my knowledge, of cheating to win, something viewed quite differently from deliberately throwing a match for a payoff. The common accusation against Khan and other Pakistani star bowlers in the 1980s was that they illegally damaged the balls to gain more movement from their delivery. Pakistani fans did not complain, no doubt confident that everyone did such things. What mattered was that Khan won. Nobody accused him credibly of missing a catch or bowling a "no-ball" on purpose. This reputation allowed him to emerge as an attractive political leader by the 2010s, building his party around an anticorruption agenda.

Pakistan cricket took a hit again in 2010 with the "spot-fixing" scandal described in the prologue. The scandal suggested the tip of an iceberg, but there were few additional bans or convictions.

For Sri Lanka, match-fixing corruption arose more recently, in 2017, when the national team lost a series to Zimbabwe. After investigations, several Sri Lankan players received bans. The national legislature then passed the first ever cricket-specific match-fixing law, establishing jail time and financial penalties for the offense. Coming into the 2019 World Cup, Sri Lanka was still recovering from the scandal. Its middling performance—in the hunt for a semifinal spot but falling short—was a good outcome under the circumstances.

Cricket Returns

In December 2019 Sri Lanka returned for matches in Pakistan, the first international test cricket in the country since Sri Lanka last appeared there in 2009. Or not the first. In January of that year, the West Indies' women had come to play Pakistan in Karachi, their team spokeswoman lauding the hospitality of their hosts and safe playing conditions. I am not writing about the women's side in this book because I did not see as much of it and it does not resonate as significantly for Pakistan's place in the politics of South Asia. I note with admiration, however, that the Pakistani women have overcome much to establish their deserved place. Their matches are well played, available regularly on cable television in Pakistan, and covered in the print media. The women's game is important in Pakistan, which is progress.

The men's short two-match test series with Sri Lanka resulted in one draw and one win for the home side, in Lahore. The results were surely less important than the venue. Pakistan was again, finally, a destination for international cricket.

WORLD CUP MATCH RESULT, PAKISTAN VS. SRI LANKA
Abandoned without a ball bowled; rain.

7   HOSTAGE DIPLOMACY

June 12, 2019, County Ground Taunton
Pakistan (1-1-1 [win-loss-draw]), 3 points, vs. Australia (2-1), 4 points

Australia is to the Cricket World Cup what Brazil is to soccer's, having won five of the twelve international iterations, including three straight between 1999 and 2007. It won its fifth in 2015, at home, beating tournament cohost New Zealand in the final. In the test format, Australia has been Pakistan's most frequent competitor after England. Pakistan's record of 15 wins against 31 losses and 18 draws is its worst against a long-standing rival.

One might assume that all this Australian winning has nurtured a lasting Pakistani grudge, particularly because Australia is easily linked to the British Empire's familiar racial issues. Australia was for three decades after World War II guarded by "white Australia" immigration preferences, and the teams today are still nearly all white. Some of its players and fans, well into the 1990s, were not above racially tinged trash talk. As Australia gradually diversified, cricket for some social conservatives came to symbolize the country's white, Anglo heritage.[1]

Australians were also akin to the English in judging their own gamesmanship as above-board and the tactics of the sport's emerging teams as "not cricket." Australian players scorned the Pakistanis for "whingeing" (complaining dramatically) and insisted Pakistani umpiring was biased.

Australia intimidated cricket rivals in the 1970s with fast bowling and "bouncers" aimed at batsmen's heads. Through the mid-1970s, the more polite "tourists" from countries like Pakistan and the West Indies tended to take the abuse—until they stopped. The West Indies recruited and developed a cadre of fast bowlers after a humiliating series loss to Australia in 1975–76, going on to win the next series and starting a period of long dominance. Pakistan also learned to dish it out. Samiuddin vividly describes Imran Khan's transformation between the first and second innings of a test match at Sydney in 1977 from a proper English swing-bowler to an aggressive pace bowler, attacking the Australian batsmen.[2]

Despite the salty match history, however, I heard little Pakistani animus toward their Australian rivals. One reason is that Pakistani cricket fans admire success as much as any, and Australia has maintained an unsurpassed winning standard in cricket, the most consistently successful team since World War II. That Australia often took the English down a peg could not have hurt in Pakistani estimations.

Throughout the Cold War and into the "global war on terrorism," Australia was as close as any country to the United States, an unpopular stance in Pakistan. The country's small diplomatic and military footprint probably mitigated much blowback. As did diplomacy. My Australian counterparts were excellent and engaging diplomats who put themselves out into the Pakistani community. Finally, somewhere in the calculus, Pakistanis have a warm association with Melbourne, the site of Pakistan's most important international triumph, at the 1992 World Cup.

Melbourne Glory

For Imran Khan, a superstar past his prime, 1992 was a final chance, as it was for the great batsman Javed Miandad, who, like Khan, had played on all the previous Pakistan World Cup teams—1975, 1979, 1983, and 1987. It was in the previous Cup that expectations had been highest for the team. India and Pakistan had cohosted that tournament, the first played outside England. It was a watershed moment, when the ICC had begun to share royalties more equally among the participating countries. Imran was captain of a team that had become one of the most feared of the 1980s, and Pakistan looked forward to competing for the title in the final in Kolkata.

Pakistan advanced easily to the semifinal, contested on home soil in Lahore, and then suffered a wrenching 18-run defeat to Australia. Both its bowling and batting fell short. Imran was still a stellar fast bowler at that point and took 17 wickets in the tournament, but his heroics in the Lahore match were late and muted. On the other side of the bracket, India lost its semifinal match to England, also on its own home turf in Mumbai. South Asia, having grabbed World Cup hosting rights at the ICC, had the misfortune of seeing England and Australia play for the title in Kolkata. Australia won the match, the first of its five championships.

At the next World Cup, five years later, hosted by Australia and New Zealand, Pakistan stumbled out of the gate and then crashed into the rails. After the first five matches, it had one win. In order, it had lost to the West Indies, beat Zimbabwe, escaped a losing position against England with a rained-out draw, and then lost to India and South Africa. Another loss would eliminate any chance of getting to the knockout round, and next up was the home team and defending champion, Australia. It was before that match, in Perth, that legend says captain Khan rallied his team, insisting they had "nothing to lose" and should "fight like cornered tigers." In an edgy match, Pakistan won by 48 runs. It followed that with a narrow win over Sri Lanka.

Going into the final day of group play, Pakistan needed to beat undefeated New Zealand, in Christchurch, to advance. It also needed Australia, with no chance of advancing, to beat the West Indies. Both happened, and Pakistan found itself as the fourth seed in the knockout round, facing an immediate rematch with top seed New Zealand. This time the match was in Auckland, again on New Zealand's home turf. Once again Pakistan pulled off the improbable, advancing on a clutch batting partnership of Javed Miandad and Inzamam-ul-Haq. New Zealand was out, having lost just twice in the tournament—both times to Pakistan, both times at home.

On the other side of the bracket, England advanced past South Africa on a complicated rain rule so patently unfair that the ICC jettisoned it soon afterward. The newly christened South African "Proteas," formerly the Springboks, had emerged from apartheid isolation in their first-ever Cricket World Cup, to come within a narrowly disputed margin of making the final.

Facing England in the final, Pakistan lost two batsmen before Imran and Javed steadied the team with a successful run scoring partnership of 139. Imran benefited from a dropped ball, a chance England should not have missed. (At the end of his career, Khan remained a formidable batsman.) In total, Pakistan scored 249, a good but still vulnerable target for England.

At bat, England's great all-rounder Ian Botham, long compared to Khan but also, at this point, past his best, was dismissed "for a duck" (no runs).

England then began to gain momentum to the point that Khan brought bowler Wasim Akram back earlier than planned. One of the greatest ever left-armed fast bowlers, Akram bowled two masterly balls in quick succession for wickets. England was on the ropes. Imran would give himself the challenge and honor of picking up the final wicket.

The win cemented Khan's hero status in Pakistan and allowed him to complete the fundraising to finish a national cancer hospital in Lahore dedicated to his late mother. Critics panned his victory speech for its failure to appreciate his teammates, but the win still built a foundation for his long-shot political career.

Australia and Pakistan

The Australia-Pakistan bilateral relationship is unique in that cricket is one of its biggest elements. Cricket dominates any search engine results for relations between the two countries. But there is more. For Australia, Pakistan is an Indian Ocean neighbor, bordering problematic Afghanistan and sitting close to the oil artery of the Persian Gulf. Both countries were members of U.S.-led anti-Soviet alliances throughout the Cold War. In recent years, Australia has shared the West's concern about Pakistan as an incubator of extremism.

Australia also stayed the course in Afghanistan, side by side with American soldiers. Supplies to those troops passed through Pakistan, and Pakistan's problematic role as refuge and patron of the Afghan Taliban was as concerning for Australia as for America. Afghanistan was the top issue when I met with my Australian counterparts in Islamabad.

Outside of the security relationship, and the cricket, there is a modest Pakistani expatriate community in Australia. The numbers in Australia, some 60,000 to 70,000, are not huge, though on a per capita basis the Pakistani community in Australia is larger than that in the United States.

Cutting Deals with Terrorists

While Afghanistan was the first topic of conversation with my Australian counterparts over both tours, we spent considerable time in 2018 and 2019 working for the release of Kevin King and Timothy Weeks, an American and an Australian kidnapped together by the Taliban in 2016 while working as professors at the American University in Kabul. They were held by the Taliban or by its Haqqani Network faction, the latter closely tied to Pakistani intelligence. Their captors moved them frequently within the borderlands of Afghanistan and Pakistan. At any moment, we suspected, the hostages might have been in a remote hut or even a small city in Pakistan's northwest or Afghanistan's southeast.

This constant movement in the borderlands had been the case with a prominent American-Canadian couple held by the Haqqanis between 2012 and 2017. Caitlin Coleman and Joshua Boyle had been kidnapped in Afghanistan and were ultimately discovered in Pakistan (by an American drone, according to *New York Times* reporting).[3] After the family was discovered, the United States reportedly contemplated a unilateral rescue but instead prevailed on Pakistan to mount a military operation to free the couple (and their three children, all born in captivity). The Pakistani operation was a success, with all the captives rescued unharmed; suspiciously, the Haqqani captors escaped.

The repatriation of the Coleman-Boyle family was a challenge. Boyle complicated their departure with odd demands. Most significantly, Caitlin Coleman maintains that Boyle was abusive of her while they were in captivity. She quickly divorced him following their return and took custody of their children. A Canadian court later acquitted Boyle of the abuse charges.

Although the Coleman-Boyle circumstances were unique, some of that experience informed conversations with our Australian colleagues about what would be needed when King and Weeks were freed. Discussions focused on issues such as post-traumatic stress counseling, immediate health needs (King was in his sixties with health problems), and whether they would fly together and, if so, in which direction.

The preparations for King and Weeks were an example of good bureaucracy at work—the U.S. Embassy hostage team, led by the deputy chief of mission (DCM) and run by the diplomatic security office, included the consular section (in charge of the welfare of private American citizens in the country), my political section (liaising with the Pakistan Foreign Ministry), the health unit (preparing for predeparture needs), management (money and logistics), public affairs (both fending off and appropriately informing the press), the defense attaché–military cooperation group (flight clearances, potential military airlift, coordination with the Resolute Support Mission in Afghanistan if the captives were released there), the legal attaché (FBI), in charge of liaising with families and building legal charges against kidnappers, and a number of additional embassy elements. When the Australian DCM had a quiet reception to honor the U.S. Embassy elements and Australian counterparts working for the pair's release, his house was full. Despite the sport that politicians make attacking government service (typically excepting only the uniformed military), the safety of Americans overseas is the responsibility of a range of civilian and military agencies, with committed employees setting aside everything to protect U.S. citizens.

King and Weeks's fate had become wrapped up in the Afghanistan peace talks, with their release demanded by our side as a goodwill gesture on the part of the Taliban. Pakistan signaled that diplomacy for their release should fit within the U.S.-Taliban talks led by Ambassador Khalilzad. The Taliban too wanted a release of prisoners, including the youngest son of the Haqqani Network founder, held by the government of Afghanistan.

The Taliban released King and Weeks in late 2019. Afghan authorities simultaneously released several Haqqani prisoners, including Anas Haqqani. The deal was tough for Kabul, even though the Taliban released a handful of Afghan military captives. Afghan pundits criticized President Ashraf Ghani for releasing terrorists who had victimized Afghans. He did it, he said, as an investment in the peace process.[4]

The King and Weeks negotiation was yet another proof that the United States does "negotiate" with terrorists. We try to avoid political concessions to hostage takers, but even that is not always possible. We are cognizant that any negotiation may encourage future hostage taking and try to set up guardrails to prevent the incentive from taking hold (without much success). When possible, most Americans (and her diplomats) would prefer a brilliant armed raid that frees the captives and eliminates the terrorists. But the Entebbe Option is not always available. Diplomats and legal attachés know they will not get much praise for the arduous work of negotiating a release, but most will do what is needed.

Australia Jumps on Pakistan's Mistakes

Preparing for its June 12 match against Australia, the Pakistani side knew it was important. Powerful India was up next, so Pakistan sought a win against Australia to stay close to the top of the table. Bowling first, however, Pakistan quickly let the match get away; Australia's two opening batsmen put up 189 runs between them. Amid the onslaught, Pakistan missed catches that compounded the damage, errors "criminal enough to have interested the local constabulary" in Danyal Rasool's biting ESPN review of the match.[5] Muhammad Amir steadied the contest, taking five wickets for only 30 runs in his ten overs, the best mark in the tournament to that point. All told, Australia scored 307 runs.

At bat, Pakistan was inconsistent, striking 14 "fours" between their first and third batsman but also giving up cheap wickets on overly aggressive or lackadaisical swings. A late, productive partnership between captain Sarfaraz Ahmed and Wahab Riaz gave hope, but when the two fell and only the bowlers remained in the batting order, Pakistan's fate was sealed. It lost by 41 runs, "all out." Australia moved up in the standings. Pakistan drifted down.

In beating England and losing to Australia, both in reasonably close fixtures, Pakistan seemed to underscore its middling quality in 2019. Like the country, it had recovered significantly from its disastrous match-fixing lows, but it was not as strong as hoped.

MATCH RESULT

Australia 309
Pakistan 268 (45.4 overs)
Australia won by 41 runs.

8   A DOGFIGHT OVER KASHMIR

June 16, 2019, Old Trafford, Manchester
Pakistan (1-2-1), 3 points, vs. India (2-0-1), 5 points

Cricket matches between Pakistan and India are enthusiastically anticipated and frequently disappointing. In rare test series, the draw has been
the biggest winner—64 percent of the time—as one or the other squad
played to avoid the opprobrium of defeat rather than take chances for a
win. In no other match history between test countries does the draw rate
exceed 50 percent, but then no other bilateral cricket relationship occurs
with a backdrop of national conflict on par with that of Pakistan-India:
three-and-a-half wars, countless skirmishes, and persistent allegations
of the other's support for insurgents and terrorists.

In the cricket World Cups, the disappointment has been exclusively
Pakistan's, zero-for-six against India before 2019 despite the historic
parity between the two programs. In 2019 India was again favored, but
Pakistan's surprising victory over India two years before at the ICC Champions Trophy gave some cause for hope. Once again, the match followed
a conflict, in this case the February 2019 aerial combat between Pakistan
and India.

India and Pakistan are unique among cricketing countries in that they
once played together, as British India. India inherited the colony's test
status at independence, and Pakistan had to regain it, something it did
in just five years. In October 1952 Pakistan sent a team to India for its
first international test series; it lost the series 2–1 but recorded its first
international match win, in Lucknow. The shock result led some Indian
fans to pelt their own team with stones and insults, a portent of the angry
crowds that would occasionally bedevil matches in both Pakistan and
India. National pride was at stake for citizens in both countries.

For India, it seems, cricket entrenched itself more slowly as a repository of national pride and identity, with several decades of indifferent results after independence. It remained an off-brand product at least to 1983. In the first two World Cup competitions (1975 and 1979), India won just a single match. As entertainingly portrayed in the recent movie '83, expectations were low for the Indian team heading to the third World Cup, but India shocked the cricketing world and won the championship. Their journey included winning two out of three matches against the reigning champions, the West Indies, including in the final, withstanding that team's wicked pace bowling and legendary hitting. India beat host England in the semifinals.

The 1983 World Cup was a breakthrough, but Indian cricket was slow to capitalize. Poor play in away matches and corruption scandals slowed the sport's growth. Then it changed. The team went through a transformation akin to what the West Indies and Pakistan had done earlier, setting aside niceties for a focus on winning. As the team toughened under captain Sourav Ganguly, its selectors began to focus more on merit than connections in building the national team. The results came quickly.

Among the early, epochal wins was a victory over a strong Pakistan side at the 2003 World Cup in South Africa, a victory in which batting great Sachin Tendulkar squared off against some of Pakistan's strongest-ever bowlers and scored 98, part of his record haul of 673 runs in the tournament.[1] This was the first India-Pakistan match in the wake of the bitter 1999 Kargil War, and it meant much more to home audiences than just sport. In just a few years cricket had cemented itself, as described in Boria Majumdar's history of the sport in India, into a vessel for "aggressive nationalism."[2]

The other great transformation in Indian cricket at the turn of the twenty-first century was the massive financial and media expansion created by India's economic transformation. India already possessed the world's biggest national cricket audience by far; now it was adding new riches.

In 2008 the Board of Control for Cricket in India (BCCI) and entrepreneur Lalit Modi founded the India Premier League (IPL), a short-form (T20) version of the game in which each side receives a maximum of twenty overs. The matches lasted two to three hours, perfect for busy working fans to take in at night. The league was built around a free agent model and privately owned teams bidding for the services of cricketing greats. Revenue generated by the IPL in its first year more than doubled the income of the BCCI. In 2018 the IPL brought in $1.5 billion in sponsorship revenue (compared to $938 million that year by Major League Baseball in America).[3] India was booming in the 2010s, and so was cricket.

Cricket's pride of place in the growing economy of what was fast becoming the world's most populous country has made the BCCI a powerhouse in international cricket. Where India and the rest of the world had to challenge England and Australia for influence in the ICC as recently as the 1990s, today India is the senior partner. It dwarfs Pakistan, as well, in terms of revenue and influence. In 2023 India would host the 2023 World Cup, for the first time without South Asian cohosts.

In a contest held in England, the pitch is level between Pakistan and India. The Pakistani diaspora in England is not much smaller than that of India, and the crowd was evenly divided when Manchester hosted the June 16 India-Pakistan contest, a match scheduled long in advance and the one with the most in-demand tickets before the tournament semifinals.[4] Pakistani friends had arranged trips to the World Cup in England, and this was the match they wanted to see.

Once again, however, the match lacked for drama, and Pakistan lost without much of a fight. It was too complete a defeat even for conspiracy theories to take hold. Later in the tournament, however, Pakistanis were able to scratch the Indian conspiracy itch, finding anti-Pakistan subterfuge in the result of another contest, India's match against England.

A Uniquely Unhappy Family

There is no bilateral relationship in the world today that can match the complexity and danger inherent in Pakistan-India ties. The maladies are legion and the redeeming strengths few. Territorial disputes, sectarian conflict, terrorism, and the threat of nuclear weapons top the list, but there are multiple second- and third-tier problems as well, such as disputed water rights, fishing disputes, and rampant espionage. The lack of trade and personal travel between the countries limits the ameliorative benefits of connection and dialogue.

Few Pakistanis I met in Islamabad had been to India. Cricketers were sometimes the exception, though there were stretches of years and decades when the two sides did not compete against one another. Western governments sometimes sponsored dialogue between Pakistan and India, often informal "track 2" formats, shorthand for dialogue between well-connected but unofficial representatives of the two countries, often retired military officers and diplomats. The talks were useful, sometimes paving the way for substantive progress, but the absence of broader connections between the countries meant these efforts were isolated and tenuous. Reconciliation was also hampered by a history of war and conflict. Partition was part of the story, in particular the "unresolved" status of Kashmir. This history is ever present and shaped the dangerous events of 2019.

Partition's Shadows

To an outsider new to the region, it is quickly evident that the partition of India is still present today. It was the solution advocated by the Muslim League of Pakistan's founder, Mohammad Ali Jinnah, and opposed by the Congress Party of Jawaharlal Nehru.

Partition meant different things to different advocates, but most expected it to include the separation of Muslim-dominated areas on both edges of colonial India—the western edge, dominated by the Indus River, and some part of the Bengali heartland in the east, near the mouths of the Ganges and Brahmaputra rivers. How partition would deal with Hindus in these areas, or with millions of Muslims in the center of northern India, or with "princely states" in southern India ruled by Muslims, was unclear. So too was the fate of Muslim-majority, Hindu-ruled Kashmir.[5] Once the British endorsed separation, they dispatched a team headed by a lawyer with no experience in the region to hastily draw lines.

After centuries of exploitative rule, Britain's decision to depart quickly in 1947 proved costly. No slowing could have prevented calamity, but the decision to provide just enough military force to cover its own retreat meant there was no protection for local populations. As the once intertwined cities and villages of Hindus, Muslims, and Sikhs sorted themselves out, vulnerable families and communities could find protection only through the militias of coreligionists. As in many such environments the world over, aggression often replaced defense as the way to protect the community.

The violence uprooted tens of millions as the two countries came into existence. Families moved with the complete loss of their property. Millions were killed. Violence against women was loosed, as so often is the case in intercommunal strife.[6] The two new countries also immediately fell into their first war, over the fate of Kashmir. That Pakistan and India were able to play a cricket match as early as 1952 is remarkable.

With partition, Pakistan inherited only small populations of Hindus and Christians. It immediately fulfilled the dream of a Muslim state. India retained a sizable Muslim minority and most of the subcontinent's Sikhs. For some decades, its leadership was committed formally to the promise of a state where the full range of Indian faith groups could coexist and share power. In more recent years, politically empowered Hindu nationalism has called that vision into question.[7]

One retired Pakistan Air Force general detailed to me the standard case for separation, emphasizing that his father had left family lands in India to join Pakistan at partition, traveling with only a suitcase. In the next generation, sons became generals, industry leaders, and senior government officials; across the border, where much of the family remained, the most successful cousin was a local government clerk. India, he was certain, was not a land of opportunity for its Muslim minority.

As inspiring as are the "nothing but a suitcase" stories, many of the Urdu speakers who migrated to Pakistan came with advantages of education, connections, and even class, helping them succeed. It is also likely that the lives of poor Muslims on either side of the line changed little with partition. This book will not venture a statistical study of the two Muslim communities and the variables that might have generated different outcomes. What is most germane to the politics of the subcontinent is the mythology of separation in Pakistan's popular imagination, in which partition stands as necessary, beneficial, and incomplete.

Despite the bloodbath of partition, the future relations of the two states might have gone better but for two great obstacles. One was the shape of Pakistan, divided between East (now Bangladesh) and West Pakistan, separated by over 1000 miles of India. Even though Pakistan had a smaller population and smaller army, for India the strategic prospect of a hostile power on both flanks was not a pleasant one.

India played a crucial, though perhaps not determinative, role in Bangladesh's breakaway in 1971. The separation owed more to the geographic impossibility of such a divided Pakistan, comprised of quite different peoples of equal populations. It also was fated by West Pakistan's domineering and at times abusive governance of East Pakistan. The 1971 war left another legacy of India-Pakistan grievance, to be sure, but few Pakistanis today obsess about the loss of Bangladesh—it was always a different country.

Kashmir

The second issue, Kashmir, was even more destructive of relations between the two countries and remains an issue capable of drawing the United States into an unsought mediating role. Kashmir had a long and disputed history prior to independence, ruled by Hindus, Mughals, an Afghan Empire, and Sikhs before falling under British indirect rule under the Raja of Jammu, a Hindu. Its population was about three-quarters Muslim, according to the last census under British rule. Muslims still predominate, particularly in the heart of Kashmir, the valley, radiating from the city of Srinagar.

Look on any relief map of the imposing Himalayan range running the length of northern India, and the Vale of Kashmir stands out, a flat expanse running eighty miles north–south and twenty miles wide, surrounded by rugged high mountains. It is an isolated oasis on the subcontinent, with a cool, moderate climate, well-watered and fertile. It is an orchard and a breadbasket. From its surrounds rise the great rivers of Pakistan, the Indus and Chenab. For both India and Pakistan at independence, it was a prize.

The will of its people at independence was uncertain, even among its poor and oppressed Muslim majority, with some favoring accession to Pakistan and others favoring India, or something in between, like a separate state. The Hindu prince was isolated and undecided. British governor-general Mountbatten encouraged accession to India.

With Pakistan's army at independence ill equipped and still led by a British general, Pakistan tried to force the issue by infiltrating the valley with a volunteer militia. Many of these first "freedom fighters" were from Pashtun tribes, forever cementing the Pashtuns as defenders of Islam in the national epic.

As interpreted by Pakistani journalist and historian Shuja Nawaz, the strategic goal of this first Pakistani intervention was not to seize Kashmir but to convince India that only a plebiscite could resolve the conflict—a plebiscite Pakistanis expected would lead to Kashmir's attachment to Pakistan.[8] Pressured by these incursions and swayed by Indian operatives, the prince declared for India.[9]

One Pakistani friend recounted the tale of their father among these non-uniformed, private irregulars, descending toward the valley only to see Indian military transport planes landing at Srinagar and Indian troops sent to shore up the defenses of their newly declared province. The conflict would further escalate, but both sides were playing for world opinion and diplomatic advantage as much as for battlefield victory. Near the end, Pakistan's military advantage gone, it was fighting to hold a mountainous edge of the territory in the southwest and a large but thinly populated expanse in the north.

After the UN-mediated cease-fire, which left the ultimate status of Kashmir unresolved, Pakistan administered the western reaches as Azad Kashmir and the north as Gilgit-Baltistan. India held Srinagar and the valley, as well as the city and environs of Jammu, south of the valley. The conflict has been frozen since, impervious to subsequent India-Pakistan wars and an uprising among the Kashmiri population against Indian authority in the 1990s. The United Nations has engaged in fits and starts, with its most important action the 1948 Security Council Resolution encouraging "an impartial plebiscite" to determine the region's status.[10] India has never allowed such a vote.

For the United States, Kashmir remains legally unresolved but practically settled. The pieces were long referred to as "Indian-administered" or "Pakistan-administered" Kashmir in our official dispatches, now more commonly as Indian Kashmir and Azad Kashmir.

No Pakistani leader since 1947 has recognized India's sovereignty over Kashmir, and the cause is genuinely popular in Pakistan and universally held, irrespective of religiosity or political ideology. In its less bellicose manifestation, Pakistan lobbies diplomatically for the United Nations to implement its seventy-year-old commitment to a referendum, encourages solidarity among fellow Muslim states, and presses complaints about continuing Indian human rights abuses. In this manifestation of Kashmir diplomacy, Pakistanis offer full respect to the will of Kashmiris, whatever that might be.

The second incarnation of the cause has been more damaging to Pakistan and more challenging to American diplomacy. For decades, Pakistan's army and intelligence services have supported militant groups that infiltrate Kashmir and kill Indian government officials and security forces.

Many thoughtful Pakistanis accept the arguments even for this second tactic, at least when the Pakistan-supported fighters attack Indian security forces and not civilians. There is no other way to challenge India's forceful annexation, in this view, given India's much larger conventional military forces. For the Pakistan state, the advantage of this tactic is deniability. Pakistan can deny its ties to insurgent fighters or claim they have emerged organically out of Kashmir's local population, a product of Indian oppression.

Setting aside its morality, the use of irregular warfare by Pakistan has been tactically effective: India spends a great deal to sustain massive security forces in Kashmir; its violent crackdowns to root out militants provide continuous kindling to popular unrest in the valley. On occasion, the violence draws in international, particularly American, attention, as diplomats engage against the prospect of war. In these instances, Indian critics argue, Pakistan is rewarded for the violence it foments with the international attention it desires.

At the same time, irregular warfare has landed Pakistan in several traps. The first was the permanent elevation of a security state. By sustaining a frozen conflict with India over Kashmir, the Pakistan Army nurtured a permanent excuse for its privileges, budget, and growing intercessions in national politics. In Shuja Nawaz's sharp conclusion: "The result was an unfinished war that contributed to the political instability of Pakistan." "Kashmir," he argues, "became both a reason for not allowing a democratic polity to emerge and a massive financial hemorrhage for the new state. It was to become a cornerstone of Pakistan's foreign policy and domestic politics for decades, as civilian and military leaders struggled to keep the issue alive enough to further their own careers."[11]

Other legacies included the forgone opportunities of trade and good relations with India, the subcontinent's economic powerhouse. Most damaging, however, was the elevation of covert militancy as a legitimate tool of statecraft. The large institutional presence of Lashkar-e-Taiba (LT) militants in Pakistan, with affiliated mosques and charities, remains a dangerous threat to the authority of the state. If the intelligence service's "LT handlers" pull back too hard or punish LT for a gruesome attack, the thinking goes, it could respond with violence against Pakistan. That scenario is more establishment excuse than actual probability, but regardless there is a large, armed, and popular presence in Pakistan invested in continuing the conflict with India.

A similar concern is that dropping the cause of Kashmir could lead young men to find other enemies. For years, Pakistan used anti-India militancy as a safety valve, a place to send young men inclined to violent Islamist causes. When Kashmir was too touchy, they could send them to fight alongside the Taliban in Afghanistan. With the Afghan war ending, the fear goes, denying predisposed holy warriors the outlet of Kashmir could lead them to focus on Pakistan itself.

The militancy trap has also cost Pakistan dearly in terms of its international reputation. The costliest event for Pakistan happened in 2008, the LT-masterminded attack on Mumbai. The ten attackers launched by boat from Pakistan, hijacked a fishing trawler en route and murdered the crew. Their attacks, including a hostage-taking at the landmark Taj Hotel, stretched over more than three days, as Indian security forces struggled to come to grips. All told, the attackers killed 164 people, mostly civilians, including six Americans. India captured a single surviving attacker and executed him a few years later after a trial.

Mumbai's Aftermath

During my first tour to Pakistan, the Mumbai attacks were still fresh and outrageous. At the time, Pakistan was making a pretense of pursuing court cases against the LT plotters. As the embassy's deputy political chief, I undertook several visits to the ministry of interior with our lead terrorism experts, pressing for action on the cases. The investigations, though, were stalling on easy technicalities. In April 2011, when I led a small team from our embassy to India to talk about Pakistan's terrorism threat with Indian officials, accompanied by my colleagues from U.S. Embassy New Delhi, the Indian officials were querulous, complaining about the United States' continuing strategic ties with Islamabad despite the attack.

By the time I returned to Pakistan in 2018, the meandering Pakistani prosecutions of the LT planners had come to a whimpering end. The attack's mastermind had long since been released by the Pakistan Supreme Court, and LT's founding father was a mostly free man. In 2019 one of my team attended a think tank–sponsored event at which speakers claimed, with straight faces all around, that Mumbai had been a "false flag" operation, conducted by India's own deep state to embarrass Pakistan. For some Pakistanis it was reasonable to argue that India had launched a complex terrorist attack on its own financial capital, killing scores of its own citizens, just to delegitimize Pakistan and LT.

The false flag conspiracy theory was never remotely credible, but if such an unlikely plot were true it would merit high marks for effectiveness. By 2019 Pakistan's financial system was tottering under the weight of both its own poor governance and the international restrictions placed against Pakistan for its failure to address terrorist financing.

Cue Up a Conflict

Afghanistan was the dominant American interest as the United States rebuked and then reset with Pakistan in 2018. In early 2019 an older preoccupation interceded. Washington's focus shifted to the prospect of a Pakistan-India conflict when, on Valentine's Day, a Kashmiri youth, a citizen of Indian-administered Kashmir, rammed a car full of explosives into an Indian police convoy near the town of Pulwama.

The attack killed forty and gravely wounded scores more. The attacker's "martyrdom video" extolled the Pakistan-based and -supported militant group Jaish e-Mohammad (JeM), generating demands in the Indian press for a fitting retaliation against Pakistan.

It was a scenario familiar to the subcontinent. In the most recent prelude, in 2016, an attack by four militants against an Indian Army base in Uri resulted in twenty-one dead and over one hundred injured Indian soldiers. India's response, never acknowledged by Pakistan, was a brief ground offensive across the line of control into Pakistan-administered

Kashmir. India claimed its incursion targeted terrorist training and logistics facilities. One of India's points in doing so was to demonstrate that Pakistan's parity in nuclear weapons would not deter India from preventive—or punitive—military action.

For U.S. policy makers—in Washington and at our embassies in New Delhi and Islamabad—the 2019 Pulwama incident and the likelihood of an Indian response generated tensions among several important U.S. objectives: one, that we help India and Pakistan avoid miscalculation and an escalating conflict; two, that we continue to press Pakistan to end its support for anti-India militant groups; three, that we sustain Pakistan's cooperation with our effort to negotiate with the Taliban; and finally, that we continue to invest in an increasingly important U.S.-India partnership, a cornerstone of our effort to counterbalance China. These four goals were exceedingly hard to square. Key U.S. government agencies prioritized them differently, moreover, leading to uncertain policy that veered from hands-off to fully engaged.

Added to all this, I would contend, was a predisposition in American strategic (and popular) circles to look favorably on a kinetic response to terrorist attacks, whatever the actual and practical utility of the response. The retaliation is usually cloaked as "preventive"—as diminishing the capacity of a terrorist group to conduct a future act. As often, however, the timing suggests they are at best retaliation or even "retribution" (justice delivered, no court verdict required).

In the immediate wake of Pulwama, Indian sources reported that U.S. national security adviser John Bolton told his Indian counterpart, Ajit Doval, that the United States supported "India's right to self-defense." The Indian press interpreted this as a U.S. endorsement of retaliation, the nature of which, President Trump suggested, could be big.[12] As the champion of a more muscular response to Pakistan, Indian prime minister Narendra Modi, then in the final stages of a reelection campaign, seemed certain to follow through.

The Pakistan government made the usual pledges after the terrorist incident, offering to jointly investigate and promising to shut down any terrorist group found on Pakistani soil. Pakistan suggested the attacker was radicalized in Kashmir by India's mistreatment of the Muslim population. As always, Pakistan used the incident to demand international attention to Kashmir. Unfortunately, Pakistan's earlier investigation after Mumbai did not credit its sincerity.

If true that Washington signaled India its approval of a retaliatory strike, this constituted a departure from past U.S. policy. The United States typically discouraged military steps, no matter what the provocation. This was in part a legacy of the United States' long and complex alliance with Pakistan and of its twentieth-century coolness toward Soviet-supported India. By 2019 the calculation had changed: Pakistan was the brazen and unapologetic refuge for Taliban fighters attacking coalition troops in Afghanistan, while India was the huge, cautiously pro-Western democracy that might help balance the rising power of China in the "Indo-Pacific." If nothing else, great power rivalry made it more likely the United States would tilt toward India.

There was, to be fair, an argument that consenting to Indian retaliation helped mitigate the chance of broader conflict. By signaling support for India's right to retaliate, the United States allowed India the flexibility to pull its punch, to be more judicious in how and when it responded. It also could be argued that a more equivocal U.S. stance might have convinced Islamabad there was little cost to its sponsorship of anti-India proxies, leading to more terror attacks.

For the Pakistan military, however, one calculation had changed from 2016, one that made escalation more likely. After the 2016 Uri incident and India's ground foray into Pakistan-held Kashmir, Pakistan's military stood back. Some suggested this restraint had sparked discord among senior army officers. In the aftermath of Pulwama in 2019, Pakistani military spokesmen warned the country would not turn the other cheek if India attacked. The news that Washington had consented to an Indian retaliation, moreover, meant our standing as a neutral broker was diminished. Pakistan was going it alone.

Dogfight over Kashmir

On February 26, India launched its retaliatory strike. I was acting deputy chief of mission at the time, temporarily the number two and partially responsible for the safety of our large American mission. I was focused on supporting the ambassador, communicating with Washington, and considering the safety and security of our embassy as things in the neighborhood grew hot.

India chose to strike a reputed JeM training camp near a village called Balakot, claiming its bombs killed as many as three hundred terrorists (see map 3, p. 131). The strike was an escalation, but it also proved a bit abstract. It was an escalation because the Indians had struck into undisputed Pakistani territory, in Khyber-Pakhtunkhwa Province, rather than into the piece of disputed Kashmir possessed by Pakistan. Dropping bombs into Pakistan proper rather than disputed Kashmir was a step up the escalatory ladder. Second, the casualty figure of three hundred that India claimed was provocative.

Pakistan might well have dismissed the bombing, given a glaring but increasingly convincing hole in the Indian story—there were no obvious casualties. We saw not one grieving family member or smoking building in Pakistan. Even with a cowed press, Pakistan did not have the capacity to completely bury a story of dozens of casualties. The much more likely explanation—quickly borne out—was that nobody was on the mountaintop. Any JeM militants who might have been in the camp certainly had fled before the bombs fell.

In addition, the Indian bombs had missed the mountaintop. Over the coming days, Pakistan organized a press junket to the site (a madrasa, or Islamic school, in their telling) to show that no damage had been done. The European Space Agency made imagery available to the public of buildings intact and apparent blast craters on the hillside below. Analysis by the Australian Strategic Policy Institute cast further doubt on the accuracy of the strikes. Indian press and air force officials continued to insist they had hit their targets, but few neutral observers gave credence to the claim.[13]

Only in the wake of the Balakot strike did Washington begin to engage, now lighting up our phones to push a message that Pakistan should stand down and not respond. Through our protocol team, through Foreign Ministry contacts, and through military contacts, we urgently sought to arrange a call to General Bajwa from the four-star general in charge of U.S. Central Command.[14] Bajwa's staff spent the day not returning our calls. Despite the minimal impact of the Indian action, the Pakistan military remained sensitive to the fact that India had gotten away with dropping bombs on Pakistan without receiving a shot in return. The incident provoked memories of the U.S. raid to kill Osama bin Laden, when Pakistan's air defenses had been exposed. Pride and deterrence doctrine were going to dictate a Pakistani response.

The response came the next morning, February 27, when Pakistani jets fired missiles at Indian military encampments in Indian Kashmir. Cockpit videos of those strikes appeared to show Pakistani jets targeting the camps and then lowering their sights, purposefully shooting missiles just short of the targets. Pakistan was intent on showing it could retaliate, but without causing Indian casualties.[15]

There was more, however, and on what followed hinged the prospect of de-escalation or war. India scrambled fighters in response to the intrusion. In the ensuing dogfight, Pakistan shot down one of India's Soviet-era MIG-21s. The pilot ejected over Pakistan-controlled territory, where civilians corralled him and soldiers then took him away. Simultaneously, Indian Air Defenses in Srinagar activated against a suspected intrusion, shooting down its own helicopter. The "friendly fire" incident took seven lives.

The captured pilot, Abhinandan Varthaman, became a celebrity in Pakistan, an oddly antiquated figure with exaggerated mustaches and a calm demeanor. The Indian press briefly celebrated him for trying to eat sensitive papers before capture and attempting to outrun his pursuers. He would also come in for criticism for being too complimentary of Pakistani hospitality in videos that Pakistan released to prove his civilized treatment (a step that violated Geneva Convention principles against releasing a video of a captured prisoner of war). Pakistan has since memorialized Varthaman with a statue at the Pakistan Air Force Museum in Karachi.

The capture of Varthaman seemed to freeze the conflict. India might well have decided on another step, but instead claimed a fictitious shoot-down of a Pakistani plane—enough reputational victory to pause the fighting. The United States and other countries immediately called on Pakistan to return Varthaman to India. Remarkably, and certainly with the military's support, Prime Minister Khan gave the order. Varthaman was escorted across the Wagah border crossing the next day.

Before Varthaman's repatriation, rumors circulated in Pakistan that India was readying missiles for another round of conflict. One Pakistani contact said he had been tipped off by a military friend to get his relatives out of Lahore, supposedly a target. In the embassy we scrutinized our security posture and whether threats of escalation were real. Our Emergency Action Committee arrived at a consensus that the crisis was not moving up to another level. Evacuation would have been difficult at this point in any case—Pakistan had closed its air space. With the press in both countries trumpeting victory, however, the governments stepped back.

During the rest of my tenure, the Pakistan-India cease-fire was just that, with no space for actual rapprochement. I attended the large Iftar dinner hosted by the Indian High Commission during Ramadan that summer to find a strikingly empty dining hall. Pakistan's intelligence operatives had blocked traffic to the venue and discouraged Pakistanis from going. Early-arriving foreign diplomats got in, as did a few Pakistanis, some of them looking around and realizing they should not have RSVP'd.

That August, India revoked the autonomous status of Indian-administered Kashmir, causing Pakistan to ratchet up condemnations and expel the Indian high commissioner. Pakistan lost an effective advocate for India-Pakistan dialogue with the move, but the genial, pragmatic ambassador, Ajay Bisaria, was probably too welcome in some Islamabad salons for ISI's comfort in any case.

It was not until 2020–21 and the resumption of quiet dialogue between Pakistan and India that real progress ensued, including the reinstitution of a formal cease-fire along the line of control in Kashmir. The broad cease-fire ended the lethal, back-and-forth artillery shelling typical of the heavily armed border. Whether the cease-fire can hold with the radically changed regional strategic landscape caused by the Taliban victory in Afghanistan is unclear.

Lessons Learned

Cooler heads in New Delhi and Islamabad can rightfully take credit for forgoing escalation after the bracing events of February 26–28, but one can also see quite a bit of luck in how it played out. Most importantly, both sides were able to declare victory. In New Delhi, Prime Minister Modi had shown that India would retaliate and strike into Pakistan in the wake of a terrorist incident, and the world accepted its right to do so. No one at the United Nations complained about an Indian military incursion into the territory of another member state. India also claimed victory by refusing to let go of the stories that there had been scores of terrorists killed at Balakot or that India had shot down a Pakistani F-16. Most of India's media proved heavily nationalistic in sustaining its claims.

In Pakistan, the small combat victory, followed by the magnanimous release of the pilot, made for a moment of national pride. The loser in two of three large wars against India (the 1965 conflict can be called a draw), including the final one, which cost it possession of East Pakistan (now Bangladesh), Pakistanis had a deep well of insecurity vis-à-vis India. Beating India in the air, Pakistan's military had come off looking like the more professional and competent force.[16] Pakistan's honor had been vindicated, and it could afford to stand down. Pakistan also exaggerated, claiming for some time it had downed two Indian jets rather than a single MiG.

By February 28, world powers were also fully engaged. Pakistan's foreign minister, in truth, overemphasized the level and utility of U.S. diplomacy at the end of the conflict.[17] Perhaps this was because it squared with the country's goal of internationalizing crises over Kashmir. But the attention of the West and other capitals helped on the margins.

It is easy to imagine another outcome. Had Pakistan lost jets and pilots in the dogfight, another round of fighting might have ensued, leading to the use of greater and different forces. Had Pakistan miscalculated and killed Indian soldiers on the ground during its February 26 counterstrikes, India would have felt compelled to take another step.

Even with another round of shots fired, it was unlikely the crisis would have approached a nuclear threshold. Given the consequences of that threshold, however, leaders in the international community have an inescapable interest in interceding against escalation. They must do so, however, cautious to not reward Pakistan with international attention for starting the conflict through its proxies. It is no easy trick, but it is one that must be attempted.

It is worth noting, again, the argument that by supporting India's right to respond to the Pulwama incident, the United States gave Prime Minister Modi the space to step back after the embarrassing setback in the air on February 27. U.S. diplomacy might in this way have contributed to de-escalation. If championing the right to retaliate in the future, however, the United States should be vigilant about the prospects of events going sideways in the tense subcontinent. Neither side will cave in easily with

PAKISTAN AND THE CRICKETING WORLD

national pride on the line. The consequences of unintended escalation would be calamitous. At the same time, the ability of the United States to intercede as a neutral mediator may be receding—unfortunate because there is no viable alternative to American leadership in such a crisis.[18]

Another lesson from the crisis regards U.S. defense sales. The United States for decades was the source of Pakistan's most advanced aircraft, F-16 fighters, along with air-to-air missiles. In the mid-2000s, as Pakistan fought against domestic insurgents and terrorists, the Bush administration agreed to sell Pakistan a newer version of the F-16, along with 500 AMRAAM (air-to-air) missiles. The justification for the sales was Pakistan's antiterror fight, but India objected to the sales as a threat and, indeed, the U.S. maintained no control over the use of the aircraft.

The United States established a precise monitoring regime to ensure that Pakistan protected the aircraft technology, controlling access to planes on the ground. Until 2019 the United States maintained U.S. contractors at the two Pakistani bases with the F-16s, providing 24/7 observation. Pakistan accepted the protocols. After Pulwama, the monitoring was interrupted. Concerned that its greatest air assets would be at risk if sitting only at their two known bases, vulnerable to Indian missile attack, Pakistan dispersed the aircraft and the AMRAAMS. Suddenly, this advanced technology came out from under our watch.

Pakistan assured us during those weeks that it had established careful controls over access at the new sites, that they had put up fencing and video monitoring. At the same time, the U.S. Department of Defense ordered its contractors off the two principal bases, an acknowledgment that the men were not hired to risk dying in someone else's war.

Pakistan's decision to forward-deploy the jets to smaller airfields was defensible, but it was a violation of the letter of our agreement. The DOD decision to pull back the contractors was just as necessary, but it meant a reduction in our visibility. In the smoky air of conflict, the carefully constructed monitoring regime simply could not hold up. It would be stressed again in 2020 by COVID-19, when the United States again withdrew the contractors, over concerns about health.

Although Pakistan initially denied firing from one of its F-16s on February 28, India was able to display the wreckage of one AMRAAM missile on its territory after the conflict, a weapon only compatible with the F-16s.

The military public relations office had originally claimed the victory for its JF-17 fighter, a Chinese jet jointly produced in Pakistan (and available for export). Pakistan's fiction was either an attempt to market the JF-17 or a winking effort to avoid embarrassing the United States, but it wore thin. Pakistan eventually abandoned the fiction. An F-16 and U.S.-provided AMRAAM shot down the Indian MIG.[19]

India raised the issue with its friends in the U.S. Congress, asking that the United States sanction Pakistan in some way for using the U.S. aircraft against it, rather than against terrorists. This was a nonstarter. Although the sale was justified by Pakistan's counterterrorism fight, there were no written restrictions on Pakistan's use of the jets and missiles. Indeed, such restrictions would be a blow to the lucrative overseas sales of U.S. defense technology—few nations would buy our armaments if they came with an American "shutdown" veto on their use. I say this neither to defend nor condemn U.S. weapons sales, just to note that any imagined restriction on the use of our systems is illusory at best.[20]

Why Professional Diplomats Might Fear Summits

In the embassy's political and economic sections, the month of July 2019 was consumed with preparations for Imran Khan's first official visit to Washington as prime minister. The visit called for rafts of paper (information memos, issue papers, decision memos) and the usual pressure to get Pakistani concessions on key issues.

The biggest American request was that Pakistan maintain and enhance its modest crackdown on anti-India militant groups, specifically Jaish-e-Mohammad and Lashkar-e-Taiba. Pakistan had long officially banned both groups and their charitable front organizations. Nonetheless, both groups, and LT to a much larger extent, had continued to operate mosques, hospitals, ambulance services, schools, and a variety of charities. The activities of these groups were a big reason for Pakistan's "grey list" status with the global Financial Action Task Force (FATF).

Over the four months following Pulwama, Pakistan took stronger measures against LT than the U.S. government's Pakistan skeptics wanted to admit but still less than we asked. Islamabad charged its provincial governments to take over the LT-linked charities. (Most were in Punjab, with Sindh a distant second.) Eventually the provinces received budget allocations from the central government to cover some of the expenses.

Pakistan's judicial system also opened a new case against Hafez Saeed, the founder and guiding light of LT (for illegal fundraising, not for past terrorist acts). Through the Indian high commissioner, we learned that infiltrations by Pakistan-based militants across the line of control were down significantly. It was promising but incomplete. Saeed still showed up at mosques to deliver sermons, the government made few arrests, and none of the changes seemed irreversible.

Counterterrorism was another issue demanding effective collaboration across our mission, particularly among the political section's counter-terrorism unit, the economic section's finance team, our treasury and legal (FBI) attachés, other embassy security elements, and our consulates in Lahore, Karachi, and Peshawar. The core reporting officers worked overtime after Pulwama, meeting contacts and developing reports on Pakistan's compliance, teeing up points for the ambassador to make with Pakistani officials, and advising Washington on the progress. I joined my front office and interagency colleagues, through secure video link, in tense policy coordination discussions with Washington, hosted by the National Security Council. We chewed over Pakistan's actions and how they might affect our decisions at FATF, the international body whose coordinated sanctions had hobbled Pakistan's financial sectors in response to weak controls on terror financing. We debated how much credit to accord Pakistan for counterterrorism measures in the months since Pulwama.

Once again, concerns about Indian sensitivities and our burgeoning relationship with New Delhi played a role in these discussions, as did Pakistan's modest but critical help to our Afghanistan diplomacy. Said sotto voce in one meeting was a concern over the unpredictable, that President Trump might offer something outside his carefully baked instructions if he met individually with Prime Minister Khan. This was not a new bureaucratic concern—foreign policy professionals always consider the possibility that leaders will go off script when meeting in person. In the end, Washington decided it was better to talk than stall, and the Khan visit went forward. Expectedly, the president went off script.

On July 22, 2019, in a joint White House press availability with Prime Minister Khan, President Trump said that India's prime minister had asked the United States to play a mediating role between India and Pakistan. Per Trump's words, "I said, where? He said Kashmir." To Prime Minister Khan's evident delight, President Trump continued, "If I can help, I would love to be a mediator. It is impossible to believe that two incredible countries that are very, very smart with very smart leadership can't solve it . . . but if you want me to mediate or arbitrate, I would be willing to do it."[21]

His remarks were a direct challenge to New Delhi's long-standing position that Kashmir was a bilateral issue between India and Pakistan requiring no outside help. A political storm erupted in New Delhi, with the opposition pouncing and demanding that Prime Minister Modi confirm or disavow President Trump's claim that he had "requested" mediation.

With some evident discomfort, India responded through its external affairs minister, asserting plausibly that India had not asked President Trump to mediate the Kashmir dispute. U.S. officials, for their part, could not disavow the president, but "clarifications" came quickly, including one from the State Department, that while "Kashmir is a bilateral issue for both parties to discuss, the Trump administration welcomes Pakistan and India sitting down and the United States stands ready to assist."[22]

Such was the arc of U.S.-Pakistan policy from January 2018 to July 2019, from President Trump using Twitter to banish Pakistan for its "lies and deceit" to the same president warmly embracing Prime Minister Khan in Washington and then giving credence to Pakistan's longest-held and most important foreign policy aspiration, at the expense of India. In Pakistan, where elites have long chafed at the sustained reprimands of the U.S. foreign policy establishment, Trump drew lots of fans. On the idea of mediation, the U.S. government clawed back Trump's offer, but U.S.-Pakistan relations nonetheless gained a fleeting boost.

Postscript: India Disappoints Pakistan with a Loss

Pakistan's uninspired loss against India was dispiriting, but Pakistani fans would have greater reason to complain over an Indian *loss* two weeks later, against England. At that point, Pakistan's fortunes had revived, and it had a chance at advancing to the semifinals. It was then vying with

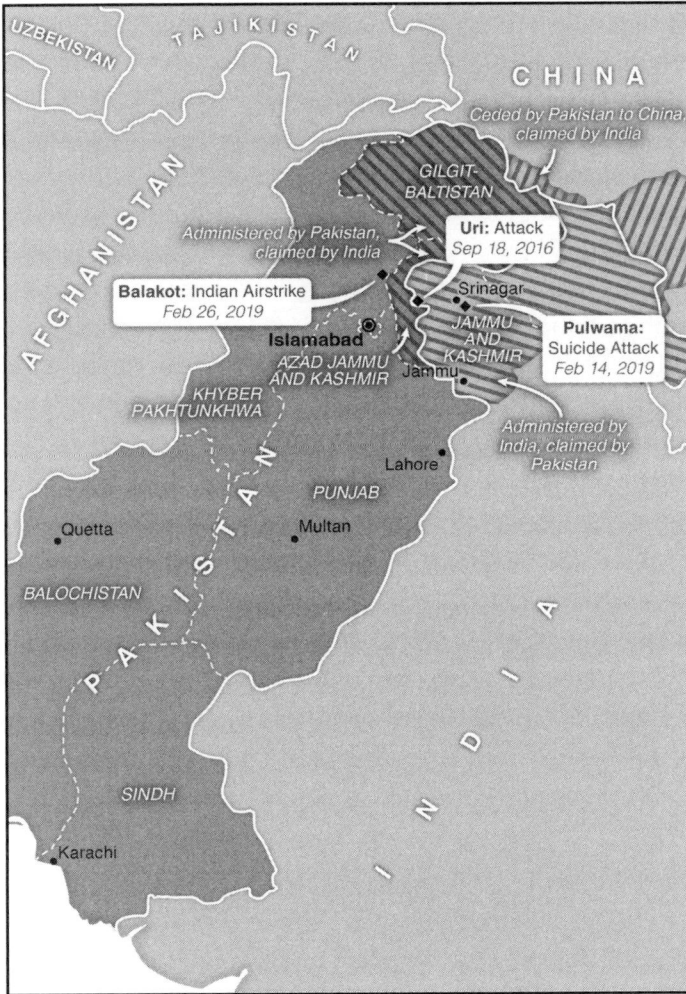

Map 3. Incidents near the India-Pakistan line of control in Kashmir.

England for the fourth and final spot. India was still undefeated and a lock to advance, so there would be no benefit to Pakistan from an Indian loss. An Indian win over England, however, would help tremendously. For Pakistanis, the uncomfortable upshot was rooting for their biggest rival.

England, however, fighting for its survival on home soil, rallied and figured out how to score against Indian bowling. It put up 336 runs. It was not an easy target for India, certainly, but the Indian team had been scoring runs with relative ease in the tournament. Pakistan still had grounds for hope.

When India fell further and further behind the necessary scoring rate over the course of the early evening, Pakistanis started to grumble. I was watching at the home of a Pakistani cricket analyst; he continued to hope that India's professionalism would win through, and they would pick up the attack. They never did. When they finished their 50 overs with only 306 runs, Pakistan's chances of making the semifinals dropped precipitously; the additional two points meant England was back in front for the fourth spot. Over its "innings," India had only five batters dismissed, suggesting a conservative approach at bat. To Pakistanis, India did not appear to be pressing for a win.

Pakistanis imagined the disappointing result was either an Indian anti-Pakistan ploy or the result of bribes and corruption. The Indians had already secured a spot in the semifinals, the thinking went, so there was no cost to the team from a loss. Given the low stakes, a player or two had taken a bribe—or, more sinister, India had thrown the match to hurt Pakistan. There was never any proof of this (and England was a good team), but conspiracies involving India and cricket required no proof in Pakistan.

MATCH RESULT

India 336/5 (50)
Pakistan 212/6 (40)
India wins by 89 runs.

9 LESSONS IN DEMOCRACY PROMOTION FROM SOUTHERN AFRICA

June 23, 2019, Lord's Cricket Grounds, London
Pakistan (1-3-1), 3 points, vs. South Africa (1-4-1), 3 points

Of the three oldest test countries in cricket, South Africa is unique for having competed in only eight of the first twelve iterations of the World Cup. The reason was apartheid, the country's former system of sharp segregation and denial of political, economic, and personal rights to its Black majority and its Asian and mixed-race minorities.

Among the many pressure tactics brought by various countries and organizations against the white minority government, sporting bans were among the more painful to the white community. South Africa's whites valued the country's competitiveness in rugby and cricket, but, over time, most teams refused to play them.

Pakistan said "no" from the outset, but well into the 1960s, Australia and England continued to engage. The Olympics, influenced by an increasingly assertive body of nonaligned, once-colonized countries, moved by 1964 to ban South Africa, but the pale states of England, New Zealand, and Australia continued to play the South African Springboks in cricket.[1] That finally changed in the late 1960s, when pressure mounted in England and Australia to bar the racist government's teams.

One of the sparks for change was the case of mixed-race all-rounder Basil D'Oliveira, a South African who migrated to England in 1960 for the chance to play professional county cricket. He was a standout in South Africa in the late 1950s but could play only in the country's "coloured" league; the authorities kept him and any other men of color off the national team. In England, after acquiring British citizenship, D'Oliveira got the opportunity to compete in international matches.

In 1968, despite some exceptional recent performances, D'Oliveira was left off the roster of an England team preparing to tour South Africa.

The English Selection Board was aware the apartheid government would call off the series if England included a South African–born nonwhite player, but the board asserted that its exclusion of D'Oliveira was based on merit. Many were unconvinced, pressing the case. When one of the selected players withdrew due to injury, the board capitulated and added D'Oliveira to the roster. As expected, South Africa canceled the tour. International cricket responded by banning South Africa from the game. The ban would last for twenty-two years, until the end of apartheid.[2]

A Boundary Then Bowled Out: Challenges to Democratization in Southern Africa

Relations today between Pakistan and South Africa are limited, though Britain imported a significant diaspora of indentured Indians (of all sects) to South Africa before the start of the twentieth century. The two countries are substantial but not hugely powerful members of the global south. Their interests intersect on some matters of global trade, climate change mitigation, and development assistance, but they conduct little bilateral trade, military cooperation, or people-to-people exchanges.

For the purposes of this manuscript, one non-cricket theme from southern Africa merits exposition: the promise and frustrations of U.S. democracy promotion. Long before Pakistan, my diplomatic career circled around southern and eastern Africa. Botswana was an early tour in the 1990s. It was a prosperous, well-governed country, whose culture had been shaped, in part, by its scant rainfall. Its currency is named for rain, and rainfall was met with happy laughter and even spontaneous dance. The desert climate also instilled thoughtful stewardship of natural resources. Thrift and conservation—along with diamonds—helped overcome the minimal infrastructure left at independence by the British.

When I served there, the country's second president, Quett Masire, had made clear his intention to abide by the country's two-term limit and cede power to a democratic successor, which he did in 1998. The United States was not a heavy influence on that decision, but we had modest programs designed to bolster Botswana's young but culturally grounded democratic norms.

Next door, in South Africa, Nelson Mandela had just assumed the presidency, a powerful moment for the advancement of democracy. The

United States had a spotty record on South Africa, to be sure, with a long U.S. government history of abiding the apartheid regime as a Cold War ally, balanced by a grassroots African American–led civil society movement that eventually won the day, forcing change in U.S. foreign policy. Western sanctions against South Africa wore down the white nationalist regime, but Black and some white South Africans orchestrated the transition. The United States contributed on the margins and borrowed hope from the triumph of majority rule.[3]

I later served as the senior South Africa desk officer in Washington and then on the secretary's policy planning staff, responsible for sub-Saharan Africa. It was enough tenure on the accounts to see Botswana and South Africa hold to democratic norms despite populist challenges. It was also an opportunity to engage over many years on Zimbabwe, a classic policy failure where Western demands for democratic change stalled against a determined autocrat and his supporters. The long campaign for change, again undergirded by economic sanctions, contributed to ruinous economic deprivation for ordinary Zimbabweans.

The Zimbabwe story is complex, and most of the blame for what happened adheres to the late president-for-life Robert Mugabe. But the West contributed, producing too little financial support in the 1990s for a just land reform and too much support for structural adjustments and trade liberalization that decimated local manufacturing.[4] The economic orthodoxy benefited mostly white commercial farmers with a bent toward exports—and, secondarily, government coffers through taxation. The economic imbalance of structural adjustment, misaligned along racial lines toward the small white community, inheritors of the benefits of white minority rule up to 1980, was a politically toxic outcome. Mugabe turned a corner and began targeting the white landowners for populist political benefit with mob-led, illegal land seizures.[5] The IMF and World Bank's policy prescriptions, often right on paper, can easily founder when applied to an underdeveloped political system that cannot handle the stress, and when the international advisers pay too little heed to colonial and racist legacies.

The land seizures resulted, predictably, in the collapse of commercial agriculture and the disappearance of its tax revenues for an insolvent government. The new landowners lacked titles and collateral needed to borrow for seed and fertilizer. Most lacked experience in high-value commercial farming. Once a breadbasket of cereals production, Zimbabwe fell into hunger.[6]

With the land redistribution card played so poorly and the economy sinking further into despair, Mugabe's playbook for retaining power in the 2000s soon devolved into old-school political repression, including jailing Black political opponents and critics, shuttering newspapers, stuffing ballot boxes, seizing more properties, and unleashing violence. The West responded with sanctions targeting Mugabe and his cronies, steps that further hurt the economy and provided Mugabe with a scapegoat for the country's economic ills.

I had the chance to press a few South African politicians and non-government leaders about the situation across their northern border during these years, asking if South Africa would use its moral weight and economic influence to press for political reform and fair elections. Mostly, they demurred. South Africa's leading labor confederation was sympathetic to the plight of oppressed Black trade unionists in Zimbabwe, but its public criticisms were mild. Thabo Mbeki, head of the African National Congress and the successor to Nelson Mandela as president, was Mugabe's junior in African liberation circles and clearly reluctant to say a word. His successor, Jacob Zuma, was too scandal plagued himself to lead on Zimbabwe.

Mugabe's end came much later than many had hoped, indeed later than insurance actuarial tables might have predicted for a man born in 1924. It was not until his much-younger second wife moved to succeed him that the old guard of the Zimbabwe military deposed Mugabe, in 2017.

Nobody could conclude from the outcome that targeted Western economic sanctions had proved useful in bringing about democratic change (or that what followed Mugabe would be truly democratic). Zimbabwe had suffered almost two full decades of Western scolding and sanctions by the time Mugabe fell. Zimbabweans were the victims of Mugabe, primarily, but also the sanctions. It was a case study, among many historical examples, of the potential costs of the U.S. proclivity to pursue "regime change" overseas. (Apartheid, featuring racial exclusion and minority rule, was in my view unique—an entirely appropriate effort at regime change. There, the policy could build on the absolute clarity of self-determination for all.) Sanctions and IMF structural reform were ready tools in the West's relations with Pakistan as well. Though I came late in my career to Pakistan policy, I came with a skeptical view of the usefulness of sanctions and an inclination to expect political damage from structural adjustment programs.

South African Cricket Highs and Lows

For at least two decades after the end of its apartheid isolation, South Africa was one of the strongest cricket teams in the world, but one that fell just a little short in the World Cup contests. It has dominated Pakistan in the test match format, winning twice as many as it has lost, and Pakistan has yet to win a match in South Africa. Still, South Africa has underdelivered, and by 2019 it was a weakening side.

In the World Cup, South Africa offers a history of "almost." It debuted in Australia in 1992, and if not for an unfair rain rule might have made the finals against Pakistan, rather than England. Pakistan might still have prevailed, but a postapartheid South Africa in its first World Cup would have changed the narrative and perhaps the cricket karma. Counterfactual historians might wonder if a Pakistan loss in that final would have altered the political prospects of the then–Pakistan captain, Imran Khan.

In the 1996 Cup contested in South Asia, South Africa stormed undefeated through group play only to lose in a quarterfinal knockout with the West Indies. In 1999 the South African squad, again looking unbeatable in the early tournament, lost two consecutive games against the ultimate champion, Australia. The second loss resulted from poor communication between the South African crease runner and batsman. Australia rather than South Africa advanced to face Pakistan, a game Australia captured with suspicious ease.

Last Chance at Lord's

By June 23, 2019, neither Pakistan nor South Africa had good odds of advancing further. Sitting at three points each in the standings, the two teams were ahead of only sophomore World Cup qualifier Afghanistan, which was winless. For both teams, a win was essential.

My impression was that Pakistanis were inured to their team at this point. The losses to Australia and India were hardly shameful given the strength of those teams, but the cumulative impression of three losses against just one win left my friends with not much passion for watching more. Happily, this was the point at which Pakistan's play improved.

Pakistan batted first and built to a steady run rate, with Haris Sohail the surprise difference maker. The team had not played him since the dismal first match against the West Indies, but he came through with a massive 89 runs on just 59 balls. A cumbersome runner, Sohail nonetheless stoked the pro-Pakistan crowd to a frenzy with his delicate, slicing, cutting, and sometimes powerful shots. It was an epic outburst, coming late in a tournament that was close to slipping beyond Pakistan's grasp.

Mohammad Amir, not the lightning bolt many had hoped to see but still Pakistan's best bowler in the tournament, asserted himself to ensure South Africa's chase never really got going. He caught South Africa's lead-off man, Hashim Amla, "lbw" for only 2 runs and later induced a high pop fly by South Africa's captain, Faf du Plessis. His run rate of 4.9 in ten overs kept South Africa well off the pace. Pakistan won by 49 runs, still alive, while South Africa was mathematically eliminated from a semifinal spot.

MATCH RESULT

Pakistan 308/7 (50 overs)
South Africa 259/9 (50 overs)
Pakistan wins by 49 runs.

10 NEW ZEALAND AS THE BEST OF THE WEST

June 26, 2019, Edgbaston Cricket Ground
Pakistan (2-3-1), 5 points, vs. New Zealand (5-0-1), 11 points

Generating even a short chapter on Pakistan–New Zealand relations is a stretch, but during my time in Islamabad, New Zealand achieved something of an exalted status in the minds of the Pakistanis. New Zealand achieved that special place in the wake of tragedy, but it was a place earned through what seemed to be societal grace.

On March 15, 2019, a murderer, inspired by the hothouse grievances of white nationalism, killed fifty-one people at two mosques in Christchurch, New Zealand. The news was shocking but continued two marked trends in terrorist attacks in the late 2010s—globally, the greatest number of terrorism victims have been Muslims, the biggest numbers killed by coreligionists from another sect but more than a handful killed by white Christian men. In the United States, the trend has been both racist and antisemitic: victims have been targeted for being Brown, Black, Jewish, and Muslim. The terrorists have been white Americans with semiautomatic weapons.

The Christchurch images were incongruous. The suburbs stuck in the news cycle looked not much different from some low-key, prosperous neighborhood in the American Pacific Northwest. It seemed an odd place to find blood rage, but then so had Bali, Utoya, and Sousse.

In Islamabad we learned much about two of the Pakistani victims, Naeem Rashid (age fifty) and his son Talha (age twenty-one). Reports credited Naeem with charging the mass murderer during the first attack at the Al Noor Mosque, creating the time and space that allowed a few more to escape. In all, the attack killed nine Pakistanis.

The first reactions in Pakistan were familiar, focused on the hypocrisy and moral failings of the West. Particularly in the era of Donald Trump, a common narrative focused on the mistreatment of Muslims by Western law enforcement, governments, and businesses. Pakistanis were suspect wherever they went, ran this narrative, yet they were often the first victims of prejudice or even violence. Christchurch was the aberrant act of one individual, certainly, but Pakistanis saw it as part of a larger trend. In this telling, New Zealand was lumped together with the Western Anglo world, a fifth eye of the British-American-Canadian-Australian crypto-alliance that mistreated Muslims.

Quickly, however, sharp distinctions emerged in the New Zealand reaction. Led by a young and charismatic prime minister, Jacinda Ardern, New Zealand collectively rose to the occasion. There was an open outpouring of support to families of the victims, many scattered throughout the British Commonwealth. Authorities arranged visas so that family members could come to bury or mourn their loved ones. New Zealanders showed their solidarity with the country's small minority Muslim population. The country banned assault weapons, as if such a sensible decision could be a measure taken by a responsible government rather than the touchstone of a culture war.

The Christchurch murders immediately took me back to another horrible act of terrorism, this one during my first tour in Pakistan: the July 22, 2011, slaughter of seventy-seven people by a young Norwegian right-wing extremist similarly driven by a desire to rid his country of Muslims. In step with many mass murderers of the right, he also considered feminism an enemy ideology. This was further proof, if more were needed, that a strong motivation in that space is the perception of diminishing relative power among insecure white males.

After detonating a bomb in Oslo that killed eight, the murderer took a ferry to Utoya Island, where he targeted a gathering of the National Labor Party youth wing, methodically killing sixty-nine, mostly young men and women, some children. The killer blamed the Labor Party for its embrace of multiculturalism and immigration. The Norway victims were mostly white Norwegians, and there was a moment of international speculation of Islamic terrorism before the identity and ideology of the killer was released. During both of my tours in Pakistan, the greatest acts of terrorism in the West were perpetrated by Westerners.

These two mass murderers have become iconic personas in the violent white nationalist virtual world. Their manifestos and irredeemable political thought continue to inspire. If eradicating terrorism remains an American priority, we will need to invest much more in policing these fervid swamps of conspiratorial, aggrieved, racist thought, terrain that some personally nonviolent politicians of the right have protected for political gain. In the wake of the defeat of Donald Trump in the American election of 2020, his fake fraud claims quickly assumed the status of canon in these same swamps.

A Dependable Test Victim Becomes an ODI Star

There is little trade between Pakistan and New Zealand, not surprising given New Zealand's small size and distance from Pakistan. New Zealand's diplomatic representative to Pakistan was resident most of the year in Tehran rather than Islamabad. Though both countries remain members of the British Commonwealth and were brothers in arms in both World Wars, their different colonial histories and paths to self-rule or independence set them apart.

New Zealand achieved international test status in 1930, just two years before colonial India. Still, New Zealand was not a strong side for its first fifty years in the ICC. For Pakistan, the rare tour to New Zealand or visit by a Kiwi team was an opportunity to win, and Pakistan often did just that. Still, Pakistan was the site of New Zealand's very first international test series victory, a 1-0 win in a three-match series over the new year in 1969-70.

Stephen Wagg's valuable account of cricket culture around the world, *Cricket: A Political History of the Global Game, 1945-2017*, suggests two distinguishing features of New Zealand's cricket trajectory.[1] The first element was its limited popularity. Home to the most successful international side in rugby, the All Blacks, New Zealanders long imparted less importance to cricket. The Anglophile cricket subculture was more committed to cordial ties to England than to winning matches. It was slow to schedule regular fixtures against even its closest neighbor, Australia, much less the countries of the Indian subcontinent.

A second notable feature is that New Zealand became more progressive in recruiting for diversity. Like all the white settler countries, New

Zealand carries the historic stain of wars of dispossession against its Indigenous people (the Māori), but its post–World War II national dialogue on the issue has been better than that of the United States or Australia. Wagg concludes that "debates about national identity and access to the game, while not without controversy or racial stereotyping, have on the whole lacked either the crudeness or the divisiveness evidenced elsewhere in the cricket world."[2]

In contrast to its middling record in test play, New Zealand has been a star in the one-day (ODI) format, particularly at the World Cup. It has qualified for every World Cup tournament and achieved the semifinals a record eight times in the first twelve iterations, failing to advance out of group play just twice.

Going into the match against Pakistan, New Zealand was riding high, undefeated and on track again for the semifinals. Although all five of its wins were against teams that would occupy the bottom half of the table, New Zealand looked like a serious obstacle for the desperate Pakistan team.

Holding Their Nerve

Again playing before what was in many respects a home crowd of expatriate Pakistanis in Birmingham, Pakistan bowled first and kept the match close. The young lefty Shaheen Afridi starred, taking three wickets and allowing just 28 runs in his ten overs. Pakistan's target was set at 237.

Batting after the break, Pakistan briefly stumbled, its first and second batsmen losing their wickets with only 28 runs contributed. In the third spot, Babar Azam steadied the chase, batting carefully and then picking up the pace, gaining a century with 101 runs scored, not out. Sohail Harris followed up his exceptional performance against South Africa with 68 runs. In the end, partnering briefly with Azam, captain Sarfaraz Ahmed got the winning hit, smashing a four to the boundary on the first ball of the second-to-last over. Now just one point behind England in the standings and tied with Bangladesh with seven points, Pakistan was back in the tournament.

JUNE 26 MATCH RESULT

New Zealand 237/6 (50)
Pakistan 241/4 (49.1)
Pakistan wins by six wickets.

11 AMERICAN AND PAKISTANI MISADVENTURES IN THE GREAT GAME

June 29, 2019, Headingley, Leeds
Afghanistan (0-7), 0 points, vs. Pakistan (3-3-1), 7 points

Afghans gave the British little time to teach them cricket. It was probably played a little in Kabul from 1839 to 1842, when forces from the quasi-governmental British East India Company invaded and occupied. That ill-considered bid to block Russia in Afghanistan would end in one of the British Empire's greatest defeats. Isolated outside Kabul by an angry population, the British-Indian force, along with soldiers' wives and families, were annihilated while retreating from Kabul to the Khyber Pass in January 1842. Tribal marksmen and traditional swords would take the lives of all but a few of the 16,000 interlopers.[1]

A brief British invasion later that same year—named an *army of retribution*—saw British forces kill adult males wantonly. Rape, looting, and purposeful destruction in Kabul would mark neither the first nor the last use of "collective punishment" in the region.

British influence in Afghanistan would flare at different points in the nineteenth and twentieth centuries, but its cultural imprint was never long or deep. Instead, Afghanistan's enduring cricket roots came as an outgrowth of the Soviet invasion of Afghanistan in 1979. That war and those that followed pushed Afghan refugees into Pakistan, as many as three million residing in camps, towns, and cities. In all those places, young Afghans grew up amid Pakistani enthusiasm for cricket, at a time when the Pakistan national team was reaching its zenith.[2] Many of the refugee camps, which famously became centers of conservative Islamic teaching and militancy, also became incubators of cricket.

Afghans launched a national cricket board in 1995, in Pakistan. As the Taliban gained control of Afghanistan in the late 1990s, it banned most games (and music and girls' education). It reversed itself only in

2000 with an exception for cricket, by then immensely popular.[3] Pakistan invited the Afghan national team to play in its B league.

With U.S.-led regime change in Afghanistan just a year later, opportunities for cricket expanded. War and terror were a hindrance, but Afghanistan cricket thrived. The team climbed quickly in the world rankings, first past the third tier of international cricket, the Ugandas and Bahrains, and then—by the early 2010s—past the second, the Canadas and Kenyas. In 2015 Afghanistan qualified for its first World Cup (in an expanded field of fourteen teams). It even earned a victory in its debut, over Scotland.

With the Afghan war and casualties growing worse every year, Afghanistan's team began dividing its "home" matches between cricket pitches in India and the Persian Gulf, balancing the financial and political opportunities offered by these two centers of Asian cricket. (Pakistan was not an option due to its terrorist violence.) For Afghanistan, India offered the richest cricket market, but cricket officials were surely aware of Pakistani paranoia about Indian influence and did not overcommit.

By 2017 Afghanistan cricket had arrived. The ICC admitted it, along with Ireland, as a full test member. Afghanistan's admission bent the ICC's rules—not because the men's game was unworthy but because Afghanistan had, to that point, failed to develop a women's game.[4] Militant threats and other forms of resistance had stymied earlier efforts at creating a women's league. By late 2020, Afghan officials reported halting progress toward putting together a women's side, but the country's continuing turmoil and conservative political currents remained a challenge.[5] After the Taliban took Afghanistan in August 2021, it was impossible to imagine the women's game thriving, creating a new quandary for the ICC.

Leading up to the 2019 World Cup, the Afghan men looked competitive. In the 2018 Asia Cup, they had beaten two test nations, Sri Lanka and Bangladesh, and achieved a tie with India. They lost a close match against Pakistan. In qualifying for the selective 2019 World Cup field, Afghanistan had crossed into the global top ten.

For the Afghan team, the accomplishment of making the tournament would have to suffice. By the date of its match against Pakistan, Afghanistan had gone zero-for-seven, losing by often large margins. It had played close against India, however, just seven days before its Pakistan match. The danger for Pakistan was that Afghanistan might not be an easy win.

"History Starts Today"

America's intervention in Afghanistan, and its bloody exit two decades later, owed much to a deadly brew of idealism, hubris, and cultural ignorance. I met dozens of smart Americans over the years who understood Afghanistan and therefore the weak foundations of U.S. aspirations there, but those many smart and experienced soldiers, diplomats, and aid workers could never compensate for the mistaken assumptions that fed our involvement and colored our exit.

Richard Nixon and Henry Kissinger knew where Afghanistan was, but for many Americans the country did not imprint until the 1979 Soviet invasion. With the romanticized mujahidin struggle, moreover, Afghanistan was shoehorned into the Cold War with little thought to the intricacies of a country we would one day invade.

In the immediate aftermath of the 9/11 terrorist attacks, then-deputy secretary of state Dick Armitage, based on his own recollections, convoked the visiting Pakistan spy chief to lay out the unequivocal American demand for Pakistan's support in Afghanistan. When the Pakistani, Lt. Gen. Mahmud Ahmed, tried to divert the conversation toward the complexities of U.S.-Pakistan relations, Armitage responded that the past was not at issue, that "history starts today."[6] Twenty years later we could say with confidence that was not the case—the region's history exerted a substantial weight on the outcome.

One freighted term from that past was the "Great Game," a British conceit for securing British India against Afghans, disruptive Pashtuns, and, most importantly, Russian encroachment. Rudyard Kipling popularized the phrase as the animus for the quaint spy craft in *Kim* (1901). In 1979 the Soviet invasion revived the game as the United States worked with Pakistan and Saudi Arabia to frustrate their occupation. In 2001, after the attacks on New York and Washington, America opened another iteration of the game. This time, Pakistan was on the other side.

In the 1980s the Pakistan military, American spies, and even jihadist Pashtun militia aligned in opposition to the Soviets. The border was the staging ground for America's most successful (and damaging) Cold War move, the funding and arming of the "mujahidin" guerrilla fighters.

The United States did the work in league with the military-run government of Pakistan, a government turned religious conservative under military ruler Gen. Mohammad Zia-ul-Haq. It was done in close coordination with Pakistan's ISI, propelling that former backwater of military service into the domineering intelligence service it remains today.[7] The work was funded with government and private money from Saudi Arabia; some of the allied fighters from the Middle East would later morph into international terrorist threats to the United States. And it was done in collaboration with the Haqqani Network, the family-based group of mujahidin built by patriarch Jalaluddin Haqqani in the 1970s to oppose Soviet-influenced secular governments in Kabul, even before the Soviet invasion. Years later, the Haqqanis were the most lethal attack planners against U.S. troops in Afghanistan.

In the 1980s American officials and private citizens could venture toward the border with some degree of Pakistani forbearance, although even then there were conflicts between the intelligence services over which militants to favor and with how much assistance. Those disputes were exacerbated in the Soviet endgame, as the United States came to favor a soft defeat for the Soviets while the ISI aimed at a quick takeover in Kabul by Islamist, Pashtun allies.

Hussain Haqqani describes this critical juncture of the Soviet endgame as a point when American strategists did not see quickly enough the Pakistan plan to use Afghan and other Islamist proxies to project power in central Asia and against India, a strategic or even ideological commitment that would lock in Pakistan policy for decades.[8] Some Pakistanis saw the massive explosion of an ammunition depot near Islamabad in 1988 as an indicator of CIA-ISI tension, the possible result of a CIA plot to slow down the mujahidin advance on Kabul. The depot was a transshipment point for U.S.-funded arms bound for the anti-Soviet fighters.[9]

Where once the American and Pakistani sponsors of covert action worked in concert, by the 1990s Pakistan was operating on its own. America and the international community had left the field, leaving Afghanistan to its warring. Pakistan and other neighbors scrambled to preserve their interests and exploit the vacuum. In the civil war that ensued, Pakistan identified the most promising faction to be the austere, obscurantist, cohesive Taliban clerics out of Kandahar. It was an opportunity, and a threat, for Pakistan. The threat, mitigated through good relations with the Taliban, was that the movement's more extreme ideology might spill over to Pashtuns in Pakistan. The opportunity was the chance to neutralize the Indian-funded, non-Pashtun militias from the north of Afghanistan, the "Northern Alliance." More than a few international observers in the 1990s were tolerant of the Pakistani view that the Taliban might be an antidote to the disorder, bloodshed, corruption, and drug trafficking that had consumed the country after the Soviet exit.

Pakistan's deal was a risky one. Pakistan suffered reputational costs for its ties to the Taliban. It found it had little sway against the group's more extreme practices. More importantly, the group's seizure of most of the country by 2001 meant inevitable leakage of the radical ideology back into Pakistan madrassas, refugee camps, and villages. Until 9/11, however, this devil's bargain seemed manageable.

The American invasion after 9/11, a low-manpower venture built on airpower and support to opponents of the Taliban (some Pashtun, many not), quickly defeated the Taliban, but the planners had little vision about what was to follow. The United States almost immediately sent Pakistan over to strategic paranoia as it failed to abide by a commitment to keep Northern Alliance forces from occupying Kabul.

In a comprehensive and balanced rendering of the U.S.-Pakistan relationship and the many errors by both Washington and Islamabad in managing the challenge of Afghanistan, Pakistani journalist Zahid Hussain, in *No-Win War*, enumerates many mistakes in the initial months. Most notable was the decision to spurn those defeated Taliban willing to participate in the new political dispensation. America insisted on "unconditional surrender," an ambitious goal for a U.S. war plan that had originally envisioned only several thousand U.S. troops. The victors quickly assembled a conference in Bonn to set a new course for the country, but it inadequately represented diverse ethnic communities. Hussain argues that: "The absence of the Taliban, whose main support base was in the Pashtun-dominated areas in southern and central Afghanistan, had left a big void in the ethnic balance in the new dispensation in Afghanistan. There was a strong view that if moderate Taliban had been included in the Bonn negotiations, the insurgency that developed in later years could have been minimized."[10]

Mistakes were legion. The Western powers failed, early on, to fund and implement a program for demobilization, disarmament, and reintegration of fighters. It squandered an opportunity to work with Iran, also then a Taliban opponent, after the administration decided to describe it as part of an "Axis of Evil" along with Iraq and North Korea. Finally, after taking a hands-off approach to Afghan governance, the United States began to indulge the warlords.[11] Only later, as the Taliban insurgency reemerged, would it shift reluctantly to nation-building, pumping in money and military supplies and creating, in the process, a corrupt and ineffective client state.

Pakistan was a critical player in the early days, the indispensable route into landlocked Afghanistan for coalition supplies and air cover. It provided sometimes robust support against the thousands of al-Qaida fighters that soon pushed into Pakistan. But Pakistan would not entirely forsake the Taliban. Alex Strick van Linschoten and Felix Kuehn offer deep research on the Taliban, al-Qaida, and Pakistan during this period and conclude that "Musharraf managed what the Taliban had not: as Pakistan would continue to do, it became all things to all people."[12] It supported the American invasion, while "groups within the ISI had not stopped supporting the Taliban." After the Taliban defeat, it allowed the shell-shocked survivors to take refuge in Pakistan. It eventually encouraged their reorganization into a guerrilla resistance.[13]

The Bush administration seemed only moderately concerned about Afghanistan after the Taliban fell. Iraq was the favored target, and Washington took its eyes off Afghanistan in 2002 to build up for that terribly ill-conceived invasion, squandering a time of relative peace in Afghanistan, when it might have encouraged a more effective and representative government there, perhaps one that Pakistan could have seen as less hostile to its interests.

Even accounting for the many mistakes of the original mission, it is difficult to imagine a fully successful trajectory in Afghanistan. Almost any conceivable dispensation overseen by Westerners would have sparked a degree of militant resistance. And Pakistan, in 2002, seemed to view the matter in absolutes: any government welcoming of an Indian diplomatic presence might have provoked GHQ's resistance. It is possible there was a narrow counter-historic path to victory among all the permutations, but it would have been exceedingly difficult to discover.

2001–10: Collateral Damage in All Directions

Much of the dysfunction in U.S.-Pakistan relations over Afghanistan was evident by the time of my first diplomatic deployment to the region in 2010. Under military chief–cum–president Pervaiz Musharraf, Pakistan had been threatened and cajoled into providing support to the U.S. invasion of Afghanistan in 2001.[14] It gave approval for the use of its airspace, the only reliable way to fly in, and for use of its roads and ports to supply the troops. In short order, however, it chose to simultaneously shelter the Taliban, a massive hedge against Indian influence in Afghanistan.

Pakistan was unmistakably the victim of the great American misstep of December 2001, the failure to deploy significant blocking forces to prevent the vanguard of al-Qaida, Osama bin Laden included, from escaping the mountain cave complex of Tora Bora into the remote reaches of Pakistan. U.S. political and military leaders jointly owned the failure. They famously chose to avoid small risks and consigned the world to another decade of bin Laden–hunting.

Only late in the Tora Bora operation did the United States put in a rushed request to the Pakistan Army to seal a hundred remote valley defiles between the countries. The request was well beyond Pakistan's means, and the U.S. had no organizational support to offer—resources were fully committed to the buildup against Iraq. Pakistan rounded up scores of foreign al-Qaida fighters and turned them over to America, but hundreds more melted in among the Pashtun communities and cities of Pakistan, a massive virus dump of international jihadist thought and experience among the most restive communities of Pakistan. As Steve Coll aptly concludes: "Al Qaida's arrival created conditions that would further destabilize Pakistan. It connected the country's indigenous radical networks with Al Qaida's international ideologists. It deepened resentment among Pakistan's generals, who would come to see their country's rising violence as a price of American folly in the fall of 2001."[15]

After the Americans spurned the Taliban, moreover, the movement slowly regrouped—securing senior leaders in Pakistan's towns and cities and rearming at the tribal bazaars. Within the remote Pashtun tribes of the border region and the fervid preaching of certain Pakistani madrassas, sympathy and support for the displaced Taliban ran high; new recruits came to join the cause.[16]

Pakistan was alarmed by the hundreds of al-Qaida veterans escaping into Pakistan, but its reaction to the displaced Taliban was more complex. The army captured a few high-profile Taliban, but most were left alone, overlooked by the local constabulary. Pakistan had begun what Washington long decried as its "double game": maintaining its logistical support for U.S. operations in Afghanistan and cooperating against al-Qaida, but simultaneously allowing the Taliban a safe haven and eventually abetting its lethal operations across the border. Pakistan had made its strategic calculation—it would rather earn the enmity of the West than alienate the thousands of Taliban fighters in its midst, and it would rather see Afghanistan at war than in a peace that allowed for an Indian presence.[17]

The ISI maintained ties to the Taliban in deniable compartments. The service worked through retired military officers, but there was some level of communication between the top generals and the Taliban leaders. Pakistan's material assistance was modest, supplying only weapons that were available and untraceable in local markets.[18] Still, Pakistan's role was an open secret rather than a state secret. This support remained constant even as Pakistan-U.S. and Pakistan-Afghanistan relations went through highs and lows of détente and hostility. Throughout the years, Pakistan made successive bids to improve ties with Afghan presidents Karzai and then Ghani but also encouraged challenges to their viability and independence.

It may be that Pakistan had little in the way of a grand design when it decided to give refuge to the Taliban. Probably it did not envision a twenty-year conflict in which NATO forces would take thousands of casualties and the Taliban would emerge strong and completely victorious. It hoped to avoid guerrilla warfare in Pakistan by appeasing the Taliban, but it got that anyway from Taliban cousins: the Tehrik-e Taliban Pakistan (TTP), which had coalesced by 2007. Pakistan imagined the Taliban as a useful hedge, the way to a seat at the table and to shaping an outcome in Afghanistan that preserved Pakistan's core interests. Possibly it did not envision the Taliban's total victory.

Whatever the long-term thinking, America's invasion and Pakistan's decision to shelter the Taliban was the beginning of nearly two decades of stalemate and acrimony between the two countries. For the United States it was a stalemate because we depended on Pakistan's roads and airspace. We could do only so much to pressure Pakistan. Pakistan muddied the waters by denying support to the Taliban, but it in effect launched a sustained proxy war against U.S. and NATO forces.

The costs of these policy quagmires have been high for all the main actors (the United States, Pakistan, the Afghan government and army, and the Taliban), but most of all for the Afghan and Pakistani civilians subjected to unceasing violence and insecurity. For the U.S. side of the U.S.-Pakistan bilateral relationship, the toll of killed and injured U.S. (and allied) soldiers dug a deep well of anti-Pakistan belligerence across the Washington policy community.

For many tribal Pashtuns, the Pakistan Army's clumsy work in rooting out al-Qaida terrorists and its modest support for U.S. efforts against the Taliban spurred resentment, leading thousands into open rebellion against the state. The TTP insurgents, the "Pakistan Taliban," as discussed in chapter 6, targeted government agents, noncompliant local leaders, and educators, launching bloody terrorist attacks to accompany more conventional insurgent tactics. Pakistan was awash in violence, and the economy sputtered in its wake.

For years, Pakistan and America cooperated against the TTP even as they were at loggerheads over the Afghan Taliban.[19] The U.S. military presence at U.S. Embassy Islamabad was big in 2010, a three-hundred-person operation hot-seating in the cramped spaces of our old and inadequate chancery.

While still focused on attacking Pakistan, including a brazen assault on GHQ in Rawalpindi and an assassination attempt against Musharraf, the TTP also began "to embrace al-Qaida's message of an expanded, global jihad."[20] In May 2010 a Pakistani citizen with ties to the TTP came close to detonating an explosives-laden car in the middle of Times Square in New York. Both America and Pakistan feared terrorism running amok; both sides blamed the other. The bilateral relationship was not great.

2010: A Peace Process Not to Be Spoken Aloud

President Obama had campaigned differentiating the explicable Afghanistan from the unjustified invasion of Iraq. Given the Taliban regime's unwillingness to hand over al-Qaida after 9/11, the reasoning went, the invasion of Afghanistan was necessary and inevitable. The Bush administration's great error had been to take its eyes off Afghanistan while building up troops, throughout 2002, for an invasion of Iraq. By the time of President Bush's reelection in November 2004, our soldiers were fighting resurgent militants in both Afghanistan and Iraq. Both wars would become less popular in the United States, though up to 2008 most Americans seemed to accept the Washington consensus that Afghanistan had been necessary. Neither Democrats nor Republicans wanted to cut and run from the Afghan conflict, despite its steadily mounting costs.

Faced with tough choices over how to deal with a war going badly, the Obama administration chose to surge troops to Afghanistan, seeking to apply the successful recipe of the Iraq surge of 2007–8 (but, in retrospect, without much of an underlying strategy). It also increased drone strikes in Pakistan's northwest against terrorists and militants. The United States was upping the pressure, but also moving inexorably toward the idea of a negotiated settlement. Simultaneous to the military surge, Obama assigned star diplomat Richard Holbrooke to work with Pakistan, Afghanistan, and international partners to find a solution to the conflict.

Despite the bluster of well-paid consultants in the counterinsurgency industry, evidence was mounting by 2010 that even a fully resourced military solution was not going to work. The world's best soldiers, American army and marines, backed by the most precise air support imaginable, could achieve only incremental, costly gains in counterinsurgency offensives. Part of the problem, as Holbrooke wrote to U.S. secretary of state Hillary Clinton in 2010, was that counterinsurgency "does not work against an enemy with a safe sanctuary—and I do not believe we can get Pakistan to see its strategic interests as being symmetrical with ours."[21] The Taliban could not be defeated because the Taliban could retreat to safety in Pakistan, returning to ambush and attack when it suited their interests. Another weakness in the surge was its famously delineated endpoint: the Obama administration announced when it would end, eighteen months hence, thus inviting the Taliban to stick it out.

Other factors mitigated against counterinsurgency success: a remote and fractured geography that complicated "clear and hold" operations; family, clan, communal, ethnic, and confessional schisms; corrupt, venal leadership by our partners in the government, fueled by our excessive spending; and a national identity built on resistance to outsiders. The

Obama administration tried new directions, including a strategy of sapping the Taliban by turning local commanders or even individual soldiers. Pakistan's chief of army staff Ashfaq Parvez Kayani rejected the "bottom up" approach as doomed, pressing for reconciliation with Taliban leadership.[22]

It was evident by 2010 that the Taliban had seized on the two things that unite Afghans—fighting foreigners and Islam. Even if most Afghans disagreed with aspects of the Taliban's interpretation of Islam, resisting their vision was risky. Educated, urban Afghans were ready to accept the idea of women's rights, or even democracy, but these were not causes that could rally the countryside the way that conservative Islam and nationalism could. In the end, the Taliban cornered the "fight, kill, and die" causes that produce committed foot soldiers—and suicide bombers. The Taliban was also notoriously ruthless—murdering and maiming any who stood in its way—undergirding its claims to national causes with pernicious intimidation.

For all the many factors leading to the failure of the Afghan military and of U.S. peacebuilding, however, it is impossible not to return to that first cause: Pakistan's sanctuary for the Taliban. This safe haven let the Taliban move back and forth across the border at will and allowed the Taliban-affiliated Haqqani Network to plan and implement mass casualty attacks in Kabul and other cities.

Successive U.S. administrations railed against this reality, but our pressure had limits. Anything more than harsh rhetoric risked Pakistan shutting off our lines of access to Afghanistan. It was a no-win calculation, and the war's ultimate, bloody outcome in 2021 assumed aspects of Greek tragedy—fated from the start by the very nature of the American intervention and the Pakistan military's core strategy. In this author's view, only an American war against Pakistan could have changed the outcome in Afghanistan, at a cost far out of proportion to U.S. strategic goals, and with risks too numerous and profound to enumerate.

American governments were reluctant to come clean about the no-win prospects. As thoroughly reported in the *Washington Post*'s "Afghanistan Papers" revelations, military and civilian officials under presidents Bush, Obama, and Trump were aware that the counterinsurgency and nation-building projects in Afghanistan were not succeeding even as spokespersons put forward cherry-picked progress statistics for public consumption.[23] I do not believe these assurances ever found much purchase. A still influential percentage of the American public remembered Pentagon claims of success during Vietnam. Among the majority too young to remember Vietnam, plenty were born skeptical and well aware when the government was selling a bill of goods.

Holbrooke was an excellent choice for the diplomatic effort in the early Obama administration. The lead diplomat behind the Dayton Accords, which ended the Balkan Wars of the 1990s, he was capable, headstrong, and aggrandizing, all good characteristics for the Afghanistan assignment. Still, at least during his lifetime, the opponents of negotiation would be stronger—swaths of the Pentagon and CIA and even the White House opposed a deal or even talks with the Taliban. In any case, the Taliban was not ready. Nor was Pakistan.[24]

Holbrooke's title was special representative for Afghanistan and Pakistan (SRAP, pronounced "S-wrap"), and he took the inclusion of Pakistan in his title seriously. SRAP came to mean the man and his office and, for the State Department at least, SRAP ran diplomatic policy toward Pakistan and Afghanistan in 2009–10. The titularly responsible Bureau of South and Central Asian Affairs at the State Department became mostly a facilitator to SRAP, exercising little authority. The bureau naturally tilted toward its area of residual responsibility, guarding the increasingly important U.S.-India relationship.

If the advocates for negotiation made only marginal progress at first, the proponents of massive U.S. assistance were more successful, arguing that we might win over Pakistanis and Afghans through generous development work. For Pakistan, the Kerry-Lugar-Berman Act of 2009 authorized $1.5 billion per year. Advocates described it as an effort to address the socioeconomic disparities thought to foster militancy, an effort to win "hearts and minds," and a bid to convince Pakistan to reconsider its security policies. We made little progress on any of these key goals.

Pursuing economic development in Pakistan is a tall order. Even hundreds of millions of dollars in American assistance could go only so far in a country of over two hundred million people, particularly when programs ran up against corruption, infrastructure gaps, poor public education, and a class-bound society in which privileged elites exercise stifling control over most sectors of business. Our strategy never overcame these barriers. We also passed on the old-style signature projects (infrastructure) that might at least have registered with the Pakistani public. Holbrooke helped channel assistance through the Pakistan government, a way to reduce the overhead costs of American subcontractors, but this choice made assistance vulnerable to chaotic and politicized Pakistani governance.

The huge inflows of American assistance in 2008–15 did little to win over Pakistani sentiments. In late 2010, for example, we poured unprecedented amounts of humanitarian aid into Pakistan during catastrophic flooding on the Indus River. I participated in biweekly meetings on the effort, briefed every so often on our polling numbers, which were expected to climb with this American generosity. At best it was a blip, from something dismal like 8 percent favorability to something dismal like 11 percent. We simply could not budge Pakistanis' strongly held perceptions that we had done them a series of bad turns: abandoned the region to radicalized Islamists after the Soviets departed, punished Pakistan unfairly with sanctions for going nuclear, and then compounded the chaos by invading Afghanistan in 2001 and pushing al-Qaida and the Taliban into Pakistan.

Even if the aid and diplomacy made only marginal improvements to U.S.-Pakistan relations, and concrete talks with the Taliban remained distant, Holbrooke made incremental progress at surfacing and testing the idea of a negotiation. This built awareness among allies, Pakistan, the Taliban, and the U.S. bureaucracy.

Holbrooke's death in December 2010 sapped hope for accelerated negotiations. It left Cameron Munter, a career ambassador about to embark on a difficult 2011, with little bureaucratic support in Washington against a more punitive approach to Pakistan. The respected career diplomat Marc Grossman replaced Holbrooke as "SRAP." He was unable to check much of the Pakistan-bashing in 2011–12, but he was serious and would effectively advance toward substantive talks with the Taliban.[25] It would turn out to be a marathon. By the time talks got substantive, seven years later, the diminished American presence in Afghanistan had degraded American bargaining power.

Politics mitigated against risk-taking in early Obama foreign policy. The Democrats lost big in the 2010 midterm elections; the Tea Party was growing and constraining Republicans' willingness to work with the administration. International events compounded the risk, particularly the Arab Spring uprisings. Although in most cases these popular rebellions across the Arab world produced little lasting change—most of the autocrats survived—the fall of Hosni Mubarak in Egypt and the brief rise of a Muslim Brotherhood government there enraged both the House of Saud and its allies in the U.S. Congress. Critics blamed Obama for being soft against Islamist rebellions and too critical of our traditional friends in power. Against the script, it was the CIA and special operators who bought President Obama a little breathing room in 2011.

Zero Light Seven: Bin Laden Is Dead

Like colleagues from all parts of the U.S. mission, I spent much of February and March 2011 dealing with another cratering in U.S.-Pakistan relations, this one brought about by the shooting of two young Pakistanis on the streets of Lahore by an American contractor, an incident recounted in chapter 3. Amid the national outrage, Pakistan's military establishment pressured the embassy to reduce personnel—too many were spies building networks of informants, according to ISI. In tit-for-tat pressure campaigns, a reporter in Pakistan blew the cover of the American station chief, a move that had the imprimatur of the ISI. Later in the spring, the embassy sent home a political section colleague after a minor fender bender, intent on avoiding another dustup. What I did not know was that our work to prevent further ruptures after the Lahore incident was critical to another effort, one known to only a few in the embassy.

I returned to Islamabad the morning of May 1 from a visit to my family in Buenos Aires, Argentina. In the office to catch up on work that Sunday, I saw a tech team laying cables across the floor, from a nameless office to the ambassador's suite. I did not think too much of it—the old embassy was jerry-rigged that way at the best of times. I would speculate the next day it was the video feed, the same one President Obama and secretaries Clinton and Gates were famously viewing from the White House situation room.

I woke the next day to newscasts revealing a downed U.S. helicopter in the military-garrison town Abbottabad. Word quickly emerged that the

United States had raided Pakistan, flying in from Afghanistan undetected by Pakistan's air defenses, and had killed the 9/11 spiritual leader in his three-story residence.[26]

Pakistanis were not ecstatic. The news was a body blow. Many felt a sense of betrayal by their government, as most had believed its long-standing assertions that bin Laden could not be in Pakistan. Whether or not any official Pakistanis were complicit in his hiding, the embarrassing truth was he had lived comfortably in a military town for years.

Tougher still was the black eye to their air force. Pakistan's military is the only widely respected institution in the country. It had been caught out, unable to detect or stop U.S. attack helicopters flying deep into the country.

Finally, Pakistanis directed a grievance at the United States for going it alone. Pakistan was nominally an ally, yet we had withheld the intelligence on bin Laden. We had denied Pakistan the possibility of cooperating in a kill or capture, a chance to soften the reputational damage from bin Laden's comfortable hideout. Both governments spent the first day trying to spin the operation as a product of previous U.S.-Pakistani intelligence cooperation, but it was not much of a fig leaf.[27]

Our Pakistani colleagues in the embassy suffered most acutely. When Ambassador Munter convoked a community meeting to explain what had happened, I could sense the concern and disappointment. These Pakistanis, loyal to their country but great professional colleagues, knew that their association with the embassy would expose them to even more government harassment and tough questions from family and friends.

The government, including chief of army staff Kayani, conveyed disappointment, asking why the United States had betrayed Pakistan rather than trusting its leadership. Despite our differences over the Taliban, Pakistan argued its record in combating al-Qaida was strong.

Unfortunately, the only honest answer to Pakistan's complaint was that the U.S. government was unsure about possible Pakistani complicity in hiding bin Laden. Even if most analysts and U.S. leaders were willing to believe that Kayani and other senior leaders did not know bin Laden was in Abbottabad, a majority were not prepared to trust Pakistani security services with the secret. They held a profound fear that if the United

States confided the information to Pakistan, bin Laden might be tipped off or spirited to a new hiding place by a rogue Pakistani colonel.

President Obama made the only choice possible. He would have risked his presidency in telling Pakistan. It was, moreover, reasonable to speculate that something could have gone wrong in a joint operation. The damage to U.S.-Pakistan cooperation would have been greater had we tipped Rawalpindi and then failed in the operation.

As it was, Pakistan launched an intense campaign to expose and arrest any Pakistanis who had helped the United States locate bin Laden.[28] A Pakistani doctor remains in prison today for his sin of helping America locate and kill the author of 9/11, an unforgiveable bit of Pakistan military vengeance.

The killing of bin Laden changed the politics around our engagement in Afghanistan. By 2011 al-Qaida had been much reduced as a threat and had not pulled off a mass casualty attack in the West in years. Its briefly formidable network centered on Karachi had wreaked havoc in the early 2000s, but the United States and Pakistan had rolled up much of it by 2010. Al-Qaida sometimes "inspired" attackers in their countries of residence, but this was much less threatening than the complex training and preparation behind the 9/11, Bali, Madrid, and London attacks. Even after ISIS emerged with its own branch in Afghanistan, the counterterrorism justification for staying in Afghanistan was less acute. Bin Laden was dead. America had avenged its losses.

The Wayward Private

One additional chapter from the Obama years played a role in peace-making in 2019. This was the case of Bowe Bergdahl, an army ranger private who walked away from his base in Afghanistan in 2009 and soon became an abused hostage of the Haqqani Network. The circumstances of Bergdahl's capture would remain the stuff of controversy, but by any credible account he deserted his unit. Commanders had to put Afghan and American forces in danger searching for him.

For the Obama administration, Bergdahl was an immediate headache. It was impossible to ignore the fate of an American soldier held by the Taliban and Haqqanis, even a deserter (and we could not really know the circumstances of his disappearance and capture until we spoke to him). From the political section in Islamabad, we consistently raised his case with Pakistani interlocutors, encouraging the government to prevail on the Taliban to release him. By the time I departed Pakistan in mid-2011, the army had promoted Bergdahl to sergeant while in captivity.

Over the ensuing three years, the Bergdahl case would emerge as a central piece in the Afghanistan peace process. Not until 2014 was the deal made. The Taliban released Bergdahl in Afghanistan to U.S. Special Forces, and the United States released five Taliban from the Guantanamo Bay detention facility, transferring them to Qatar. Qatar agreed to keep the five under observation and prevent their leaving the country for at least a year. (They remained well beyond that year, contrary to dire warnings from critics of the deal.)

Pre–presidential candidate Donald Trump, along with many Republicans, laced into the deal that got us only a "dirty, rotten traitor" while releasing five Taliban killers "back to the battlefield."[29] These attacks were misguided. The "Guantanamo Five" were hardly global terrorists—most had been in civilian roles in the Taliban government.[30] All were part of a brutal, undemocratic Taliban government that had failed to turn over al-Qaida, but they had not been terrorist plotters against the West. The United States had shipped them to Guantanamo Bay, Cuba, and held them there without trial for over a decade. A better nomenclature than "terrorists" is simply that they were our "enemies" in a war, and if you cannot vanquish your enemies on the battlefield, you will eventually have to talk to them.

This criticism of the Bergdahl deal also misses its central objective. The release of the five was designed to build a channel for communication with the Taliban, quietly and discreetly—and away from Pakistani eyes.

Just over three years later, the Trump administration held preliminary talks with the Taliban Political Commission in Qatar—a commission that included members of the Guantanamo Five. By late 2018 the released prisoners were a part of our regular diplomacy. There was little criticism in conservative social media. What would have been appropriate from the Trump team would have been a "thank you" for Obama's investment in diplomacy.

Political parties, naturally, take the opportunity to score cheap points while in opposition, exploiting issues they would keep quiet about if in the party of government. Mostly we expect and accept this behavior. Still, it was striking how the GOP's response to the Guantanamo Five–Bergdahl deal was quickly set aside when it came a Republican president's turn to try diplomacy.

Af-Pak, Round Two: Lies, Deceit, Surrender

President Donald Trump put a premium on ending the Afghanistan war. In its first chaotic year, his administration's foreign policy trod a familiar but fruitless path, imagining that by being tougher than its predecessor it could generate a military victory or a favorable climate for negotiations. It ramped up precision bombing in 2017.[31] His team also sought greater Indian commitment to Afghanistan.[32] It did this despite the absolute limits to India's ability to project power there and despite the certainty this approach would drive Pakistan further into its hedging policy. In his first tweet of 2018, Trump announced an aid freeze to Pakistan, an effort to force Pakistan to eliminate the sanctuary afforded to the Taliban. Trump announced the policy with a certain verve:

"The United States has foolishly given Pakistan more than $33 billion in aid over the last 15 years, and they have given us nothing but lies & deceit, thinking of our leaders as fools. They give safe haven to the terrorists we hunt in Afghanistan, with little help. No more!"[33]

The aid cut did not alter Pakistan's relationship with the Taliban, but it did get attention, and by the time of my return to the country in July 2018 as head of the political section, there was a more energized constituency in Pakistan for improving ties to Washington. By that time, as well, the tough Afghan policy had run its course, and the Trump team moved to embrace a negotiated end to the conflict; they would ask Pakistan to facilitate.

This outreach built on a meeting with the Taliban in Doha during the summer of 2018, led by the State Department's senior official for South and Central Asian affairs, Ambassador Alice Wells. After that start, the administration selected Zalmay Khalilzad to return to the game, though Wells and her National Security Council counterpart, Lisa Curtis, would play essential roles in enabling the process. Washington launched

Khalilzad's effort by sending him with the new secretary of state, Mike Pompeo, on the latter's first visit to Pakistan. Making an early and effective introductory call on Pakistan's new prime minister—and, of course, army headquarters—Pompeo brought along and "introduced" Khalilzad as the newly appointed special representative for Afghan reconciliation.

Pakistan's intelligence service was a key channel to the Taliban, potentially a point of leverage given its long relationship and the support and shelter it had provided the group, and chief of army staff (COAS) Qamar Javed Bajwa exercised ultimate authority over Inter-Services Intelligence (ISI). It was obvious we needed his support. Pakistan's security services could communicate with the Taliban and potentially apply pressure.

For Pakistani foreign policy experts, Khalilzad was familiar. He had been a Bush administration ambassador to Afghanistan, the country of his birth and youth, and then ambassador to Iraq and to the United Nations. As an ambassador, and later in his think tank incarnation during the Obama years, he frequently condemned Pakistan's support for the Taliban. Pakistan government officials had reason to be skeptical that he could play an honest broker and acknowledge Pakistan's influence and concerns.

Khalilzad visited multiple times over the next eighteen months, bringing different iterations of his team of advisers and staying anywhere from a day to a week. Gen. Austin Miller, the commander of U.S. and NATO forces in Afghanistan, frequently flew down from Kabul to join the talks. The longer visits were waiting games, holding out for a promised meeting in Islamabad that the Pakistan security establishment might or might not deliver. As an Afghan Pashtun, raised in Kabul, the naturalized Khalilzad was able to see into the regional culture and politics in ways that a non-native foreigner could not. Nonetheless, he had his critics, some of whom viewed him as ready to amplify Taliban promises for the sake of a deal.[34]

Despite initial skepticism in Pakistan, Khalilzad gradually won credibility as he described the American government's acceptance that there was no military victory on the horizon in Afghanistan and that a negotiated settlement would have to include power-sharing with the Taliban. Prime Minister Khan, a longtime and vocal advocate of American negotiation with the Taliban, had reason to feel vindicated.

General Bajwa and the three successive ISI directors we engaged over the next year also seemingly agreed to the opening, although they and Islamabad think tankers now consistently warned against too "precipitous" a U.S. pullout. When President Trump announced, around this time, his decision to pull over one thousand special operators from northern Syria, despite advice to the contrary from the American security establishment, Pakistan awoke to the prospect that the United States might really cut and run from Afghanistan as well. It was a potential earthquake after eighteen years of U.S. and NATO presence.[35]

Pakistan, to be sure, saw positive aspects of a U.S. withdrawal. Only under the umbrella of the U.S.-supported Afghan National Defense Forces was India able to sustain its robust diplomatic presence in Kabul and other Afghan cities, for example. Pakistan had long alleged that India was using its diplomatic posts in Afghanistan to support Baloch separatists and other terrorists operating against Pakistan. A Taliban-controlled government would curtail or eliminate India's presence.

On the downside for Pakistan, experts feared that a quick American withdrawal could mean a return to full-scale civil war in Afghanistan, with more refugees fleeing to Pakistan. More importantly, the absence of U.S. attack helicopters, drones, and special forces might create an opening for the expansion of al-Qaida (friends of the Taliban) and ISIS (enemies). The Taliban also had ties to the Pakistan Taliban, the TTP, and Pakistan had reason to fear that their Afghan Taliban friends might be soft on their TTP enemies once in power. Ideally, the Afghan Taliban would press the TTP to negotiate a peace with Pakistan; in the worst case it might use them as a proxy against Pakistan. In short, there were aspects of the imminent Taliban-led Afghanistan that could be problematic for Pakistan.

So it was that after years of Pakistan encouraging the United States to negotiate and end the war in Afghanistan, Pakistanis like General Bajwa were urging Khalilzad to go slowly and carefully. He warned, moreover, that President Trump's open enthusiasm for a withdrawal was weakening the U.S. negotiating position and encouraging the Taliban to be recalcitrant in the talks.

Whatever Pakistan's calculus, Bajwa and company came to accept the inevitability of a U.S. withdrawal and began to work with Khalilzad's diplomacy. They pressured the Taliban to talk and even to accept the occasional ceasefire, thus satisfying the minimal U.S. "asks." They would not push meaningfully against the Taliban's goal of seizing power. As United States Institute of Peace visiting analyst Zachary Constantino described the calculus, reflecting key steps during my time in Pakistan:

"The demands from the United States have now favorably moved in Pakistan's direction. Islamabad need only facilitate talks with the Taliban rather than extirpate the group, which affords Pakistan wide latitude to sidestep the sanctuary question. To satisfy US requests, Pakistan has thus far taken modest, low-cost actions to advance negotiations, such as releasing Mullah Abdul Ghani Baradar, the Taliban's top envoy, in 2018 and convening other engagements between the Taliban and US diplomats."[36]

I will leave it to Khalilzad and his staff to author the book on the negotiations, as is their due and responsibility. My view, primarily of engagements with Pakistan, could only be partial. The center of gravity for talks with the Taliban quickly moved to Doha, Qatar. There was an advantage for both the Taliban and the United States in relying on talks in Doha—it kept Pakistan intelligence at a remove and increased the flexibility of the Taliban Political Commission. This proved a tactical rather than strategic benefit, given the outcome.

Our chief of mission, Ambassador Paul Jones, became a trusted intermediary for Khalilzad, engaged in almost daily outreach to Bajwa, his lieutenants, and the ISI. I accompanied him on multiple trips to army GHQ in Rawalpindi and the ISI's office park in Islamabad and then moved to empower more junior officers in my section to join when possible.

A disconcerting part of our duties required establishing connections to ISI counterparts through messaging apps, to quickly exchange details on logistics and other matters. I was a bit uncomfortable getting messages directly from the notorious ISI. No doubt it was as strange for my counterpart. Whether American or Pakistani, we were all worried about jeopardizing our government security clearances.[37] Visits were another matter, and I stressed my favorite embassy driver with one unscheduled midnight visit to ISI.

We also met extensively with government officials, politicians, and think tank luminaries, taking information from that feedback loop and sending it to Washington in the form of State Department "cables." We reported on and interpreted the occasional curve in the road, as in the spring of 2019 when Prime Minister Khan impolitically suggested that Afghanistan needed to set up an "interim" government to facilitate the peace talks.

There was arguable merit to the suggestion, but it was deeply troubling to Afghan president Ashraf Ghani, producing an amusing diplomatic dustup. Ambassador Khalilzad quickly took a high road to defuse things, tweeting that the United States appreciated Pakistan's help in facilitating talks with the Taliban but that the formation of Afghanistan's government must be for Afghans to decide. Mini-crisis averted, or so we thought. Hours later, our career ambassador in Kabul, John Bass, jumped into the fray, giving Ghani a more robust bucking up by tweeting:

"Some aspects of #cricket apply well in diplomacy, some do not. @ ImranKhanPTI, important to resist temptation to ball-tamper with the #Afghanistan peace process and its internal affairs."

This little snippet is a remarkable haiku of the crazy form diplomacy has evolved into in the social media age. In my view, it was too clever by half with its cricket reference. In a 1996 biography, written soon after Pakistan's World Cup triumph, Khan had admitted to using a bottle cap to scuff a ball in a 1981 English county cricket fixture (to give it greater spin when he was bowling). The seemingly offhand remark, at first little noticed according to a later Khan biographer, Christopher Sandford, soon exploded into an event in the British media, a proof for those who diminished Pakistan's cricket success against England with accusations of cheating.[38] As always in the world of cricket etiquette, there seemed to be a double standard: although Khan was likely suggesting that everyone did it in the English league, the reaction was one of Anglo tabloid outrage at the devious Pakistanis.

In resurrecting ball tampering, the drafter in Kabul had just had our ambassador reference an old accusation that Imran Khan was a cheat. While loads of Pakistanis differed with Khan on politics, he remains the national hero in cricket. It was one tweet perfectly designed to unite Pakistanis, and it unleashed a Twitter storm in response. U.S. Embassy Pakistan did not clear the language in advance, as would have been appropriate when an embassy to another country chose to comment on the government to which we were accredited. Given the sorry ending to

Ghani's government in August 2021, moreover, it is hard to say in retrospect that Khan's suggestion of a different political arrangement in Kabul might not have been worthwhile.

A second small detour arose in July 2019, when we got word from Embassy Kabul that key members of the Afghan political opposition were receiving invitations to a think tank–sponsored conference in Pakistan. The obscure Lahore-based think tank listed on the invitation had little experience with this type of conference, though a former foreign secretary of Pakistan was listed as its president. The conference was not in itself a terrible idea, but it was scheduled just a week before Afghan president Ghani was to visit Islamabad to improve the frosty relations between the governments. We feared that Pakistan hosting Ghani's main political opponents might undermine the upcoming leaders' summit.

I went to the Foreign Ministry to ask about the initiative and received a plate full of misdirection. The official in charge of Afghanistan said his ministry was not involved and the ministry had no plans to attend at a senior level. When I pressed him to confirm that the government of Pakistan was not involved, he deliberately clarified: he was "not aware" of any Foreign Ministry involvement; what other parts of the government might be doing he could not say, leaving open the possibility that the ISI was involved.

A contact who attended the conference described it as poorly organized as a discussion forum but successful in its undeclared purpose of building ties between the Pakistan establishment and the potential political challengers to President Ghani. The Lahore think tank played little role, with management handed over to a better-known Islamabad outfit with overt ties to the ISI. In the audience, up front, were several young, attractive "interns" who might or might not have been "honey traps" for the Afghans. In the back rows were two ranks of well-suited men, what you come to expect from ISI operatives. We speculated they were there to hand over bags of cash to grease the backroom talks. Despite the Foreign Ministry's denials of participation, foreign minister Shah Mahmood Qureshi delivered the keynote.

In all, the Murree Conference represented an annoying but not unprecedented diplomatic feint. Despite the unnecessary deceit, we saw positives in Pakistan gaining a better understanding of Afghanistan's civilian leaders. It was a good thing if Pakistan spread its eggs to more than the Taliban basket.

Ghani still came to Islamabad a week later, and the meetings were positive, the rhetoric flowery, the promises of increased Pakistan-Afghanistan trade and other good things sweetly spoken. There was minimal follow-up.

To the Exits

A major sticking point in talks with the Taliban was the group's long insistence that peace dialogue in Afghanistan would come only after a U.S. military withdrawal. The Taliban derisively referred to the Afghan president as the "mayor of Kabul," a reference to his limited writ beyond the capital. They characterized the Afghan Army as a dependency of the United States and suggested it would collapse following the American departure. The United States, meanwhile, argued that the Taliban should talk to the government elected by Afghan voters and that U.S. withdrawal would follow progress in such intra-Afghan talks. In retrospect, the U.S. government's insistence on the authority of Afghanistan's elected governments seems naive.

The process of overcoming these incompatible "redlines" was at the heart of Khalilzad's diplomacy. His approach amounted to continuously nudging the Taliban toward contact with the government in Kabul even as the U.S. troops remained. There were false starts, including attempted "proximity" meetings (with the Taliban in one room and the government representatives down the hall, not meeting directly but conversing via an intermediary).

Ultimately, the demonstrable intent of President Trump to quit Afghanistan persuaded the Taliban to give a little, and they found their way to joining minor talks with the Afghan government (if in a forum where the government's role was watered down by the presence of other societal representatives). Khalilzad could take credit for getting the Taliban past a redline while U.S. troops were still in the country.

This proved not enough, however, as there was no way to enforce Taliban sincerity or compromise in this intra-Afghan dialogue. It may be that years of U.S. diplomacy focused on getting the Taliban into a dialogue with the government had exhausted all our creativity and leverage. We got the Taliban to a starting point, not the end point, and then we agreed to leave, which was reasonable if we assumed the Afghan army and government possessed the will and capability to fight long enough to induce Taliban negotiation of a final settlement. Instead, both institutions collapsed as U.S. forces departed.

Officially, Khalilzad and the Taliban elided their fundamental disagreements by concluding a deal that promised a phased U.S. withdrawal contingent on positive steps between the Afghan government and Taliban, including a "reduction in violence" and the commencement of intra-Afghan negotiations. Prisoner exchanges were part of the package and continued to be a tortuous sticking point.

As the agreed withdrawal date of May 2021 approached, the new Biden administration had to deal with an intra-Afghan dialogue going nowhere and a Taliban priming to take the country after the American departure. If Washington abrogated the agreement, conversely, it faced the certainty the Taliban and its Haqqani Network would launch complex, deadly attacks on U.S. troops, something the Taliban had foregone for most of three years to encourage negotiations. Biden, it seems reasonable to speculate, was not opposed to the idea of an American withdrawal, but the lack of a U.S. presidential transition during those months of false electoral challenges meant that the incoming administration received no briefs from the outgoing one on how the U.S. withdrawal was supposed to work just three months after Biden's swearing-in.

In Kabul, politicians and the citizenry viewed the February 2020 U.S.-Taliban deal with alarm—though perhaps not enough. Afghans were rightly worried about the prospect of the Taliban returning to power, about how the Taliban would curtail democratic and social rights and threaten those who had collaborated with coalition forces or served the Afghan government. Kabul and other cities had remained dangerous places throughout the long conflict, but they also had grown accustomed to improved rights for women and girls, freedom of speech, and other personal protections. Many of those freedoms are now absent under the Taliban, which knifed through the corroded regime and military without pause to claim power.

The reputational consequences of America's having left tens of thousands of Afghan civil servants, military, press, educators, and elected representatives to the tender mercies of the Afghan Taliban were significant.

Thousands of American diplomats and soldiers, moreover, are suffering the double blow of having sacrificed for a lost war and seeing the Afghans who trusted them lost to potential retribution under the Taliban. The outcome was to nobody's liking, particularly as it was punctuated by the ISIS attack that killed thirteen Americans and scores of Afghans at the Kabul airport.

Despite the costs, it may be that the strategic gain of stepping away from a resource-draining and unwinnable war will overshadow the losses over time. It may be that rather than finding opportunity in post-America Afghanistan, the Chinese, Russian, Iranian, and Pakistani governments, which undermined coalition efforts, will taste their own bitter fruits of sowing Taliban rule. This author suspects that we all will.

The dangers to the United States from Afghanistan remain real. Throughout the long conflict, the Taliban, although equal parts Afghan nationalist and "Islamist," continued to utilize foreign fighters from outside the region, including those attracted to the banner of al-Qaida. At least in public (I cannot speak to all that might have been said to Ambassador Khalilzad in private), Taliban members were vague about how they might enforce their promise that Afghan soil would not be used for planning and implementing terrorist attacks against other countries. There was history to suggest that the Taliban would not interpret this promise to mean kicking out either al-Qaida or other regional terrorist outfits that had aided them in their fight: the Islamic Movement of Uzbekistan, Lashkar-e-Taiba, Jamaat Ansarullah (Tajik), and, perhaps, even the Pakistan Taliban.

The Taliban may be sincere in a belief that they can harbor these "guests" but prevent them from organizing international terror attacks. At a minimum, though, veteran members of al-Qaida who have long resided alongside the Taliban in Afghanistan and Pakistan are likely to have a secure place in the new Afghanistan. There are fears the Taliban could go further, creating a "rest and relaxation" safe haven for al-Qaida fighters from the Middle East and further afield. At this writing, however, it is not evident that jihadists are flocking to the new Taliban Afghanistan, nor that the Taliban would welcome them.

We can feel more confidence that the Taliban will crack down on al-Qaida's global rival ISIS, but there remains a risk that the group will find space in Afghanistan to attract recruits and plan regional attacks. The Taliban has consistently opposed and fought against ISIS, but without U.S. military and intelligence capabilities they may find it difficult to fully dismantle or even contain the group. ISIS-Khorasan is also a check on the Taliban politically, a group that could attract Taliban defectors who find Taliban leadership too moderate or compromising. With an even more radical jihadist rival, the Taliban may feel it necessary to remain harsh and puritanical, which has been the initial verdict on their rule.

After departing Afghanistan, the United States and like-minded allies may try to manage the al-Qaida and ISIS risks by maintaining intelligence networks outside the country as well as a means for launching strikes into the country. This will be a challenge. Afghanistan is landlocked, so our aircraft carriers and submarines cannot access its air space without intruding on that of another nation. None of Afghanistan's neighbors is likely to offer the United States the presence and operating freedoms it long enjoyed at Afghan bases, though Pakistan will probably offer limited access for U.S. aircraft and cruise missiles if it can maintain plausible deniability. In accepting the Trump peace deal, the Biden administration made a gamble that it can manage a return to the pre-2001 status quo of a Taliban regime permitting al-Qaida's presence, in part because our homeland and global vigilance is much greater than before. As we considered the emerging Taliban deal in U.S. government circles, including during my time at the embassy, there was a bit of magical thinking about how the Taliban might allow a residual U.S. military presence in Kabul, a force that would have a strictly counterterrorist mission.

After the withdrawal, critics made much of the Defense Department's advocacy for this outcome, as if President Biden's team had simply failed to follow up on this bright idea. It was never viable. I saw nothing to suggest the Taliban would permit the United States to maintain such a role after they took power. And to maintain 2,500 counterterrorism operators in Kabul *against* the wishes of the victorious Taliban, we would have needed ten or twenty thousand more troops to protect them. For the Taliban, it would have been the end of the agreement. We would have taken casualties and the war would have continued. The dispiriting outcome in Kabul in August 2021 was both inevitable—because we could not win—and a choice—because we were exhausted, but there was no easy option left unexplored by the Trump or Biden administration.

With the Taliban takeover, the United States has only limited tools for demanding Taliban political moderation and vigilance against terrorist plotters. One lever is the Taliban's access to the international financial system and humanitarian assistance. In power, however, the Taliban can survive significant economic hardship, pain that in any case Western capitals may decline to impose for solid humanitarian and pragmatic reasons. If the West pushes the Taliban regime to the point of state failure, the security consequences for South and central Asia could be substantial.

Another lever is Taliban leaders' strong interest in convincing the United States and the United Nations to remove them from international "no fly" lists, and for the United States to scrub their names from "Rewards for Justice" bounty lists. They have become accustomed to traveling to foreign capitals and hanging out in opulent Doha and Dubai. The West should be cautious about clearing these leaders to travel. Our decisions should hinge on Taliban actions against the terrorists in their midst and their moderation domestically.

Other countries may exert influence: Russia and China appear inclined to work with the Taliban, though both have concerns about terrorism. The Taliban is interested in Chinese investment, but it is unclear whether China will demand more than that the Taliban contain Uighur militants, some of whom were long-standing Taliban allies. Iran has important trade routes into Afghanistan and is host to hundreds of thousands of Afghan refugees. Although it now views the Taliban as a hedge against the more violent anti-Shia ISIS, it will be cautious with the Taliban because of the group's own anti-Shia bias.

Finally, Pakistan, which retains real influence with the Taliban. Taliban leaders maintain substantial family and business ties in Pakistan, which Rawalpindi could restrict in a pinch. Pakistan is Afghanistan's most important outlet for trade and commerce. The ISI has a variety of connections with Taliban fighters and leaders, most famously with the Haqqanis. Pakistan can use this influence, and the United States should ask that it do so for the most serious matters—against terrorism, reprisal killings, or the wholesale violation of gender or minority rights. But if the

1990s are a precedent, Pakistan's demands may carry limited heft. This time around, moreover, the Taliban still has in its midst thousands of armed Pashtuns interested in fighting Pakistan. Pakistan will be cautious in how it pressures the new "Islamic Emirate" in Kabul.

My residual hope is that the twenty-year presence of American and Western soldiers, international aid workers and educators, brave journalists, and occasional sportswomen will have left a lasting imprint in Afghanistan that the Taliban cannot eradicate. Despite the many American mistakes in Afghanistan, the ideas planted may be hard to fully eliminate. To this end, the selfless efforts of our soldiers and diplomats who gave their last full measure may have made a lasting difference. Any such liberal impulses appear firmly suppressed for now under Taliban rule but may reemerge when that unjust theocracy proves incapable of delivering either justice or jobs.

If, however, the Taliban gets away with murder again, imposing a horrific and violent theocracy, then a small consolation will be that the images of Afghans living under the extreme and self-interested jurisprudence of the Taliban will serve as an inspiration to Muslims living in more moderate polities to fight for their rights. It could be that rather than serving as a great inspiration to Muslims around the world, the Taliban's Afghanistan will be a complete turnoff.

Back to the World Cup: Pakistan Fights On

At the time of its eighth match, Pakistan was still alive with a shot at qualifying for the tournament's semifinals. A loss to Afghanistan, however, would mean de facto elimination from that hunt. Afghanistan's winless campaign only added to the pressure on Pakistan—a defeat would have seemed ignominious.

Afghanistan could be a challenge, moreover, particularly its trio of spinning bowlers, playing on a pitch that favored their skills. Scuffles between fans of the two countries during the match spoke to the bilateral tensions.

Afghanistan batted first, grinding to a total of 227. As had been the case the entire tournament, its top-of-the-order batsmen scored runs but surrendered wickets too easily. Pakistan fast-bowler Shaheen Afridi amplified this trend. Brought in for the fourth over to stem a spate of

Afghan runs, Afridi gave up another 14 but took two wickets on consecutive balls, retiring Afghanistan's second and third batsmen. In all, the first half of the match had been a mixed affair—Afghanistan getting to a decent, undisciplined total, and Pakistan bowling strong but not stellar "innings."

Joining the chase after the break, Pakistan again stumbled. Leadoff man Fakar Zahman was "bowled" on the second ball. Imam ul-Haq and Babar Azam would march to solid totals of 36 and 45 runs, respectively, before making their own impatient mistakes against the tricky Afghan spin bowler Mohammad Nabi. Forced to conserve wickets, Pakistan batsmen slowed the pace, managing a steady run accumulation through the middle order.

Still the Pakistan wickets fell, plunging Pakistan into its lower order batsmen with runs still needed. The final four overs would be nail-biters—big hits for Pakistan batsmen juxtaposed, in the 48th over, by a masterful stand by Afghan spinner Mujeeb Ur Rahman. In the final over, Pakistan won with a boundary on the third-to-last ball.

It was a disappointing loss for Afghanistan, their closest approach to a win in the tournament. For Pakistan, the win put the team into fourth place on the tables—a qualifying position for the semifinals. At that point, with Pakistan the fourth seed and India the first, it was possible to envision a Pakistan vs. India rematch in the knockout round. Getting there required that India defeat England. India did not oblige.

In October 2021 Afghanistan was again competing, this time at the Cricket T20 World Cup in the Persian Gulf. The new Taliban authorities allowed and even encouraged the men's team, part of its rebooted, image-conscious 2021 manifestation, interested in international recognition and the support of cricket fans at home.

The inclusion of Afghanistan is controversial. The Taliban assuredly will not promote a woman's game in the country, meaning the ICC must abandon its gender inclusion policy to accept the men's team. Whether cricket authorities should abandon the principle of gender equality in favor of the expected moderating benefits of engaging Afghanistan in sports takes us back squarely to the issues confronting world cricket with the apartheid teams of South Africa. Then the decision was to ban. Today, it seems, the inclination is to let them play.

There is no choice but for the West to engage the Taliban regime to address security issues of high import. While that unelected government represses women so severely, however, it seems unjust to bend the ICC's rules and let the Afghan men's team play cricket internationally. The countries of the ICC should use this leverage, and soon, to communicate at least one price for the Taliban's repressive and archaic approach to women.

MATCH RESULT

Afghanistan 227/9
Pakistan 230/7 (49.4 overs)
Pakistan wins by three wickets with two balls remaining.

12 AN EMBARRASSING ECONOMIC DIVERGENCE

July 3, 2019, Lord's Cricket Ground
Pakistan (4-3-1), 9 points, vs. Bangladesh (3-4-1), 7 points

Bangladesh is a conversation killer in Islamabad. The country was once the eastern half of Pakistan, the lesser half in Punjabi estimations. Its loss was a national disaster but quickly absorbed.[1] Its comparative economic ascent today, however, is an indictment of Pakistani failures. Some Pakistanis are starting to draw lessons from the comparison.[2]

When Pakistan split in 1971, the east and west were starkly different places. East Pakistan, today's Bangladesh, was the poorer of the two halves, and government resources had significantly favored West Pakistan from the moment of independence, in 1947. This included a huge difference in military resources.[3] At partition, West Pakistan attracted the lion's share of educated and monied Muslim refugees from what became India.

East Pakistan was asked to conform to a national language, Urdu, that few of its people spoke. It was an agrarian society with a large population squeezed onto fertile but flood-prone land, with little built-up industry or infrastructure. Militarily, it was weak. Pakistan's military had recruited heavily among Punjabis and Pashtuns in the west; Bengalis were underrepresented and formed only a small part of the officer corps by the time of independence.[4]

A Bitter Divorce

Compounding the challenges for the emergent Bangladesh were the heavy costs of separation. Most damaging was the shocking intensity of Pakistan Army repression, frequently called a "genocide" because it was perpetrated by an army of one ethnicity against a population of another. Anywhere from 200,000 to 500,000 Bengalis died, whether protesting, fighting, or just trying to survive. The crackdown, Operation Searchlight, remains an embarrassment to Pakistan.

There would be scant justice meted out for these atrocities. After Pakistan's ultimate defeat against the Bangladeshi irregulars and the Indian Army, which had entered the conflict on Bangladesh's side, India purposefully moved Pakistani prisoners from East Pakistan to India, where they were safe from reprisals. The prisoners would be bargaining chips in India's peace talks with Pakistan, not subjects of investigation and punishment for war crimes.[5]

A commission of inquiry briefly empowered in Pakistan after the war, led by a former chief justice, castigated soldiers "who indulged in these atrocities, brought a bad name to the Pakistan Army and alienated the sympathies of the local population by their acts of wanton cruelty and immorality against our own people." The recommendation of trials, however, was set aside, and the prime minister, Zulfiqar Ali Bhutto, ordered all copies of the report burned. A found copy of the Hamoodur Rahman Commission of Inquiry was leaked and published in 2000–2001.[6]

An important legacy of 1971 was the deep and lasting nature of the Pakistan-Bangladesh breakup. The two did not remain friends. Bangladesh, of necessity, became a close economic partner with India. It kept none of Pakistan's commitment to vindicate the rights of Kashmiri Muslims by challenging India. Pakistanis and Bangladeshis, meanwhile, remain distant today despite having shared a national passport for twenty-three years. Only slowly has this separation eased. One place that Pakistanis and Bangladeshis do meet is on the cricket pitch.

Bangladesh's Slow Rise to Cricket's Test Elite

Cricket had a similarly unequal history between the two halves of post-independence Pakistan. The game had a slow start in Bengal during colonial times, coming first to Kolkata (Calcutta) and then slowly (as did the colonizers) to the floodplains of East Bengal (today's Bangladesh). After independence, the government and cricket authorities concentrated resources for the game in West Pakistan; West Pakistani athletes dominated the roster. Dacca (later Dhaka), in East Pakistan, boasted a first-class cricket pitch, however, and Pakistan hosted its first home test there, against India in 1955 (a draw). There were no East Pakistanis on that team. Only in the late 1960s, as East Pakistan careened toward separation, did Pakistani selectors include a few Bengali players.[7]

Matches in late East Pakistan were politicized, fraught affairs. In 1969 British authorities assured England's visiting Marylebone Cricket Club that it would not have to travel to East Pakistan, already in full agitation against the military government. The British Foreign Office then changed its mind, sending them to signal support for a unitary Pakistan. Oborne notes that "for the majority of the MCC players, the tour would provide the most terrifying days of their lives."[8]

In February 1971, on the cusp of a crackdown and then war, Pakistan cricket selected a young Bengali nationalist to join a Pakistan "eleven" playing in Dacca. The man, Roqibul Hasan, sported a map of the future Bangladesh on his bat and told his Pakistani teammates they would need a visa the next time they visited Dacca.[9]

After separation, Bangladesh required most of three decades to join the ranks of first-class cricket nations. Soccer was already a popular sport in the country, seen as more egalitarian and in line with the original socialist ethos of the new nation. Wagg notes that some in the new government thought to eliminate cricket altogether.[10]

Pakistan's national team, presumably with the required visas, first returned for matches in Bangladesh in 1975, soon after the country's founder, Sheikh Mujib, had been killed as the Bangladeshi Army overthrew his government. The Pakistani team escaped a stadium in riot in Chittagong and then had its Dacca match canceled.[11] It was a rough beginning for Pakistan-Bangladesh cricket.

Bangladesh eventually caught the rising tide of Indian cricket and by 1999 obtained test status.[12] That same year, it competed in its first Cricket World Cup. It failed to advance beyond the group stage but claimed a great boost to national morale by beating Pakistan. As it had across South Asia, cricket became a repository of national pride in Bangladesh.

What's Wrong with Pakistan?

Beyond their difficult history, Bangladesh has become a challenging topic in Pakistan due to its relative economic success. In 2020 it surged past Pakistan in per capita gross domestic product. Pakistan's rival India had long since done so, transforming in the 2000s into a global economic

176 PAKISTAN AND THE CRICKETING WORLD

force, but the comparative success of Pakistan's poor younger relation was an entirely new embarrassment.

Born in greater poverty, with fewer natural resources, having lower educational attainment, and crowded into a great floodplain that may one day disappear with sea-level rise, Bangladesh has nonetheless outpaced Pakistan. Social indicators in Bangladesh are still lagging, and some are even behind those of Pakistan, but by many measures of future potential, including childhood education, Bangladesh has caught up and surpassed Pakistan. It has done so despite a raft of its own governance issues, including high levels of corruption.

Pundits, businesspeople, politicians, and academics have many explanations and a few excuses to explain Pakistan's decline relative to Bangladesh. Several point to noneconomic drivers, including terrorism and India. All offer a glimpse at what ails Pakistan.

The first explanation is Pakistan's wrenching years of instability, violence, and terror, particularly from 2001 onward. In this telling the United States and al-Qaida get much of the blame, and in that order.

For two decades Pakistan was synonymous with terror. Go to Pakistan to make shirts, the thinking went, and you might land in a hostage video. Never mind that the odds of this happening were always lower than the odds of having a car crash on the way to the airport departing for Pakistan. Terrorism wins from irrational fear, not from reasoned statistical analysis. But there was *something* to this fear. When terrorists blew up the Marriott Hotel in Islamabad in 2008, the economic consequences were immediate. It was a hotel favored by business travelers.

Bangladesh has had a few terrorism incidents as well, with radical Islam gaining a foothold in the mid-2010s and ISIS making a singular splash in 2016 with the livestreamed Holey Bakery attack. Still, Bangladesh remains more synonymous with cyclones and cheap manufacturing (sometimes with terrible occupational safety outcomes, as with the Rana Plaza collapse in 2013). The latter are not great images for investors either, but more easily dismissed than terrorism.

Related to but separate from the problem of insecurity, Pakistanis also point to Bangladesh's homogeneous population and unitary form of government as beneficial to its focus on economics. They contrast this to

Pakistan's charged ethnic map and independently governed provincial administrations.[13]

Terrorism, insurgency, and ethnonationalist agitation are powerful but not entirely sufficient explanations for Pakistan's relative stagnation. Businesses, particularly low-wage-seeking manufacturers, will often find a way to deal with danger if the other fundamentals—trade and monetary policy, infrastructure, education—are good. Pakistan's fundamentals have not been good.

As with terrorism, Pakistan's foreign and security policy can be blamed for another oft-cited problem: the country's failure to develop a trading neighborhood, particularly as regards India. Unlike Bangladesh, which of necessity trades with its rapidly growing neighbor and has developed a symbiotic relationship with it in some industries, Pakistan conducts most of its limited business with India through expensive middlemen in the Persian Gulf. Any exports to India, beyond those in a few sectors carefully managed and restricted by both capitals, go to the UAE or Qatar or Oman to be rebranded, the higher prices captured by middlemen and reducing the returns to Pakistan manufacturers and growers.

With a huge land border, ethnically related populations, and historical ties, Pakistan and India could trade a great deal, it is thought, but in fact trade little. It is as if the United States conducted little business with Canada or Mexico, at a cost of tens of billions in lost wages and profits. On closer inspection, however, this often-cited theory takes you only so far.

It is true that formal Bangladesh-India trade is at least three times higher than that of Pakistan-India, $9.42 billion compared to $2.76 billion in 2018.[14] That healthy figure for Bangladesh, however, disguises two dynamics: First, Bangladesh runs a huge trade deficit ($7.66 billion), exporting only $883 million to India. Second, while the deficit owes in part to typically brutal Indian import barriers, it is even more the product of Bangladesh's export imperatives, which point it to developed-country markets in the West. Imports from India are primarily raw materials (mostly cottons) that Bangladesh's factories transform into its predominant global export (ready-made garments). While this trade flow is vital to Bangladesh's overall success, it is not what we typically imagine of a robust and balanced bilateral trading relationship.[15]

Setting aside India, Bangladesh has no great trade ties within its South Asian neighborhood. Bilateral trade with Pakistan was $853 million in 2018, hugely tilted toward imports of raw materials as well. It trades little with Myanmar, its only land border other than India.

Pakistan, conversely, enjoyed something of a captive market with its immediate neighbor Afghanistan, exporting $1.67 billion and importing just $518 million in 2018. Turning to slightly more distant neighbors, Bangladesh and Pakistan trade equal amounts with the Persian Gulf countries and with the members of the Association of Southeast Asian Nations (ASEAN). Bangladesh's great advantage in trade is not the neighborhood. It is its focus on exports to developed economies, an area where it outperforms Pakistan by better than two-to-one.

In all, it seems a stretch to credit much of Pakistan's economic stagnation to bad relations with India or its neighborhood. Bangladesh has far better relations with India but exports only twice as much as Pakistan there, and that is only a small fraction of its overall exports (1.8 percent). It is true that Pakistan and India would both benefit from fewer barriers and more trade, but even without the political barriers, India's protectionism would remain a hurdle to Pakistan.

Once they account for these two noneconomic factors (terrorism and frozen relations with India), Pakistanis tend to look inward for deficiencies, an uncomfortable exercise. My acquaintances and academics cited four additional reasons for Pakistan's gradual decline relative to Bangladesh: inconsistent and statist economic policies; corruption; military aggrandizement of the budget and business; and conservative social norms, particularly around gender. Each one is a credible factor and, combined, they explain much of Pakistan's economic malaise.

Critics of bad economic policies tend to start with Zulfikar Ali Bhutto, whose quasi-socialist policies in the 1970s bequeathed cumbersome, noncompetitive state industries, full of protected ghost workers, who were not required to show up on the job. Despite halting free-market reforms and privatizations, this statist legacy endures. Government protections have bloated industries like power, water, railroads, and steel, raising the costs for other businesses that need their inputs.[16]

A favorite example is Pakistan International Airways (PIA). It was a leader in the developing world in the 1950s and 1960s, a proud flagship of the nation. Its pilots trained the first tranche of pilots in several Persian Gulf countries. By the 2000s it was a mess, an old fleet losing money hand over fist, overstuffed with protected workers, real or imagined. Politically connected but poorly qualified managers filled its ranks.

By the turn of the twenty-first century, PIA was rumored to be open to crime. Unscrupulous officials and workers were rumored to smuggle people and goods on its international flights. Worst of all, the airline skirted safety protocols. When a PIA flight crashed early in 2020 in Karachi, the cause being pilot error (killing 97 of the 99 passengers and crew), reports quickly surfaced that 262 out of Pakistan's 860 active pilots had not taken the pilot exam.[17] Most of the unqualified pilots worked for PIA.[18]

Beyond the unresolved, protected roles of state industries, Pakistan extends preferences and protections to the companies of its elite—subsidized water to sugar mills and cotton farmers and tariff protections to select manufacturers. A wide range of explicit and unwritten benefits drain national and provincial budgets and discourage innovation and competition. Tax avoidance is rampant and successful, further starving the government of resources for essential public investments.

Pakistan has also failed to incubate and sustain the most promising and job-creating industry: textiles and apparel. One friend in the business described on-again, off-again incentives in the sector, a marked contrast from Bangladesh, which has consistently promoted its growth. Over the years, some leading Pakistani investors in the sector have shifted operations to Bangladesh.

Amid this economic policy incoherence, fiscal crises have forced Pakistan repeatedly to approach the International Monetary Fund (IMF) and other international financial institutions for support. Since 1988 the IMF has granted Pakistan twelve major program loans.[19] With the loans, international lenders have demanded a slate of free-market-oriented policy reforms, including privatization and trade liberalization. Whether or not the IMF medicine was really the right cure, the Pakistan government has been consistently inconsistent in implementing the reforms. The stop-start nature of economic reforms and policy initiatives has bedeviled Pakistan, driven by an absence of real vision about Pakistan's place in the world economy and by the fragility of governments, whether civilian or military.

Marked throughout the fleeting political dispensations has been "rent-seeking" behavior, the desperate clawing of family heads and political bosses to gain a portion of the returns from government programs, established companies, union contracts, or housing development schemes. Some of this is corrupt, some not illegal, but altogether it speaks to an economic mindset of exploitation rather than creation. This, I would emphasize, is not my outsider's judgment; it is a conclusion I heard frequently from thoughtful Pakistanis.

Bangladesh and India have also suffered bouts of instability and economic mismanagement. Like all societies, they feature rent-seeking politicians and corporations. Cutting through this miasma, however, both Dhaka and New Delhi came to pursue pro-growth and pro-export economic policies over the past twenty years. Pakistan, by contrast, has been a hot mess of policy reversals and briefly serving economic teams. Investors have not known Pakistan's intentions and, with Imran Khan at the helm after 2018, they still did not.

Compared to Pakistan and most global peers, Bangladesh has remained "all in" on pushing exports. It created more labor market flexibility (fewer restrictions on hours, wages, and occupations) than its peer competitors and ensured the import of necessary raw materials for its primary sector, apparel.[20] As a result, Bangladesh continues to grow as a popular source of ready-made garment manufacture, exports of which constitute the great bulk of its $44.9 billion sent abroad (to Pakistan's paltry $26.7 billion) in 2018.

Pakistan's exports remain weak for a variety of reasons, including its poorly trained and male-dominated workforce, a lack of modern technology, and a failure to meet global quality standards.[21] The low rate of exports has meant Pakistan suffers a substantial trade deficit. With its exports lagging and imports dominated by a tidal wave from China, Pakistan's foreign exchange reserves have plummeted, standing at about one-quarter of those held by Bangladesh (before the global disruptions of COVID and Russia's Ukraine invasion).[22] Through much of 2019 Pakistan had reserves sufficient for just two or three months of imports, a weakness noticeable to any international business.

Closely related to the challenge of poor and inconsistent economic policies is the second explanatory factor, corruption. It is pervasive, prevalent where any business encounters a government regulation or a government contract. Imran Khan made fighting it the motivating principle of his political movement, with a focus on the role of politicians.

Pakistan's corrupt elite have sucked up state resources, exploited the courts and government regulators to protect sagging business ventures, and avoided paying taxes. The enfeebled, elite-captured state then failed to invest in infrastructure, particularly a dependable power supply, or in education and health. With an undernourished and undereducated workforce, power blackouts, and undependable courts, Pakistan had little basis for attracting productive foreign or domestic investment.

Many other countries, some successful, have also had entrenched corruption. Pakistan's may have been more damaging due to a proclivity of its beneficiaries to send the proceeds offshore, into properties and bank accounts in safer places. Fearful of confiscation by the state or the military, worried about security, or just pessimistic about economic prospects, elite Pakistanis prefer an investment in Dubai or Britain. This behavior is contrasted with the corrupt corporate elite of 1960s South Korea or even today's India, for example, where the more unscrupulous capitalists have plowed their gains into more domestic investment, building economic empires at home. For Pakistan, the siphoning of wealth out of the country creates another vicious cycle. The country, so enfeebled by corrupt practices and tax avoidance, is not a secure place to invest. Individual moves to protect money offshore make sense; collectively, they are a disaster.

For all the power in this explanation—and there is a great deal—it has some limitations in explaining Pakistan's versus Bangladesh's and India's outcomes. Corruption is pervasive in Bangladesh as well. (It often rates worse than Pakistan on Transparency International's Corruption Perceptions Index.) India has its own problems with both high-level and petty corruption.[23]

Bangladesh's corrupt actors, however, had a less dominating jumping off point. The country limited the power of the landed gentry, leading to slightly more egalitarian ownership of land and less opportunity to translate land-wealth into corrupt power and influence. This may have slowed the reach of rent-seeking capitalism into other sectors. The more egalitarian approach to land dovetails with other positives on the Bangladeshi ledger, including the financial empowerment of women and greater investment in education. Even with corruption, then, there appears to be a societal focus on expanding economic opportunity.

Closely related to corruption in explanatory power is the Pakistan military's heavy take from the economy and government revenues. Pakistan's armed forces command a big slice of Pakistan's resources, whether human, fiscal, or material. Pakistan diverted some 4 percent of its GDP to the military in 2019, but the greater damage might come from crowding out more productive state investment.[24] For the fiscal year 2020–21, military spending represented 18 percent of Pakistan's national budget plan.[25] These figures are like those of the United States (3.4 percent of the GDP and 15 percent of government spending), but these numbers are high for a country with the developmental challenges faced by Pakistan.

By contrast, Bangladesh allocated just 1.3 percent of the GDP to the military in 2019. It cannot hope to match the Indian military, and accepting this disparity proved a developmental advantage. The net result on the budgets of Pakistan and Bangladesh is that the latter put more into productive investment, particularly the health and education of its population.

The cost of militarization in Pakistan goes beyond the diversion of state resources to buying military hardware and paying soldiers' salaries. The military has fanned out across the economy, taking additional state resources and skewing business investment. Shuja Nawaz identifies the brief military government of Yahya Khan as a point at which the "culture of entitlement" among the officer class took deeper root. Under General Zia's regime in the 1980s, it grew out of all proportion.[26]

Quasi-state corporations run by the military or pensioned retirees are now found in every sector of the Pakistan economy. Commonly referred to as "fauji" companies after the name of just one of the official conglomerates, the companies win contracts, crowd out competitors, and run roughshod over the free market. In her seminal 2007 study of the Pakistan military's economic reach, Ayesha Siddiqa describes in detail the breadth of the four principal "military welfare trusts," including their major stakes in "cement, fertilizer and cereal production. In addition, some of the foundations are involved in the insurance business, information technology, banking and education. In recognition of the fact that the armed forces have a better reputation than a number of civilian institutions, the link with the parent services is advertised to attract business."[27]

The last point is critical: the military has exploited its standing as Pakistan's most essential and most trusted institution—a reputation it has shaped through manipulation of the press and a policy of perpetual resistance to India—to gain its broad foothold in the economy. The competitive distortions extend beyond consumers preferring "Fauji Flakes" to a civilian breakfast cereal. Most importantly, investors view the political connections of military-linked companies as an asset, favoring them as partners and suppliers. A military welfare trust partner means an inside track to a favorable regulatory determination or better odds of winning a government contract. The cost of that political goodwill and regulatory certainty may be a noncompetitive price for cement or insurance or shipping services. In sector after sector, the distortions add to Pakistan's cost of doing business, making the country less competitive.

In addition to the reach of the welfare trust foundations, there are economic enterprises run directly by the military. One is the Frontier Works Organization, the largest builder of the country's roads; it takes on major projects that in other countries would be competed out to private companies. Another is the National Logistics Cell (NLC), begun to ensure smooth transport of military supplies to the border with Afghanistan but now a major competitor to private shipping companies (and, ironically, to the civilian state-run national railways). The NLC, per Siddiqa's analysis, benefits from free land for its logistics and storage. Its vehicles "do not face checks and controls that a normal transportation company is likely to encounter at the hands of customs, police, and other authorities. The private sector transporters must carry the costs of corruption by these officials, and the NLC does not."[28]

The bottom-line performance of all this military business activity in Pakistan is obscured. Much of the companies' budgets are off-book, their accounts rarely laid open to the public. Given this opacity, it is impossible to credit the popular assertion that the military-linked companies are more efficient and therefore worthy of their economic predominance. Siddiqa, moreover, presents sufficient evidence from her research to suggest that inflated payrolls, pilferage, and business losses bedevil many of these enterprises.[29] When Pakistani politicians like Imran Khan promise to spearhead anticorruption drives, it is understood that any investigations or corrective actions will overlook the military business sector. Given their dominance, this means an enfeebled anticorruption campaign.

In 2019 our embassy's economic and political sections worked up a critical look at the breadth of the military's economic enterprise and its deleterious effects on economic outcomes. Pakistanis do not like this scrutiny, but understanding this distorting economic force was critical as the U.S. government developed its approach toward a new IMF rescue package.

Ironically, as the Pakistan military uses the threat of India to justify its role in politics and the economy, its distorting impact on economic growth has rendered the country vulnerable to its growing and more prosperous neighbor. India can invest less of its gross domestic product (GDP) in its military and still substantially outspend Pakistan. In 2019 India spent 2.3 percent of its GDP on the military, less than Pakistan's 4 percent, but the take came from a GDP almost ten times larger. India's defense budget of some $65 billion dwarfs that of Pakistan. These comparisons are not exact: India's budget includes a much larger distribution to veterans and administrative salaries, and it masks shambolic military procurement policies that eat up gobs of money.

Nonetheless, the bottom-line strategic truth remains as a threat to Pakistan: its much smaller economy is not growing as fast as India's. The military can demand only so much from a smaller budget. The Pakistan Army is undermining the economic foundation required for national defense.

Taken as a whole, the Pakistan military's distorting role in the economy is a significant burden and a major factor explaining the disparity of outcomes between Pakistan and Bangladesh.[30] Bangladesh's armed forces also intrude on the economy, to be sure, including benefiting from favorable land-development deals and infrastructure projects, but the reach is considerably less pervasive than in Pakistan.

Poor economic policy, corruption, and the military's role, taken together, present convincing reasons for Pakistan's underperformance compared to Bangladesh. A final, powerful factor flows both from government policy and society: gender bias and the limited role of women in the economy. Both countries fare poorly in their overall treatment of women, to be sure, with Bangladesh ranking 133rd and Pakistan a poor 154th, in 2019, in the Gender Inequality Index presented in the annual Human Development Report of the United Nations Development Programme (UNDP).[31] Both countries have long-standing societal norms mitigating against assertive women's roles in the workplace or home. More so than Pakistan, however, Bangladesh has used state policy to change these norms.

As Bangladesh has put more emphasis on education and health, it has also worked harder than Pakistan to ensure that women benefit from its programs. In Bangladesh today, females are expected to complete 12 years of schooling compared to 7.6 for Pakistan. According to UNDP's Human Development Report, 39.8 percent of Bangladesh females have received some amount of secondary schooling, compared to 27.6 percent in Pakistan.

Microfinance in Bangladesh, a global leader, was another key tool in the empowerment of women. In his insightful study of Pakistan and Bangladesh published in 2009, former U.S. diplomat William Milam identified this area as another key difference explaining the relative performance of the two countries, with Pakistan's microfinance efforts poorly targeted and less impactful.[32] Since 2009, moreover, Pakistan has retrenched significantly in the access granted to international nongovernmental organizations (NGOs), shutting off what could be an important avenue for progress. Developmental NGOs remain substantial contributors in Bangladesh.

Beyond the weakness of its development budget, the Pakistan government has played a more nefarious role in holding back women. Both military and civilian administrations have indulged movements promoting traditional, limiting visions of Islam, systems that relegate women to secondary roles. Per Georgetown University's *Women, Peace, and Security Index* for 2020, Pakistan trails Bangladesh badly in terms of women's cell phone use (34 to 73 percent of the respective populations) and in terms of women's access to financial instruments (only 7 percent of women in Pakistan, compared to 36 percent in Bangladesh).[33]

Overall, the greater discrimination in Pakistan means a significantly lower level of women's participation in the economy compared to Bangladesh. The UNDP Human Development Index records 2019 labor participation rates as equivalent for men in the two countries, but for women it is 36.3 percent in Bangladesh compared to 21.9 percent in Pakistan. This is not to say that almost 80 percent of Pakistani women are not working. Most are, but in poorly remunerated informal roles—tending crops and animals, securing drinking water, caring for children. But the low level of women's participation in the formal labor force costs Pakistan. Were it to approach Bangladesh's modest rate of women's labor force participation, Pakistan would benefit from millions of additional workers generating income and entrepreneurship.

A foreign diplomat posted to Islamabad can easily fail to see the impact of theocratic and societal sexism in Pakistan. There are many remarkable female leaders and thinkers in Islamabad, occupying prominent positions in a few niches, speaking freely, and showing no tolerance for mansplaining from less capable raconteurs. But these are the exceptions that underscore the loss Pakistan suffers by marginalizing millions of women constrained by poor education, conservative social norms, closed doors, and glass ceilings. Through some remarkable leadership, Bangladesh has made greater strides in empowering women, providing greater access to capital, education, and opportunity—far from equal, to be sure, but significantly ahead of their former compatriots in West Pakistan.

Bangladesh's empowerment of women and intentional family planning have also tamed its population bulge, at least compared to Pakistan. Both countries are overpopulated and growing, featuring "youth bulges" of those under age twenty-five. Bangladesh remains the most densely populated large country in the world. Since independence in 1971, Bangladesh has added an astonishing 100 million people to reach its current population of 160 million. Pakistan, with no discernible effort to control growth, has added at least 150 million in the same period. Its population has grown fourfold to well over 210 million today. Bangladesh has overcome Pakistan in per capita income due to both better economic growth rates and the slower rate of population growth. Pakistan, carelessly, has bequeathed itself a vast number of young people to employ and feed.

Educated Pakistanis see most of the glaring economic weaknesses described above when confronted with the mirror that is Bangladesh. Bangladesh was dealt a poor hand at its second independence. Despite the handicaps—few resources, great vulnerability to flooding, and a desperately insufficient government sector in 1971—it has gradually over-come its circumstances, getting ahead with consistent steps. In the mirror that is Bangladesh, Pakistanis see the costs of unreliable governance and their long obeisance to a military praetorian class.

Today, both Bangladesh and India grapple with their own forms of assertive religious extremism—Muslim varieties in Bangladesh and Hindu nationalism in India. These trends may yet damage the economies of both countries. To this point, however, both remain better economic bets than Pakistan.

More worrisome, Bangladesh today is also suffering a gradual back-sliding in democratic norms. In power since 2009, the secularly oriented Awami National League government increasingly exploits its power to diminish and prevent the return of their rivals, the Bangladesh National Party. It uses judicial harassment, exploitation of a digital security law, and even more nefarious aspects of policing to limit democratic rivals, the free press, and academics. Now flush with power, the Awami League government may place fewer restraints on its rent-seeking politicians and might ultimately degrade its positive economic climate. Bangladesh is not out of the woods.

Tough Prospects

Pakistanis confronted by economic decline placed much hope for an economic turnaround on the China-Pakistan Economic Corridor (CPEC), a raft of Chinese investments in infrastructure like power, roads, and the Gwadar Port. To date, eight years in, CPEC has not proved decisive at lifting Pakistani incomes. Some of the investments, in power for example, seem to have been beneficial. Others were white elephants, infrastruc-ture projects that continue to sap Pakistan's foreign exchange reserves to pay for Chinese inputs, loan repayments, and salaries. I took one of the expensive toll roads and enjoyed the wide-open lanes—much of the traffic continued to use the old road, which was poorly maintained and crowded but free of tolls.

Gwadar Port has fallen short. It may yet be a major transit point for Chinese goods heading to the Persian Gulf and the Suez Canal, but the turmoil in Baluchistan and western Pakistan's small population mitigate against Gwadar catalyzing industrial production in Pakistan. Infrastructure without viable economic return is a doubtful path toward growth. At a minimum, CPEC is not a silver bullet to the country's woes.

As CPEC was revealing its limits, Imran Khan's anticorruption drive was also falling short. The money grafted by former rulers was at best difficult to repatriate, and any amounts returned, even in the best case, were going to be small against the overall Pakistan economy. Less corruption in government would be a boon to investor confidence, no doubt, but in the absence of sound programs for social investment and export promotion, it is hard to see it making much of a difference. If the large and distorting military-linked segment of the economy remains off-limits to reform, moreover, the economy will remain entombed. In short, Khan's central economic program lacked the vision required to make much difference, and this more than anything probably lead to his government's military-assisted collapse in 2022.

There are some glimmers in Pakistan described earlier in this book—some recognition of the need to improve education and women's rights and improve the performance of state industries. A peace in Afghanistan, even under the Taliban, might give Pakistan a boost, if the uptick in terrorism that follows can be contained. As yet, however, most of Pakistan's maladies remain. Despite my best hopes for Pakistanis with entrepreneurial drive and sharp ideas, the country's governing elite have yet to do enough to enable their success.

Last Act on the Pitch

In the final World Cup match for both teams, the outcome was low stakes but for bragging rights. Pakistan entered the contest with an infinitesimal chance of making it to the Cup semifinals, a chance that would evaporate if it even lost the coin toss and batted second. Under tournament rules, Pakistan could advance only by overcoming New Zealand's much better tournament run differential. It needed to run up a massive score batting first and then hold Bangladesh to next to nothing in its innings. If it batted second, it would stop scoring once past Bangladesh's mark, leaving no chance to make up overall runs on New Zealand.

Pakistan won the toss and put up a strong score, 315 runs. Imam ul-Haq recorded his sixth century in ODI competitions with a perfect 100 before dismissal, and Babar Azam added 96, claiming the highest cumulative run total for any Pakistani batsman in a World Cup.

Despite this fine total, Pakistan had no chance. The Pakistani run total left it with a nine-run edge over New Zealand. Bangladesh erased the margin by its second over. In the end, Bangladesh went meekly with just 221 runs, all out. Amid this modest total, Bangladesh's Shakib al Hasan scored his seventh half-century in the tournament and surpassed 600 runs, putting him third on the all-time list of scorers in a single World Cup. For Bangladesh, the tournament was a relative disappointment, finishing with three wins, five losses, and a rainout.

For Pakistan, the young bowler Shaheen Afridi recorded his finest performance: six wickets taken in 9.1 overs with just 35 runs allowed. In all, Pakistan had shown steady improvement after a dismal beginning in the competition. With wins in its final four matches, it reclaimed a fair degree of respectability and came close to advancing. Pakistan's 5-3-1 record included wins against both tournament finalists, England and New Zealand. Tied with New Zealand in fourth, Pakistan became the first team to win its final four games and still fall short of the elimination rounds.

MATCH RESULT

Pakistan 315/9
Bangladesh 221
Pakistan wins by 94 runs.

Part 3

OVER THE HORIZON

13 THE WORLD CUP FINAL

July 14, 2019, Lord's, London
England (6-3, 12 points, 3rd place) vs.
New Zealand (5-3-1, 11 points, 4th place)
Semifinals: England defeats Australia; New Zealand defeats India

England has had countless triumphs in cricket and soccer, but until 2019 just one in the designated global competitions, the World Cups. It won a single soccer World Cup, at home in 1966. In recent decades, it has been far from the top of that sport. In cricket, England can claim multiple victories in multiple formats against every cricket-playing country. But before 2019 it had not won a World Cup.

I asked a few Pakistani friends in the lead-up to the England–New Zealand final whether they might be pulling for England, sentimental that the progenitors of the game deserved to hoist the trophy at least once. The answers were unanimously "no." All were pulling for New Zealand. Few of these Pakistanis followed Kiwi culture or aspired to visit New Zealand, but all favored it strongly against the English.

Some of this support owed to New Zealand's forthright and empathetic response to the mass killings in Christchurch just months before. New Zealand had come to represent for Pakistan what the Western democracies should be. Some of it was the light anti-England animus that still colored relations with the old colonial power. Most importantly, probably, New Zealand had knocked out India in the semifinals.

For the cricket fan, New Zealand had an equal "past-due" claim: it had been a semifinalist in the World Cup eight times and runner-up once but had never taken home the trophy. It has been a consistent performer in the past two decades, while England was absent from the top ranks of the sport.

Whatever sentiments and biases a fan might have, though, the final delivered as much drama as cricket can conjure, which turned out to be quite a bit. The match was impossibly close and offered a riveting final hour. The outcome was decided by inches, and then by inches again.

An Extraordinary Final

The final at Lord's was played before a loud and partisan crowd sprinkled with New Zealand supporters. Pressure on the English side was intense.

Batting first, New Zealand posted a solid 241 runs. It was a reachable target for England, but the team quickly surrendered four wickets from its top batsmen with just 86 runs to show. Third batsman Joe Root, and the fourth, captain Eoin Morgan, were out with just seven and nine runs to their credit. Fortunately for England, the fifth batsman, Ben Stokes, would last until the end of the match. At the end he was partnering with England's bowlers from the lower end of the order, not its best batsmen. He needed to protect his wicket and stay in the game, but he also needed to hit for power and collect runs. Fours and sixes were the best way for him to stay in the crease.

Stokes was a compelling recipient of an entire country's cricketing hopes. Born in New Zealand, Stokes nonetheless played for England, the country of his father's citizenship. He had bowled England to a famous loss against the West Indies in a "Twenty20" tournament in Kolkata in 2016. With a 19-run cushion in the final over, Stokes had surrendered an unheard of four consecutive sixes to the West Indies' number eight batter. Just a year later, he was arrested after a barfight; he had broken his hand in the melee. At Lord's in 2019, though, now relied on for his bat rather than bowling, he remained entirely within himself, every stroke calibrated to take just as much as the delivery allowed.

Even with Stokes's exceptional self-control, it would take two great bits of luck to avoid defeat. In the second-to-last over, Stokes hit a ball in the air, just short of the boundary. One of New Zealand's surest fielders, Trent Boult, settled under it and made the catch. Out—and certainly the end of England's chances—but then it was not out. Boult could not control his backward momentum and tripped against the boundary rope, ball still in hand. By rule, the out became 6 runs. England was still breathing but needed 16 runs off the eight balls remaining.

The final over began with Stokes jabbing two balls to close fielders for no runs. England needed 15 runs off the four balls remaining, or 14 to tie. The betting odds at this point would have dipped low for England.

Stokes swept the next ball across the boundary on one knee, a brilliant six. At this point came another almost incomprehensible trick of fate: Stokes struck a groundball that New Zealand's Martin Guptill scooped up easily—it was a sure single but doubtful double. Stokes and his running partner, Adil Rashid, had to try for two, however, so that Stokes could return to bat. They pressed their luck. Guptill took aim at the wicket, a good chance to throw out Stokes and end the contest. Indeed, Stokes appeared beat as he dove, bat outstretched toward the pitch line, in desperation. And then, repeated on every replay, Guptill's throw struck Stokes's bat rather than bouncing into the stumps. The deflected ball skittered away, all the way to the boundary. By rule, England gained four more runs for the inadvertent boundary, the umpire ruling that Stokes made no change of stride or bat angle to purposefully block the throw. The judgment seemed accurate enough. Stokes raised his hands in an offer of apology to the New Zealand team to suggest innocent intent.

I count this as a long-delayed karmic leveling across sports, a makeup for the uncalled handball by Diego Maradona that sealed Britain's loss to Argentina in the 1982 Soccer World Cup quarterfinal. Maradona suggested that it was the "hand of God" that had delivered the victory to Argentina. Why not a righting of the scales in 2019?

England needed only three runs from the two remaining balls to win but instead scored two. After 600 balls in regulation play, England and New Zealand tied at 241. For the first time in World Cup finals play, the match would go to a "Super Over," with each team receiving six bowled balls.

England batted first and selected Stokes, the obvious choice, and Jos Buttler as a dangerous second. Stokes with eight and Buttler with seven led England to 15 runs, a good total from six balls.

Needing to protect 15 runs, England sent out Barbados-born Jofra Archer to bowl. The all-rounder, born of a British father and Barbadian mother, had come up as a teen in the Barbados system, been stymied by a back injury, and moved to Britain, where his career took off again in county cricket. England allowed him to play for the national team after just three years of residency, an accommodation to his appealing talent and his desire to play for England. Archer was capable of 90-mph balls but also had plenty of action in his arsenal.

New Zealand sent Jimmy Neesham and Martin Guptill for the final over, and Neesham held the bat for most of the over—taking a wide first ball from Archer for a free run, then scoring a double, a sixer, and two more doubles. With two balls remaining, standing on 13 runs, New Zealand needed three more to win. Two runs, and England would win the tournament on a tie score—by rule, there would be no more extra balls, victory going to the team with the most "boundaries" in the match.

Neesham took a tough shoulder-high ball from Archer on the penultimate bowl and fought it off for a single. The single run brought New Zealand to within two, and it brought Guptill to the crease. Archer treated him poorly, a tough "Yorker," the term for a ball striking the ground somewhere near the batsman's feet. Guptill fought it off valiantly, a slow strike that was an easy single but a doubtful double. The New Zealand pair gave their all, but England's Jason Roy fielded the hit cleanly and made a safe throw to wicket keeper Jos Buttler, who gathered the catch and coolly dove for the stumps, beating a diving Guptill by a foot. England 15, New Zealand 15.

On a score tied after regulation and then tied again after the Super Over, England had won its first World Cup title. The match had been perfectly even.

In Pakistan, I heard little about the English win. It was, at least, not India. Most of the attention was on Team Pakistan. In all, the tournament had been a disappointment, coming as it did just two years after Pakistan's win in London for the ICC Champions Trophy. There were some calls for captain Sarfaraz Ahmed to resign, but he endured for some time. The coach, South African–Australian Mickey Arthur, was already on his way out the door, soon picked up by Sri Lanka. Pakistani batting great Misbah-ul-Haq would take the reins for Pakistan. The team had plenty of bright talents going forward, nonetheless, and the 2019 core would turn in creditable performances in upcoming tournaments, including the T20 contests of 2021 and 2022.

As in all team sports, often the story is about the right talents coming together at the right time. In 2019, for example, Pakistan played a young teen, all-rounder Shadab Khan. His results were middling, nothing sufficient to take Pakistan to the next level. In 2022 Khan had developed to a top-tier talent, playing critical roles as both a bowler and a batsman in pushing Pakistan past almost certain elimination and into the final of the T20 tournament in Australia. In cricket at least, a rare meritocratic career path in the country, Pakistan continues to produce impressive human talent. The mind boggles at all the potential talent held back in other fields and what it might do for Pakistan if ever unleashed.

2019 FINALS RESULT

New Zealand 241/8 (50 overs)
England 241 (50 overs)
Super Over: England 15/0, New Zealand 15/1
England wins on boundary count in match

14 THE PERILS OF LEGISLATING BLASPHEMY

The case of Asia Bibi, a poor and poorly educated Christian woman from rural Punjab, was significant during both of my tours in Pakistan. When I arrived in 2010, she was already in prison, sentenced to death for blasphemy. She was still on death row when I returned in 2018. In between, I completed four State Department assignments in Washington, raised my kids through parts of elementary, middle, and high school and into college, and saw my Kansas City Royals win a World Series. Asia Bibi had been in an isolation cell. Her children, not much younger than mine, had not seen her in all that time.

The accusation against Bibi emerged from a dispute between Bibi and other female agricultural workers, all Muslim, when Bibi fetched water for them but drank first from the pail. The other women might have perceived this as a slight, based on the legacy of the caste system in India in which Christians were viewed as derived from the lowest castes. A dispute over faiths apparently arose, and the Muslim women accused Bibi of intemperate remarks about the Prophet Mohammad when they suggested she convert to Islam. Bibi and her family were attacked, local Muslim preachers stoked the story, and she was ultimately arrested and convicted of blasphemy. She was sentenced to death.

It was, in short, a conviction based on fragile evidence, principally the angry assertions of coworkers and a local imam. It was a difficult case to assess in part because journalists and government officials were reluctant to speak or print what Bibi had allegedly said. Western embassies that engaged on the case tended to be less concerned over the particular words, focusing instead on the weak evidence and on our culturally grounded ethics that rejected death penalties for expressing thoughts about religion.

Bibi was an international concern when I arrived in Pakistan in 2010 as the deputy political counselor. She was part of Pakistan's small minority

Christian community (1.6 percent of the population), a disproportionate target of Pakistan's blasphemy laws. (Ahmadis are another big target.) Bibi's Christian faith and sympathetic plight as a jailed mother drew the attention of activists and campaigners in Western capitals, and of the U.S. government—which consistently advocates against any blasphemy laws abroad.

Typically, U.S. politicians embrace the "religious freedom" cause overseas out of sympathy with coreligionists, most often Christians persecuted for their religious practice or for proselytizing. For American diplomats, it is often more an issue of human rights and freedom of expression. No matter what the motivation, ethical or faith-driven, American foreign policy has taken up the cause of religious freedom. We pushed persistently for Bibi's release but also for an end to criminalized-blasphemy statutes in Pakistan.

Two assassinations in 2011 flowed directly from Bibi's case. The first victim was the governor of Punjab and liberal thought leader in the Pakistan People's Party, Salman Taseer. He had called out the weakness of the case and visited Bibi in jail, pledging to work for her release. On January 4, 2011, his own bodyguard gunned him down at a popular coffee shop in a quiet Islamabad neighborhood. The assassin proudly claimed the murder, and many identified him as a hero. Pakistan executed him for the crime in 2016, creating a ready martyr for this reason-free brand of piety. The "martyrdom" helped launch a street movement that would help turn a national election.

Two months after Taseer's assassination, assailants killed the minister of minority affairs, Shahbaz Bhatti, a Christian, outside his mother's home. He was well known in the embassy, and we were aware of the steady stream of death threats he received as an advocate for Bibi and for abolition of the blasphemy laws. One of my officers had been spearheading conversations with Washington about getting him protective equipment, and we had raised our concerns with the government repeatedly. In the end both the Pakistan government and the United States failed Bhatti, as bilateral tensions between the countries prevented serious cooperation to improve the minister's security.

The assassinations galvanized Pakistan's hardcore religious extremists, a mix of narrow scholars, exploitative professional insurgents, and ranks of underemployed young men. The Pakistan Army for several years afterward seemed unable to contain the movement, although its black-ops propensity to leverage it for political gain undoubtedly helped it grow. Imran Khan's 2018 election and the closer cooperation between the military and civilian sides of government offered a break in this pattern, a potentially fleeting opportunity to check the bigots and see Bibi released.

The Blossoming of Religious Intolerance in Pakistan

Blasphemy laws were already on the books at Pakistan's inception, a holdover from British rule, introduced by the colonialists as a means of preventing religious insults from escalating to intercommunal strife among their Hindu, Muslim, and Sikh subjects. The laws threatened punishment of those who willfully insulted other religions, but the authorities invoked them rarely. Pakistan used them sparingly as well during its first twenty-five years.[1] When contemporary Islamic governments press the United Nations or Western countries to prevent "blasphemous" acts (satirical cartoons, Koran burnings), they use a variation of the colonial British reasoning—that it is necessary to prevent insult to keep the peace, to avoid provoking the world's Muslims.

Pakistan founder Muhammad Ali Jinnah envisioned a state for Muslims and one with Islamic elements of governance, but he aspired to a secular model of government and protection of Pakistan's religious minorities. Despite the intercommunal violence associated with India's partition, there were a limited number of incidents of religious bigotry and extremism in early Pakistan. A few Christians, Hindus, and Ahmadis even occupied senior positions in the early years of Pakistan. In the aftermath of partition, extremists found little purchase; South Asia's Muslims had won their own state, and there was little need for "othering" small minorities.

Pakistan's move away from religious tolerance to a majoritarian chauvinism has many causes—more than this outsider can understand—but state policies played an outsized role. The deep state—the military establishment—was frequently indulgent of militant Islam except within its own ranks, sponsoring proxies against other countries and indulging conservative groups to challenge the civilian political parties at home.

As Pakistan's early governments foundered and failed to address socioeconomic needs, some politicians and leaders embraced religious righteousness as a useful diversion. Ahmadi Muslims were the readiest target. Ahmadis follow Islam but recognize a subsequent prophet to Mohammad. Subsequent prophets are ever threatening to the preachers of any faith, a direct challenge to livelihoods and received nostrums. Were the Ahmadis to call themselves something other than "Muslim" the challenge would be less existential, but they continue to do so and for this have drawn the ire of the Sunni mainstream.

Anti-Ahmadi sentiment was the most significant locus of religious intolerance in early Pakistan, but it took state action to give it energy. In 1974 the populist Zulfikar Ali Bhutto engineered a constitutional amendment labeling members of the Ahmadi sect "non-Muslim." By itself, this prejudice might have been a mild affair, but Pakistan was simultaneously accelerating toward more conservative and vocal manifestations of Barelvism, its majority school of Islam, and Deobandism, the more popular school for militants. Another accelerant was provided by the military ruler Zia-ul-Haq, who made political use of religiosity throughout his rule (1977–86). The 1979 Hudood Ordinances, still on the books, made Pakistan more formally Islamist (diminishing the legal rights of women in the process). The American, Saudi, and Pakistani response to the Soviet invasion of Afghanistan—specifically the flow of CIA and Saudi money through Pakistani minders to support a religiously based guerrilla opposition to the Soviets, the *mujahidin*—further accelerated Pakistan's fundamentalist turn. Pakistanis also blame the U.S. decision to walk away from Afghanistan following the defeat of the Soviets for sowing more years of war there and for the lengthening stays in Pakistan of millions of Afghan refugees, thereby sustaining conservative itinerant preachers who targeted these stateless people.

Pakistan's deep state, moreover, found religious zealotry to be a valuable tool of statecraft. For decades, it supported anti-India militants engaged in the cause of Kashmir, a nationalist campaign infused with Muslim righteousness. It then accommodated the Taliban rise in Afghanistan as its best hedge against Indian influence there.

While the security establishment fueled militant Islam, ineffective civilian governments failed to build a secular alternative, failing young Pakistanis in the classroom and the job market. The gap has fueled extremism in a couple of ways: first, by leaving a wide demographic with limited economic opportunity; second, by channeling some students into poorly regulated Islamic schools, or madrassas. Concern over Pakistan's educational shortcomings once inspired the United States and other donors to channel hundreds of millions into the country's educational system.[2]

The impact of madrassas on extremism is a controversial topic. During both of my Pakistan tours I saw intense U.S government interest, with particular concern about Saudi funding for the teaching of conservative Wahhabism in Pakistan. The students, it was argued, left school having memorized the Koran and stomached a strong serving of intolerance, but they gained little modern knowledge and few marketable skills. These arguments are compelling to a point, but in truth only a small percentage of Pakistanis (under 1 percent of the school-age population) have received their education exclusively from madrassas. Studies have shown a higher rate of pro-militant sentiment among these students, to be sure, but in absolute numbers, the public and private schools have produced more radical alumni.[3]

The impact of education is real, but on balance the most convincing explanations of religious intolerance in Pakistan must rest with the military's instrumentalization of militant Islam and the civilian politicians' recourse to religious piety when confronted by their failings. For decades, the Pakistan Army and intelligence services have encouraged religious violence, whether in Kashmir or Afghanistan. Over time, the Pakistan state has played a role in training and equipping hundreds of thousands of young men to use violence in the name of nationalism and religion. Religion is hard to control. Some of the men, the families, the clerics, and even the towns turned against the Pakistan state.

In the Balance, the Future of a Secular State

When I left for Pakistan in 2018, the prevailing analytic view in Washington was that the country's intolerant extremists were in the ascendance, the country on a bit of a knife's edge. The army had largely defeated the Pakistan Taliban insurgency (if not its clandestine terrorists), but intolerance on the streets of the cities was a growing concern. While Washington still viewed the military as a bulwark against extreme Islamists, it was an institution thought to be drifting toward more religiosity. Younger men in the officer corps were more vulnerable to preached influences, and fewer were exposed to training in the United States or the United Kingdom.

In 2017–18 anti-blasphemy protests centering on the country's majority Barelvi sect emerged as the greatest concern. Pakistan was and still is home to a more tolerant and syncretic Islam. Shrines to Islamic "saints" are still a thing, and Barelvism verges toward Sufism, with colorful ceremonies and spiritual music, sung by women and men with backing synth music. Nonetheless, the extreme anti-blasphemy movement of the mid-2010s emerged from this Barelvi majority and not the stricter Deobandi and Salafist schools.

Formed initially by its radical cleric Khadim Rizvi to demand freedom for Salman Taseer's murderer and then to honor his "martyrdom" by pressing for maximalist implementation of anti-blasphemy laws, the Tehreek-e-Labbaik Pakistan (TLP) was by 2017 a useful weapon for the ISI's political operators. The PML-N inadvertently sharpened the blade, backing a reasonable modification in the "oath of office" in Pakistan, a change that zealots interpreted as allowing Ahmadis to declare themselves Muslims.

By late 2017 the TLP rallied marchers to shut down major roads in the capital and other parts of the country. The government appeared helpless, with police unable to break up the sit-ins as the army looked on impassively. In fact, the common view by the time I arrived (later confirmed in the courts) was that the ISI aided and abetted the protests.

The PML-N withdrew the oath-of-office proposal, sacked its law minister, and gave immunity to TLP partisans who had damaged cars or shops or scuffled with the police. In early 2018 a TLP partisan shot and injured PML-N minister of the interior Ahsan Iqbal. In this case, the TLP denounced the shooter, but there was a clear warning in the wind for those who challenged the TLP.

As described in chapter 1, the TLP's usefulness extended into the 2018 elections, when it drew conservative Muslim voters away from the PML-N of Nawaz Sharif and allowed the PTI to win multiple seats with narrow pluralities. It was useful to the military establishment's PTI project. After the election, however, the TLP became a liability.

Khan was a popular figure, setting up a government with a modest electoral mandate. The TLP saw fit to challenge him immediately when he nominated Atif Mian to a high-level economic council. Mian was an economist of international stature, and Pakistan was desperate for economic guidance, so the choice was a good one. Mian was also Ahmadi, however, and the preachers again protested and began to trickle onto the streets (this time without ISI encouragement).

The information minister, Fawad Chaudhry, spoke confidently and publicly about Prime Minister Khan's commitment to including all Pakistanis in the national project, of utilizing all of Pakistan's human capital for the greater good. A couple of days later the government dumped Mian. Two other internationally based Pakistani economists then resigned from the committee to protest the government's flip-flop. Pakistan would not be using all its talent.

Along with the public affairs counselor, I called on Chaudhry in his office just after the decision, and we took the opportunity to ask him about the reversal. Chaudhry told us he had advocated for Mian's retention, speaking out publicly, but when he "looked behind him" there was nobody else in the ruling party with him. The TLP had sabotaged the new government's first, modest economic initiative. Washington began to ask whether the state, or the army, could push back against this extremism.

Sometimes a Small Justice

It was amid the general preoccupation with the TLP that we heard something more positive. Asia Bibi's lawyer believed he saw a green light blinking at the Supreme Court, that it would finally review Bibi's unmerited death penalty. More importantly, the decision might come within months. If the Court acquitted her, we knew, it was unlikely she could find any safety in Pakistan, where an anti-blasphemy assassin would seek glory and eternal paradise by gunning her down. Between a life in hiding or foreign exile, it was evident the best choice would be for her to leave. Fortunately, Canada had already decided to take her and her family, if given the opportunity, a decision it would not make public for security reasons.

Almost immediately, I joined a small group with my ambassador, the deputy chief of mission (DCM), and three action officers from my team. We met regularly with the Canadians, through the fall, leading up to the Supreme Court hearing. Canada wanted to keep a low profile up to the moment it received Bibi and her family (and, ideally, even after). Our friends at the Canadian High Commission asked us to take the lead in communicating with Bibi's lawyer and Pakistani officials. Western human rights organizations provided support to Bibi's legal team, so the connections were easy.

On October 31, 2018, the Court published a forthright decision rejecting the conviction.[4] Bibi was innocent. The decision was not a comment on the blasphemy statute itself but on the weakness of the case, although the chief justice noted that the law had been abused. Predictably, the anti-blasphemy movement again took to the streets, blocking roads and issuing threats. The embassy's Emergency Action Committee met and limited our movements around the city.

In the face of the protests, the PTI administration once again wavered. It conceded to the protesters, promising to facilitate a legal challenge to the acquittal. The government was unable to stand up to the zealots. Threatened, Bibi's lawyer fled to Europe.

At this point, however, the calculations to which we had become resigned began to change. Unlike in 2017 the military was behind the civilian government. It did not want to see Imran Khan weakened, not then. When the TLP threatened the lives of the Supreme Court justices and, more shockingly, the chief of army staff, the military acted. Hundreds of arrests followed, and charges were laid against the TLP leadership. The protests evaporated. Just like that, when the military shifted course, the Pakistan state showed it could enforce the law, even against the pious.

Bibi's case was still under review, however, and just as Governor Taseer had been felled by one deluded bodyguard, Bibi and her family were at risk from one enraged believer. My "religious freedom" officer, in close communication with the Bibi family, shared her concerns. She and her unit chief, also an excellent and accomplished officer, worked incessantly to raise awareness of threats to the family and work for solutions with Washington.

Canada was ready to take in the family and caretakers immediately, we learned, and U.S. funding had been set aside for airline tickets. With no publicity (but most assuredly under the eyes of the ISI), the families relocated, in the dead of winter, to Canada. A Gulf country assisted with travel. From what we heard, the family's transition did not go smoothly, but they were safe—and to this point, Canada's role had been kept hidden.

Bibi's lawyer, a bit unhelpfully, kept pressure on European countries to agree to take in Bibi. U.S. members of Congress had taken up the cause as well, asking the State Department why the United States had not offered asylum. I communicated regularly with the leading congressional office to explain our approach—we had a friendly "third country" ready to take her in, I assured them. A more prominent U.S. role, taking Bibi ourselves, would be inflammatory in Pakistan and might undercut our Afghanistan diplomacy. To Congress's credit, the leading advocates let us work the process without public pressure.

In Islamabad, we also met occasionally with European diplomats on the case. We could not reveal the Canadian role but let our allies know there was a plan. Others talked of accepting her, including the UK and Italy. In a way, all these discussions were useful—it kept attention off Canada.

On January 29, 2019, under a new chief justice, the Pakistan Supreme Court confirmed Bibi's acquittal and closed the case. Bibi was formally, legally free. But would Pakistan let her leave?

Our ambassador, the defense attaché, and I met with the army chief a couple of times during this period. We were there often to talk Afghan reconciliation in support of Ambassador Khalilzad's diplomacy, but we also talked Bibi. General Qamar Javed Bajwa, proud and defensive about Pakistan's image, insisted there was no need for Bibi to flee Pakistan—the armed forces would ensure her safety. We knew she was hiding in an ISI safe house, reunited with her husband. A decade in prison had changed seamlessly to house arrest, a modest improvement but hardly freedom.

Bajwa said he feared that if Bibi went to Europe or the United States, Pakistan's critics would parade her as a lucky escapee. Governments would portray Pakistan as a place Christians had to flee. We kept the pressure on. The damage to Pakistan's image would be greater, we insisted, if a free woman were not allowed to leave. We assured Bajwa the U.S. and Canadian governments would not amplify news of her exit.

In the end it happened quickly and quietly. Pakistan intelligence dropped Bibi and her husband in Lahore, and they departed uneventfully. Pakistani streets did not explode in protest. The popular Urdu press played down her exit, but the English-language papers made her a positive headline, happy to see Pakistan credited with doing the right thing.

Most importantly, the government, civilian and military, had stood up to intolerance.

Postscript: Worse Outcomes

In late 2018 we received word through our colleagues in the consular section that an American citizen of Pakistani descent had been caught up in the anti-blasphemy web—the man had been lured to Pakistan over the internet to share in person the spiritual thoughts he was posting on social media. Naseem's comments were taken as a claim of prophecy, that he was asserting a personal channel to God. It was, by Pakistan's definition, a form of blasphemy.

Tahir Naseem's street-corner prophet act is a trope in America, looked at with a little bemused sympathy. If Kipling is to be credited, it was once so in colonial India as well, "full of holy men stammering gospels in strange tongues; shaken and consumed in the fires of their own zeal; dreamers, babblers and visionaries." In Pakistan today, the ramblings of dreamers are no longer held harmless.

Whether motivated by sport, money, or political gain, the Pakistan-based online viewer induced Naseem to travel to Pakistan and then repeat his claims on video. He was turned in to the police in Peshawar and charged with insulting Islam's Prophet and with violating Pakistani laws on the "finality" of prophethood—that there could be no more prophets after Islam's founder.

The case against Naseem was frivolous and unfair, but we knew immediately it was deadly serious. The consul general and I and our respective teams looked for a way out, something that would convince Pakistan to send the American home. We called on the country's attorney general and raised our concerns and asked for a solution, noting that he was at risk in custody. The AG picked up the phone, called Peshawar, listened, and frowned. He asked if there was a medical diagnosis, something that might be exculpatory. He promised to work for solutions.

When I left Pakistan in August 2019, there had been no movement in Naseem's case, despite various approaches to senior government officials, including by our ambassador. All our efforts were private—the best available solution at the time was a quiet intervention to remove the problem and expel Naseem from the country. The American family had encountered potholes on the legal route, as their first attorney had been ineffective.

Throughout the next year, as the embassy continued to ask for relief, a better lawyer pressed forward through the legal system. The case remained low profile both in Pakistan (a good thing) and internationally. Naseem was never going to attract the sympathy the young, poor mother Asia Bibi had, but I was left wondering if a *Christian* Naseem would have gained more popular and media global attention—and whether it would have mattered at all.

On July 29, 2020, Naseem appeared in court in Peshawar. A young man shot him six times, defending the honor of his religion from a rambling man. It was unclear how the killer got a weapon into the heavily secured courtroom. Pakistani human rights groups and public intellectuals condemned the act, but the dominant trend on social media, including from a few ruling-party politicians, was praise for the killer and threats against any move to prosecute him for murder.

By late 2020 the anti-blasphemy movement was again roiling Pakistan's streets. The state waffled between prosecuting and cutting deals with the movement. Early in 2021 it banned the group and rearrested its leader. At other times, members of the prime minister's political party seemed to inch toward appealing to the group for support. The government cut a deal later, in 2021, to release jailed members and drop charges. Meanwhile, the Pakistan Taliban militants of the Pashtun heartland began to openly praise the agitation of the Barelvi-based, Punjab-centered TLP. It was a potentially new and dangerous commingling of Pakistan's extremist currents.

In the end, Pakistan's small progress against religious bigotry and violence in 2018–19 boiled down to a decision by the deep state to limit its use of the TLP as a tool. It briefly cracked down. Since then, slippage.

If anything, Pakistani politicians in 2020 were outbidding one another to define a role for the state in protecting Islam, introducing legislation requiring that any references to its prophet include the encumbering postscript "last of the prophets." Meanwhile, the government insists on identifying an individual's religion on national identity documents and denying the right of Ahmadis to call themselves Muslim. For those

Ahmadis unwilling to fudge their own declarations of faith, this means the inability to do normal legal business in the country.

By 2020, however, harassment of the country's small Ahmadi community was proving a meal inadequate to the appetites of populist Sunni leaders. They began to target a much larger minority, Pakistan's Shia Muslims. Shia had long been the victims of violence, attacked by an alphabet soup of terrorist groups, but 2020 saw a "mainstreaming" of anti-Shia marches and bigotry.[5] Again, the foundation for the campaign was an assertion that any deviations from specific tenets of the faith sanctified by the majority are dangerous, heretical thoughts that must be checked by violence if the state will not act.

The bloody mess of this issue in Pakistan can give any thoughtful observer new appreciation for the Establishment Clause of the American Founders, prohibiting as it did government support for any one sect. It is true that the First Amendment did not prevent organized discrimination against all sorts of denominations and religions throughout American history. It is also the case that a substantial minority of Americans, imbued with evangelical Christian faith, today call for greater government acquiescence to a Christian role in public life. Nonetheless, the First Amendment remains steadfast, a durable legal check on the abuses that can arise when men decide God requires government support.

15   U.S.-PAKISTAN RELATIONS IN A NEW SOUTH ASIA

Imran Khan the athlete enjoyed a remarkably long-lasting run at the top of his sport, bowling and batting effectively into his late thirties and serving as captain of Pakistan's World Cup winning team at age thirty-nine. His run as prime minister of Pakistan, by contrast, ended abruptly in April 2022, less than four years after he assumed office.

His fall came more than a year before the anticipated general elections. Although it was repeatedly referenced in the press that his fall was the norm—that no Pakistani prime minister had ever served a full five-year term—the truth was that the previous two governments had endured for their full five years, even if individual prime ministers had been forced to resign. In the case of Khan, his fall also encompassed the removal of his party. His PTI was replaced by a coalition of opposition parties and defecting government legislators. Shahbaz Sharif, brother of three-time PML-N prime minister Nawaz Sharif, became prime minister.

Khan did not go gently. He accused a foreign conspiracy led by the United States of authoring "regime change." It was payback, he alleged, for his independence and his unwillingness to serve U.S. security interests after the Taliban seized power in Kabul in August 2021. Khan, who chafed at the cold response of the Biden administration—a contrast to the briefly star-struck response of President Trump during Khan's July 2019 official visit to Washington—also alleged the United States was motivated to replace him due to his visit to Moscow as Russia's invasion of Ukraine commenced on February 24, 2022. The U.S. State Department repeatedly and volubly denied the assertion the United States had participated in Khan's removal from power.[1]

A Cricketer's Blueprint?

As a cricket bowler, Imran Khan was a second-generation adopter of a Pakistani innovation: "reverse swing." It was a technique uniquely available to fast bowlers, though it required a team effort to impose wear and tear on a game ball over a long inning. Some viewed it as on the borderline of not being "cricket," a violation of the unwritten norms of the game.[2]

Conventional swing bowling—a curve in the trajectory produced by the angle of delivery—has been around for over a century. By rubbing or shining the ball on one side with spit or sweat or even hair gel, the team could enhance the effect. After a few overs, the ball will be ready for greater swing as the ball's shiny side experiences less friction in the air, the rougher side more drag. With "inswing," the ball may start wide of the batsman and then turn in toward his body. With "outswing," a ball may be launched in line with the batsman or the stumps but then tail away. As the ball is further worn during an inning, it becomes less useful for the swing bowler and more appropriate for slower spinners.

Swing had been a global development in bowling, considered within the English gentleman's expectations for what was "cricket." With swing bowling, at least, quick-eyed batters knew what to look for, picking up the shiny side and making rapid-fire calculations about how the ball might move. Pakistan's bowlers are widely credited with taking swing to its next and surprising level.

Pakistan's high-speed pace bowlers, including Khan, found the ball curved against the expected trajectory of spin at a high speed. This effect could be enhanced by consistent treatment of the ball. Over time, the constant application of liquid to the shiny side would begin to affect its surface, creating distinct disturbances in the airflow and reversing the normal expected swing.[3] With "reverse" swing, a ball might be induced to begin its swing conventionally and then reverse course. Developed by a Pakistani bowler, Sarfraz Nawaz, this technique was passed to Imran and by him to the key 1990s duo of Wasim Akram and Waqar Younis. These masters used the technique to pronounced effect, and it would play a part in Pakistan's 1992 World Cup victory.

Reverse swing was unconventional; over the years, it evoked accusations of illegal ball tampering from frustrated opponents. These accusations were most often targeted at Pakistani teams, although reverse swing would be picked up by bowlers from other countries.

At first glance, the election of Imran Khan in 2018 was a case of reverse swing in the country's political life. Until that point, Pakistan had vacillated between two predictable swings, one to military-led governments, the other to civilian governments of the Pakistan People's Party or the Pakistan Muslim League-Nawaz. The army, to be sure, was a constant, never far from the civilians. It cordoned off its rent-seeking, foreign policy prerogatives, and human rights abuses from political interference. But on the surface, there was almost regular rotation between two civilian parties and an occasional general at the top. Despite the frequent alternations, Pakistanis thought there was little practical difference. Whoever was in charge, Pakistan remained mired in corruption and poor economic performance.

To the hopeful, Imran Khan shattered the old system. He had become a global star on merit and then gone to the wilderness to build his political movement. His Lahori Pashtun family had been upper crust, to be sure, but not of the feudal system. He could claim a mantle of upright, incorruptible, meretricious worthiness. He focused his attacks on the civilian politicians, but in some of his stances there was a whiff of challenge to the military.

Khan the populist firebrand, with a national following that was his alone and not the property of local political princes, might indeed have posed a threat to the Pakistan Army's political authority. If any Pakistani leader had the wherewithal to withstand ISI dirty tricks it was him. Voters had long since shrugged off rumors of a child born to him out of wedlock, of womanizing, even of drug use. He was widely considered innocent of personal financial wrongdoing and therefore immune to planted stories or blackmail.

As prime minister, Khan did not embody the independence of spirit often credited him. Not only had he accepted military help to get elected, but most thought he continued to rely on the deep state to maintain his power. His election and governance did not suggest a substantial change in Pakistani politics, as neither Khan nor his institutionally weak PTI possessed the guile, willfulness, or power required to shake the army's hold. He did not have the making of a populist like Turkey's Recep Tayyip Erdoğan, capable of pushing the military back into the barracks and out of politics. Instead, the PTI coalition was held in place by compromises with past players, including the MQM and recycled officials from the pro-Musharraf Pakistan Muslim League–Quaid-e-Azam. At different points in its lifespan, Khan's government relied on the military to shore it up against challenges, until that support vanished.

Against corruption, Khan may have had some success in limiting the self-dealing of his ministers, at least compared to past administrations, but the military's vast prerogatives remained untouched. His hopes to provide more state assistance to those in need were noble aspirations, but his government lacked a convincing economic vision for how to create growth and employment. As for many a populist firebrand, the challenge of governing proved daunting.

Following Khan's April 2022 removal from power, questions arose as to his legacy and his future. His party bounced back at the ballot box, winning by-elections in 2022. It organized large rallies to protest the new civilian government and, implicitly, its military promoters. An assassination attempt against him, in October 2022, attracted more public sympathy and appeared to risk a dangerous political crossroads for the country. The government's pursuit of corruption charges against him into 2023 raised the temperature still more.

Khan is almost certain to run again in the next general election, whether held in mid-2023 or earlier, unless court proceedings prevent him from doing so. It would be foolish to predict how he and other parties will fare. Pakistan politics are too uncertain, subject to the democratic whims of voters and to deep manipulation by a variety of interested institutions. We cannot know how things will develop, but I will be watching a few key dynamics.

First, will Khan's popular following endure? He captured the enthusiastic support of millions of young Pakistanis in his long campaign to become prime minister, and he sustains an appeal to well-off Pakistanis living overseas and to conservative religious nationalists at home. He has draped himself in the flag as he blames his removal on a foreign conspiracy, threatening to chip away at the military's monopoly as defender of Pakistan's sovereignty.

Khan's unique attributes may allow him to overcome the spotty record of his rule over the course of almost four years. As head of government, he proved ineffective working within a parliamentary system, at compromising, and at developing and implementing a meaningful economic policy. His "anticorruption" stance proved to be inadequate as a framework for creating economic growth. Like all countries during this timeframe, Pakistan was buffeted by the economic drag of COVID-19, the inflationary winds of supply chain disruption, and the Russian war on Ukraine, but Khan's economic management seemed particularly haphazard apart from these challenges.

His foreign policy also came into question, particularly his too-enthusiastic response to the Taliban's seizure of power in Kabul in August 2021. When the Taliban's Afghanistan became a continuing source of terrorist infiltration into Pakistan, to an increased campaign of ISIS-K bombings and "Pakistan Taliban" attacks, Khan's alleged Taliban sympathies became a liability. Regarding Moscow, Pakistan had valid reasons for sustaining a neutral stance in the wake of Russia's war of aggression, particularly given Islamabad's geopolitical dependence on China, but there was no way to make his extended meetings in Moscow on February 24 look like smart public relations. Even for his faithful followers, Khan's record stands in need of significant improvement if he is awarded a second act.

Second, how will the military approach Khan's protests and his next candidacy? Press reports in 2022 indicated that Khan had lost the military's backing. Whether or not the military worked toward his removal in 2022, it no longer sustained him. The open breach had begun in October 2021, when Khan dallied in confirming the army's selection to replace Lt. Gen. Faiz Hameed as director general of Inter-Services Intelligence. Hameed was considered a backroom political fixer supportive of Khan, and the prime minister apparently wanted the intelligence chief to stay in place. The replacement, Gen. Nadeem Anjum, was thought by observers to be less committed to Khan's political survival.[4] It was thought that General Bajwa took offense at Khan's interference in the prerogatives of the military.

Popular movements have persisted in Pakistan even in the face of military opposition. The Pashtun Rights Movement (PTM) has endured in the face of violent attacks, press censorship, and legal crackdowns. It is not certain that Khan's "street power" will be the same in 2022–23 without implicit military backing, but his party's solid showing in Punjab and Islamabad parliamentary by-elections suggested his movement still had legs. He may stage a strong run in the next national election if allowed to run, forcing the security establishment to acquiesce or ratchet up its maneuvering against the PTI.

Significantly, General Bajwa retired as chief of army staff in November 2022, and Khan was by then out of power and so unable to pick his successor. Prime Minister Sharif chose Gen. Asim Munir, an officer Khan may have helped remove from leadership of the ISI in 2019.

A final question related to Imran Khan's legacy is whether anything he built in the PTI can persist without him. Pakistan's long-dominant political parties, the PPP and the PML-N, have been oddly dynastic affairs, parties controlled by and dependent on the hereditary leadership of a particular family. Both have a next generation in place (or at least several competing individuals in the next generation).

Khan's PTI is just as personalistic, dependent for cohesion entirely on the force of his personality and his ability to attract voters. But at sixty-nine years old, Khan has no obvious heir. None of the party's leading lights seems capable of achieving anything like his stature. He indicates that he intends to continue as the PTI leader, and he may succeed in reclaiming the national government, but without a succession plan the PTI begins to look rickety. Many midlevel politicos who flocked to his banner may see better long-term opportunities in quietly drifting back to the traditionally dominant parties.

Is There a Reverse Swing in America's Pakistan Policy?

For all the occasional bluster, U.S.-Pakistan relations were remarkably stable from the 1950s to the mid-2010s. Core pathologies were established in the first decade of the bilateral relationship and persisted. Among the most pronounced were American inclinations to see the Pakistan Army as the only sure bulwark against Islamic fundamentalism and to suspect that it might govern better than the country's politicians. The U.S. government understood that the Pakistan Army's excessive demands on the economy prevented Pakistan's economic development but accepted this as preferable to the political instability that might come with unreliable civilian politicians. Pakistan's civilian leaders and electorate suffered a related malady, it seemed, excusing all sorts of damaging behavior by their military to sustain a forever (cold) war over Kashmir.

Pakistan has been in denial about the costs of its indulgences to militant Islam, blaming America's Afghan misadventure but not its own policies for bringing an intense wave of terrorist violence to the country. It spins out excuses when its anti-India proxies escalate from insurgency to mass-casualty terrorism, as in Mumbai. Most important to the bilateral relationship, Pakistan has never stopped hedging against America's desired outcomes, whether by welcoming China's influence, developing scores of nuclear weapons, or sustaining the Taliban during the Afghanistan war.

Though the old patterns persisted—the institutional ideologies of the deep state in Pakistan and the foreign policy establishment in Washington—geopolitical changes have forced some reconsideration in both capitals. The long-established trajectory of U.S.-Pakistan relations had begun to wobble well before the U.S. pull-out from Afghanistan. Three impactful developments stand out.

First, American concerns over ties between the Pakistan Army and Islamist militants moved to the forefront of U.S. policy in the aftermath of 9/11, leaving less room for the excuses formerly given for Pakistan's dalliances with extremists. This was particularly so after American troops became directly vulnerable to extremists after the U.S. intervention in Afghanistan.

The American intervention also birthed the Pakistani "double game," in which its military and intelligence services cooperated with the United States and the United Nations' authorized actions in Afghanistan, all the while sustaining indulgent ties to the Taliban insurgency. That Rawalpindi's gambit was driven by geopolitics rather than sympathy for Taliban rule could not deflect rising concern in Washington over ties between the Pakistan Army and a range of Islamist forces: mullahs, fighters, tribal elders, charities, and terrorists. The 2008 Lashkar-e-Taiba attack on Mumbai, India, compounded the doubts strewn by Afghanistan, shattering Washington's capacity to ignore Pakistan-sponsored militancy in Kashmir.

Domestically, as well, the Pakistan military seemed increasingly comfortable with the forces of religious intolerance. This concern was amplified by ISI's use of the anti-blasphemy TLP to bludgeon the PML-N government in 2017 and 2018. True, the Pakistan Army rallied against the Pakistan Taliban throughout the 2010s and against the TLP in 2019, when it threatened the state, but Washington remained skeptical of Islamabad's commitment to eradicating militancy. Recent government negotiations with the Pakistan Taliban and concessions to the TLP caused these concerns to resurface.

A second change has been the rise of an assertive China. Where the fall of the Soviet Union had allowed the United States to diminish its attention to Pakistan but not required that it court India, the rise of China was another matter. The United States and India found that they needed one another. For Washington, India's massive population, respectable economic growth, and keystone geography astride the Indian Ocean made it important. Washington even recoined geography, shifting from "Asian-Pacific" to "Indo-Pacific" so that it could count India on the ledger against China. India meanwhile needed a strong partner and lots of bolstering as it rapidly found itself trailing China in terms of military technology, financial power, and global influence.

The impact of China's rise and the U.S.-India entente on U.S.-Pakistan relations was obscured by the legacy of the "war on terror" conflict in Afghanistan. U.S.-Pakistan relations worsened but remained intense as long as Washington sought victory—or an honorable exit—from Afghanistan. But that imperative was already losing its relative strength long before the Taliban's 2021 victory. Beijing's industrial and financial dominance and modernizing military were identified as the most significant threats to American security. India became essential. Pakistan reverted to being a distraction, albeit one capable of making America's final years in Afghanistan marginally better or marginally worse than they were going to be regardless.

With the end of the Afghan war, Pakistan's value to Washington may have dropped again. It no longer has the leverage associated with its sheltering of the Taliban. It remains America's only viable air route into Afghanistan, should the Pentagon wish to strike at a terrorist training camp there, but Pakistan is unlikely to risk upsetting the new Taliban regime by authorizing any but the most "deniable" of American air raids or cruise missile strikes on the most justifiable targets (such as the July 31, 2022, killing of al-Qaida leader Ayman al-Zawahiri).

The U.S.-India entente or alliance is still developing, but it has already ensured that the contours of U.S.-Pakistan relations have changed. It would be difficult for any American administration to replicate the decision of President George Bush in 2005 to provide new advanced F-16 aircraft to Pakistan. The bilateral military relationship has fallen off a cliff, now confined to the necessary monitoring and servicing of U.S. weapons systems and a modicum of professional exchange and training. American influence at Army General Headquarters has concurrently dissipated.

What military-to-military relationship remains is now clouded by the twenty-year bleeding of Afghanistan. Americans blame the Pakistan Army for the proxy policies that led to so many casualties and to the bad outcome in Kabul.

Although this moral dudgeon against the Pakistan Army and its Haqqani Network clients persists, most U.S. military officers I engaged with respected their Pakistani counterparts. Most significantly, they did not excuse certain actions, but they understood that their Pakistani counterparts were pursuing policies conceived to be in the best interest of Pakistan. It was a job. For this cadre, the terminology of "good" and "evil" in statecraft is rarely apt. This recognition opens a door to dialogue and a path away from the worst outcomes.

As U.S.-Pakistan military relations have diminished, China has steadily expanded its presence and support. China is the preeminent patron of Pakistan today. As such, pressure on Pakistan to maintain democratic norms has further declined—China demands stability for its investments but places little emphasis on how a government achieves these goals.

Just as U.S. influence in Rawalpindi and Islamabad has declined, Pakistan's leverage in Washington has fallen after the end of the Afghan war. Washington considers Pakistan potentially valuable against terrorist threats in Afghanistan but knows this cooperation will have sharp limits, thereby diminishing Pakistan's bargaining power. It is far removed from the imagined leverage that Haqqani bombers targeting American troops once produced, or the real leverage over thousands of tons of cargo traversing Pakistani highways for Afghanistan.

These two trends might suggest the possibility of a clash. Washington feels less need to excuse praetorian excess in Pakistan just as Rawalpindi finds less value in the American security relationship. Neither side has compelling reasons for restraint, should Pakistan and America again come into contention. On the other hand, there is far less accelerant in the troubled relationship today. And both sides have residual interests in copacetic ties.

Even with China's firm support, Pakistan's military and civilian leadership have reasons to seek functional ties with Washington. Pakistan does not wish to be even more beholden to Beijing, nor does it want to foreclose the bargaining advantages that come with having other suitors. China has shown Pakistan its limits over the past three years, moreover, providing only modest new loans and calling in some old ones. Pakistan also wants to avoid pushing the United States toward an even more enthusiastic embrace of India. Both Pakistan and the United States have reasons to keep the other side interested.

Moreover, I do not entirely dismiss the talk from Pakistani generals about enduring affinity to the English-speaking Western democracies. The army values institutional linkages to the United States, Britain, and Australia; it desires respectability and travel access for its officers and their families; and it recognizes the importance of Western governments and businesses to Pakistan's economic future. To date, China has accepted a level of Pakistani cooperation with the United States and Europe, just as China desires to sustain its own interests in India and the United States. Few governments envision benefits from a world hardening into inflexible blocs.

Given these parameters, a diminished but vital U.S.-Pakistan partnership remains both achievable and in American interests. It can advance U.S. objectives in a few critical ways:

> encouraging Pakistan to remain invested in relations with the United States rather than forcing it into exploitative ties to China
> ensuring that India not view our budding condominium against China as support for overreactions to Pakistani provocations
> sustaining connections into a Taliban-controlled Afghanistan for humanitarian or counterterrorism needs

maintaining dialogue on Pakistan's nuclear security, particularly the
safeguarding of its hundred-plus nuclear warheads

enhancing law enforcement cooperation against international terrorist networks such as al-Qaida and ISIS

sustaining pressure for Pakistan's restraint on Kashmir

Can Washington aspire to more? Beyond aspiring to a more stable and
moderate Pakistan, one that does not fall entirely into China's hands,
can U.S. foreign policy makers aim bigger? Among the goals that would
be beneficial to Pakistanis and to American interests: a Pakistan that
trades in peace with India; a Pakistan that spreads wealth and opportunity
more evenly across its population; a Pakistan that redirects some of its
military expenditure to general uplift and ends the political control by
men in uniform; and a Pakistan that allows its citizens of different sects
and religions, and even those with no desire for religion, to live lives of
security and purpose.

The short answer is that most of those aspirations for Pakistan are
beyond America's influence. They run up hard against the still dominant
ideologies of Pakistan's powerful institutions. They are, fundamentally,
goals for Pakistanis to embrace and advance rather than for outsiders.
They require that Pakistani generals step back from politics and that
moderate faith leaders, intellectuals, and popular influencers step forward against intolerance and militancy. In economics, it would require a
societal or legal check on destructive, rent-seeking behaviors. America,
with a past full of compromised policies and damaging interventions in
the region, cannot take the lead for such outcomes. Americans have far
too much work to do at home in any case.

Pakistan is also limited in what it can aspire to with Washington if its
establishment continues its dance with militancy. The ascendance of
India in U.S. calculations means Washington has little incentive or latitude
to excuse Kashmir-focused militancy. Pakistanis will rightly argue American hypocrisy as Washington soft-pedals its response to India's extremism
on the rising Hindu right, but the requirements of U.S. national security
will win out, no matter how eloquent Pakistan's complaints. Pakistan
will achieve at most a grudging détente with Washington if it supports
externally directed militants and internally focused extremists, harasses

human rights advocates at home, mass produces nuclear bombs, and excuses Chinese (and Russian) revanchism.

If our mutual opportunities for a radical reset are limited, though, Pakistan and America have good reasons to aspire to modest gains. Washington, in furtherance of those ends, should limit resorting to coercive tools and instead enhance connections and incentives.

Sanctions should be limited and targeted. In over a decade observing U.S. policy in Pakistan, I watched as threatened American sanctions, often backed by our allies, produced little to no change in the country's overarching security policies. This includes the security establishment's support for proxies in Afghanistan and its pursuit of more advanced nuclear weapons and missiles. Smaller changes could be induced, however. The tiered rankings of our "Trafficking in Persons" report or designations under "Religious Freedom Legislation" got the attention of Pakistan's foreign policy establishment like few other remonstrations. Pakistan took modest steps to address problems in both areas, in part because Pakistan seeks to be perceived as a good global citizen.

We have had occasional, if limited, success in inducing Pakistan to rein in ties to militants and terrorists. The Financial Action Task Force (FATF), an international mechanism to sanction countries that fail to act against terrorist financing, causes real concern in Pakistan. The FATF's "grey listing" of Pakistan, and its potential "blacklisting," which could sharply limit Pakistan's access to international capital markets, forced some concrete measures against terrorist finance after 2019. This led to Pakistan's removal from the list in October 2022.

Pakistan's steps against terrorist "front" organizations and militant networks have been far from complete, but FATF and other levers led Pakistan to take steps against fundraising for Lashkar-e-Taiba, forcing more of this activity underground and making it a bit more difficult for the militants. The steps have been more significant than in the past, prompting some to question whether Pakistan has begun to jettison its long-standing ideological commitment to Kashmir militancy. It is too early to reach such a verdict, and skepticism is always in order on this issue.

Against other behaviors of the military establishment, U.S. tools have produced little. We sharply curtailed our military assistance to Pakistan in recent years over concerns about its support to the Taliban, but Pakistan's tolerance for the group continued, in part because Pakistan feared the Taliban's ability to increase violence in Pakistan if truly confronted. That consideration remains in place given the Taliban regime's deep ties to the Pakistan TTP.

The issue of human rights presents a similar story. The "Leahy Law" requires the State Department to deny U.S. military training to Pakistan units that have engaged in a pattern of human rights abuses, including extrajudicial killings of dissidents. It is good policy for the United States, but it has produced only limited change in Pakistan. Pashtun troublemakers still "disappear," allegedly at the hands of the Pakistan security forces. Limiting the influence of any restrictions on U.S. military cooperation is China, ever present, ready to increase military sales and training to Pakistan.

It is fair to argue that the United States should avoid again giving substantial amounts of military assistance to Pakistan if the country's security chiefs insist on policies antithetical to U.S. interests and values in the region. Our military assistance should be confined to what is adequate to sustain U.S. connections. Sales are another question. Washington should consider transferring weapons that will ensure a relative conventional balance between Pakistan and India if Pakistan wishes to make a purchase.

If targeted sanctions can achieve only modest gains, the conceptual opposite of sanctions—that is, linkages—have some potential. The United States gains much from every Pakistani who visits or studies in the United States, and we benefit from the ties between Pakistani Americans and their cousins back in Pakistan.

There will always be outliers—expatriates who study or work in the West and come to reject its tolerance and materialism, a handful to the point of violence—but a huge majority among students and visitors take back something of American values, traditionally defined: religious tolerance, economic opportunity, individual freedom, democratic governance. It is difficult to demonstrate a macro-level impact from exchanges, but I am constantly reminded that one step common to authoritarian regimes is to limit their citizens' travel and exposure to Western democracies. Hard-headed autocrats fear something in the exposure. Our moves to cut off visas or reduce professional exchanges with such countries are ill-considered, holstering our best weapon, our greatest source of influence. Beyond reopening our doors to visitors from Pakistan, America should relaunch a robust program of military training with every officer the Pakistan military is willing to send.

A third tool, incentives, requires more intention and strategic thought. Within this basket, I imagine utilizing international monetary assistance or small capital funds more forthrightly to generate individual opportunities and foster competition in Pakistan. Economic opportunity is, in my view, a more powerful transformative tool than even voting. Helping Pakistanis push against the gates of privilege and monopoly can be wildly subversive, inculcating opposition not to the Pakistan military's legitimate roles but to its stifling interference in business. At a minimum, Western finance should not undergird the worst maladies of Pakistan's political economy.

The suite of foreign policy tools proposed here will strike sharp readers as inadequate to align Pakistani and American interests. This point is a given. Pakistan will be transformed only if Pakistanis themselves desire it. It will require those currently privileged to gradually cede power, and it will require those now on the "outs" to demand reform rather than just a place at the corrupt table for themselves.

Pakistan can chart a future that makes it more difficult for the United States to turn its back. Pakistan and Pakistanis have plenty of strengths. Their best bet to exploit their virtues is that a gradual reduction of regional conflict will allow them to be more forthright in opposing the ideologies of militarism, militancy, and intolerance. Circumstances have left Pakistan vulnerable to weak politicians, assertive generals, and intemperate preachers, but this is a fate its people can change. The challenge for the United States is to help on the margins, do no harm, and, if Pakistan makes a case for improved ties, be open to the pitch.

An Afghanistan Afterward, August 2022

From the perspective of grand strategy, the Trump-Biden withdrawal from Afghanistan was the success it needed to be. As Washington galvanized the Western alliance to oppose Russia's brutal invasion of Ukraine, planners enjoyed greater flexibility without the burdens of the formerly "forever" commitment to Afghanistan. Washington had extra air assets and personnel with which to bolster eastern Europe.

There was alarming talk at the Afghanistan denouement that, because the United States had proved an unfaithful ally to the Afghan army and government, other countries would doubt America's commitment. Taiwan, for example, would see in Afghanistan its own future abandonment in the face of China. Even treaty allies in NATO would come to doubt America's commitment. Commentators and politicians suggested that the U.S. withdrawal from Afghanistan "emboldened" Russian leader Vladimir Putin to fully invade Ukraine.

Ironically, the subsequent Russian invasion of Ukraine offered a tonic to talk of the West's faltering commitment to defending itself and democracy. Putin's disastrous Ukraine invasion reminded Western audiences of the World War II–era brutality and wars of conquest that many thought had been relegated to history texts. It convinced a broad swath of the European and American public that an active and committed NATO was a vital security guarantee. The invasion has been a continuing humanitarian disaster, to be sure, but it was ameliorative to a shaky West.

Geopolitics aside, the Afghanistan withdrawal must still be assessed for its impact on the threat of global terrorism. Through its first winter, the Taliban was distracted with issues of governance, including sorting out its own power structures and dealing with an economy in crisis. It sustained a robust effort to deal with the threat of ISIS-Khorasan, its fierce jihadist rival, but it continued to disappoint Pakistan by not effectively restricting the several thousand "Pakistan Taliban" (Tehrik-e-Taliban Pakistan, TTP) fighters using Afghanistan as a refuge for attacks in Pakistan's Pashtun heartland. Its apparent effort to press the TTP into ceasefires and negotiation with Pakistan so far has been insufficient to change the view that the Taliban is not doing enough.

Some commentary suggests that Afghanistan, no longer policed by NATO, is fast becoming a platform from which threats to the West are bound to emerge.[5] A sober assessment by Pakistan security scholar Joshua White noted in early 2022 that terrorist groups "will find themselves less vulnerable to monitoring and targeting by the United States and its coalition partners; will be able to take advantage of a huge pool of experienced armed labor drawn from former Taliban, Afghan security forces, and other militant ranks; and will have increased space to forge new collaborations and plan operations in the region and further afield."[6]

The need for caution and concern is irrefutable. Though the Taliban have said repeatedly that they understand their international obligations to include preventing terrorists from attacking other countries from Afghan soil, it is not apparent that they feel obliged to eliminate militant groups that are resting and refitting in Afghanistan. The strike killing Zawahiri in Kabul in late July 2022 underscored the concern about legacy al-Qaida members still hanging out under Taliban protection. The United Nations' 1267 Committee, basing its conclusions in part on consultations with member states, reported in February 2022: "There are no recent signs that the Taliban has taken steps to limit the activities of foreign terrorist fighters in the country. On the contrary, terrorist groups enjoy greater freedom there than at any time in recent history. However, Member States have not reported significant new movements of foreign terrorist fighters to Afghanistan."[7]

Despite the justified warnings, however, the Cassandra cries tell only half the story. For in the long and unwinnable war waged in Afghanistan, there was consistent fertilizer for global terror, a conflict that motivated young martyrs and churned resources over to jihadist outfits. Though air strikes and U.S.-supported Afghan raids into the hinterlands should be credited with disrupting many malevolent actors, the long war nonetheless fueled persistent terrorist threats in Pakistan and fed a global narrative that helped both al-Qaida and ISIS prosper. The terrorists in "Af-Pak," moreover, had access to porous borders long before the Taliban assumed responsibility for border control. The dangerous Taliban dispensation of today did not replace an ideal yesterday.

In terms of global terrorist threats, variously defined as threats against the West or simply terrorism projected beyond a group's area of safe haven, a verdict on the consequences of the Taliban takeover is still far off. Unfortunately, we may not know the worst until an Afghan-borne terrorist attack explodes somewhere in the world. Or we may not know because global terrorism will continue at a low ebb.

It may be that safe havens do not matter as much to global terrorist plots today as they did in 2001. The world is more electronically connected. Would-be martyrs can be spun up through online propaganda and influence, with no need to visit a far-off training camp. If the goal is merely to inspire attackers in the West, either ISIS or al-Qaida can achieve that objective from any internet café in the world. In short, the potential ISIS or al-Qaida safe haven in Afghanistan should be a concern but may not match the uniquely menacing threat the al-Qaida base there posed in the late 1990s.

For Pakistan, however, the threat from Afghanistan has grown more acute following the Taliban takeover. The TTP continues to operate from Afghanistan with apparent impunity. The Taliban, focused on ISIS-K and the possibility of more nationalist resistance emerging from the vestiges of the old Northern Alliance, seems reluctant to act against the TTP. It is constrained by a fear that TTP fighters could join ISIS-K if pressured too hard. It is also constrained by real ties of kinship and loyalty.

An American observer is likely to feel some schadenfreude in seeing the pickle the Pakistan security establishment has landed in while dealing with the TTP threat. For years, American soldiers died and the Afghan government teetered because Pakistan allowed the Taliban a refuge. Today, Pakistan soldiers in Khyber-Pakhtunkhwa die because the TTP can infiltrate Pakistan with fighters from relative safety in Afghanistan.

But a dangerous outcome in Pakistan is not positive for the United States. The continuing insecurity in northwest Pakistan is a danger to Americans in the region, but it could go further. This instability can sustain the networks of jihadists and radical ideology that seep out of Pakistan.

It is hard to see exactly how the TTP insurgency ends. The Pakistan military sacrificed a great deal to beat back the threat from 2008 to 2018. It should be unwilling to cede significant autonomy to the self-proclaimed Islamist leaders of the remote Pashtun lands today. Citizens of this region must enjoy the same democratic and secular legal rights as those in the rest of the country. Absent a concession of such autonomy, however, it is unclear whether TTP will be motivated to settle. Fighting is a multi-generational occupation, so that absent an apparent victory, certainly, families and tribes may just continue at it.

One path forward is that the Taliban gains firmer control in Afghanistan, with success in sweeping out the ISIS-K threat. Once secure on that front, the Taliban may be more inclined to challenge the TTP, settling groups of them away from the border or forcing their capitulation or exile back to Pakistan.

The new Taliban regime requires amicable relations with Pakistan to prosper. It needs the outlets for commerce and travel and family connection. Pakistan's security establishment can only hope that the Taliban will come to bear the sacrifices required to contain the TTP sooner rather than later.

Pakistan's TTP problem creates a modest additional opportunity for improved U.S.-Pakistan ties, if it persists. The United States can offer some assistance to the Pakistan military as it takes on this renewed militant threat. Both sides, however, would be ill-served to again push terrorism to the forefront of the relationship. Washington and Islamabad, and even Langley and Rawalpindi, need to operate toward a multifaceted, mutually beneficial bilateral relationship, building up multiple stakeholders to sustain ties in the face of Chinese assertiveness and Islamist provocations. This outcome would help India as well, as a strong U.S.-Pakistan relationship is a force for moderation in the region.

To a significant extent, the Biden administration has adopted this approach of positive but cautious engagement in Pakistan after the fall of Kabul. Bureaucracies in both capitals were in motion to establish new levels of dialogue. Modest security packages had gone forward. It is a justified approach, and diplomats in both capitals are to be applauded for choosing this course.

Storm clouds nonetheless continue to loom over the bilateral relationship, particularly from the chaos of Pakistan's internal politics. The contest may continue among the army, the populist Imran Khan, and the tottering old parties, casting a shadow over the desired rapprochement between capitals. A victory by the army or Khan that diminishes still further Pakistan's political pluralism will make Pakistan a less appealing partner for America. These challenges call for smart diplomacy and careful choices, but with less conflict baked into U.S.-Pakistan ties, there is a fair chance that the United States can navigate through the turbulent waters and maintain a working relationship with its legacy South Asian ally. For Pakistan, the vagaries of American politics are less significant. It most likely can find an interested audience in Washington if it continues to invest in the West.

Notes

Prologue

1. See an impressive recent study by South Asia peace researcher Christopher Clary, who demonstrates the power of "leader primacy theory" as a robust explanatory tool for periods of progress in Pakistan-India relations over the past seventy years. Christopher Clary, *The Difficult Politics of Peace: Rivalry in Modern South Asia* (New York: Oxford University Press, 2022).

1. Pakistan's Elections

1. It did not always work well, even in the early days. During a tour as deputy political and economic chief at our embassy in La Paz, Bolivia, in the early 2000s, I watched as our millions in support to democratic institutions and rule-of-law programs were gradually and then quickly swamped by the emergence of a leftist political movement coalesced around a coca-grower's union leader. U.S. Embassy mistakes contributed to his rise to power, which ushered in an era of revolutionary rule allied to the Bolivarian movement of Hugo Chavez in Venezuela. The Bolivian experience of those years is nicely chronicled first in an excellent documentary and then a feature film starring Sandra Bullock, both titled *Our Brand is Crisis*.
2. Outright military dictatorships remain rare, but in recent decades the backsliding has taken on aspects of "competitive-authoritarian" rule, described by academics Steven Levitsky and Lucan Way as signifying democracies that have been hollowed out by the executive branch or other forces. Steven Levitsky and Lucan Way, "The New Competitive Authoritarianism," *Journal of Democracy* 31, no. 1 (January 2020): 51–65.
3. Thomas Carrothers, "Rejuvenating Democracy Promotion," *Journal of Democracy* 31, no. 1 (January 2020): 117.
4. Hussain Haqqani, *Magnificent Delusions: Pakistan, the United States, and an Epic History of Misunderstanding* (New York: Public Affairs, 2013), 315–20. Haqqani was Pakistan's ambassador to the United States during this period. He has been a public critic of the Pakistan military's political role.

5. Zahid Sahab Ahmed, "Fighting for the Rule of Law: Civil Resistance and the Lawyers' Movement in Pakistan," *Democratization* 17, no. 3 (May 2010): 492–513.

6. Ayesha Siddiqa, *Military Inc.: Inside Pakistan's Military Economy*, 2nd ed. (London: Pluto Press, 2017), 298–304.

7. "Text of the Charter of Democracy," *Dawn* (Pakistan), May 16, 2006, https://dawn.com/news/192460/text-of-the-charter-of-democracy.

8. As in any Pakistani election, there were grounds for complaint. Most telling was the leverage wealthy landowners (sometimes called "feudal lords") exercised over tenant farmers and other employees. Commonly referred to as "vote banks," these clusters of thousands of votes meant that local campaigns depended on handouts or threats to mobilize voters.

9. Siddiqa, *Military, Inc.*, 308–9.

10. Siddiqa, *Military, Inc.* presents the most comprehensive and well-known counterpoint to the benign take on the Pakistan military's economic role. Although the operations of the various welfare foundations are opaque and many of their contracts involving state entities unaccountable, Siddiqa martials available evidence to paint a portrait of extensive damage caused by the military's intrusion into the economy. See chapter 9, "The Cost of Milbus," 256–82.

11. Kate Musgrave, "Censorship in the Name of Security: Pakistan's Dawn Leaks Case," *Center for International Media Assistance*, June 6, 2017, https://cima.ned.org/blog/censorship-name-security-pakistans-dawn-leaks-case.

12. Hasham Cheema, "How Pakistan's Panama Papers Probe Unfolded," *Dawn*, updated December 24, 2018, https://www.dawn.com/news/1316531.

13. Niloufer Siddiqui, "What's behind the Islamist Protests in Pakistan," *Washington Post*, December 8, 2017, https://washingtonpost.com/news/monkey-cage/wp/2017/12/08/whats-behind-the-islamist-protests-in-pakistan.

14. M. Ilyas Khan, "Why Was Pakistan General Giving Money to Protesters?" BBC, November 29, 2017, https://bbc.com/news/world-asia-42149535.

15. Aqil Shah, "Pakistan: Voting under Military Tutelage," *Journal of Democracy* 30, no. 1 (January 2019): 135.

16. Maria Abi-Habib and Salman Masood, "Military's Influence Casts a Shadow over Pakistan's Election," *New York Times*, July 21, 2018, https://nytimes.com/2018/07/21/world/asia/pakistan-election-military.html.

17. "General Election 2018: FAFEN's Preliminary Election Observation Report," Pakistan's Free and Fair Elections Network (FAFEN), July 27, 2018, https://fafen.org/fafens-preliminary-election-observation-report.

18. Memphis Barker, "EU Piles Pressure on Imran Khan after Pakistan Election," *The Guardian*, July 27, 2018, https://theguardian.com/world/2018/jul/27/pakistan-election-imran-khan-official-results-win-coalition.

19. Heather Nauert, "Pakistan Election Press Statement," July 27, 2018, U.S. Embassy and Consulates in Pakistan, https://pk.usembassy.gov/pakistan-election.

20. Zahid Hussain, *No-Win War: The Paradox of U.S.-Pakistan Relations in Afghanistan's Shadow* (Karachi: Oxford University Press, 2021), 114.

21. Simbal Khan, "Geostrategic Policies and Their Impact on Human Security: Lessons from Pakistan's Peacebuilding Approach to Afghanistan," in *Conflict Prevention and Peacebuilding in Asia: Lessons in South-South Cooperation*, ed. Anthea Mulakala (Sejong City: Korean Development Institute, 2019), 72–74. Khan describes Pakistan's engagement as motivated significantly by its desire to salvage then-cratering U.S.-Pakistan relations.

22. Pakistan Supreme Court, "In the Matter of the Tenure and Extension of the Chief of the Army Staff," November 29, 2019, https://supremecourt.gov.pk/downloads_judgements/const.p._39_16122019.pdf.

2. On Cricket

1. Osman Samiuddin, *The Unquiet Ones: A History of Pakistan Cricket*, Kindle ed. (Noida, India: HarperCollins India, 2014); and Peter Oborne, *Wounded Tiger: A History of Cricket in Pakistan* (London: Simon and Schuster, 2014).

2. Oborne, *Wounded Tiger*, 42.

3. Oborne, *Wounded Tiger*, 43.

4. Samiuddin, *Unquiet Ones*, 26–34.

5. On the uncertain popular expectations about citizenship in the postpartition dispensation, see Yasmin Khan, *The Great Partition: The Making of India and Pakistan* (New Haven: Yale University Press, 2007), particularly 193–98.

6. Stephen Wagg, *Cricket: A Political History of the Global Game, 1945–2017* (London: Routledge, 2018), 92–93.

7. Samiuddin, *Unquiet Ones*, 77.

8. Samiuddin, *Unquiet Ones*, 240

9. Samiuddin, *Unquiet Ones*, 91–97.

10. Oborne, *Wounded Tiger*, 143.

11. Mohammad Isam, "Hanif, and the Old-Time Jolly in Dhaka," *ESPN Cricket Info*, August 11, 2016, https://espncricinfo.com/story/hanif-mohammad-and-some-old-time-jolly-in-dhaka-1045015.

12. In C. L. R. James's seminal *Beyond a Boundary*, the Trinidadian author makes a case for the universal appeal of cricket based on its consistent focus, throughout the match, on the drama of "two individuals . . . pitted against each other in a conflict that is strictly personal but no less strictly representative of a social group." C. L. R. James, *Beyond a Boundary*, 50th anniversary ed. (Durham NC: Duke University Press, 2013), 196.

3. China and America in Pakistan

1. Shuja Nawaz, *Crossed Swords: Pakistan, Its Army, and the Wars Within* (London: Oxford University Press, 2008), 92–121.

2. Hasan-Askari Rizvi, "Pakistan's Nuclear Testing," *Asian Survey* 41, no. 6 (November/December 2001), 945.

3. Pakistan was one of the few countries not to have signed the Nuclear Non-Proliferation Treaty and so did not break an international commitment in developing nuclear weapons. It also had a convincing strategic rationale for doing so, given India's early development of an atomic bomb. Nonetheless, illegal activities associated with Pakistan's effort, led by A. Q. Khan, discredited the effort. These included cooperation with rogue states like North Korea and Libya and violations of a variety of export-control laws around the world. Still, Pakistan had some grounds for feeling victimized by its post-test U.S. sanctions.

4. Zahid Hussain, *No-Win War: The Paradox of U.S.-Pakistan Relations in Afghanistan's Shadow* (Karachi: Oxford University Press, 2021), 142–45.

5. Ayesha Siddiqa, *Military Inc.: Inside Pakistan's Military Economy*, 2nd ed. (London: Pluto Press, 2017), 76–77.

6. Cameron Munter, "Imagining Assistance: Tales from the American Aid Experience in Iraq in 2006 and Pakistan in 2011," *Brookings Local Orders Paper Series*, March 2016, https://brookings.edu/wp-content/uploads/2016/07/cmuntersv7-1.pdf. Munter, my ambassador in Pakistan in late 2010 and 2011, describes many of the challenging dynamics associated with this massive aid flow into national and provincial governments, which had limited capacity and sometimes used unscrupulous approaches. Also, Shannon K. O'Neil, "Critiquing U.S. Aid to Pakistan: A Second Take," *Council on Foreign Relations*, October 15, 2015, https://cfr.org/blog/critiquing-us-aid-pakistan-second-take.

7. Steve Coll, *Directorate S: The CIA and America's Secret War in Afghanistan and Pakistan* (New York: Penguin, 2018), 520–29.

8. Hussain Haqqani, *Magnificent Delusions: Pakistan, the United States, and an Epic History of Misunderstanding* (New York: Public Affairs, 2013), 5.

9. Salman Masood and Pir Zubair Shah, "CIA Drones Kill Civilians in Pakistan," *New York Times*, March 17, 2011, https://.nytimes.com/2011/03/18/world/asia/18pakistan.html.

10. U.S. Central Command, "Release of Pakistan/Afghanistan Cross-Border Fire Investigation Report," December 26, 2011, https://scribd.com/fullscreen/80616338?access_key=key-26rt0xtpw7icq41c5zat.

11. Farhan Bokhari, "With China as Its Mentor, Pakistan Triples Arms Exports," *Nikkei Asia*, November 9, 2019, https://asia.nikkei.com/Politics/With-China-as-its-mentor-Pakistan-triples-arms-exports.

12. This is sometimes called the "Pressler" generation, named after the Senate amendment (sponsored by Senator Larry Pressler) that prevented military aid to Pakistan if the president could not certify that the country did not possess a nuclear weapon. The nonproliferation objective was surely noble, but the mistake was to include IMET in the basket of restricted items. IMET serves American interests. Beginning in 2022 we may see several years of Pakistani military leadership by senior officers with little exposure to the United States.

13. "Pakistan Trade," World Integrated Trade Solution (World Bank), https://wits.worldbank.org/countrysnapshot/en/pak.

14. Shamil Shams, "Pakistan's U-Turn on China Economic Corridor?" *Deutsche Welle*, September 18, 2018, https://dw.com/en/is-new-pakistani-pm-khan-backtracking-on-chinas-economic-corridor/a-45539991.

15. Daniel Markey, *China's Western Horizon: Beijing and the New Geopolitics of Eurasia* (New York: Oxford University Press, 2020), 53.

16. Avery Goldstein, "China's Grand Strategy under Xi Jinping: Reassurance, Reform, and Resistance," *International Security*, 45, no. 1 (2020), 196. Goldstein notes the debt-trap charge was not sustained by "analysts who examined the evidence more systematically."

17. Goldstein, "China's Grand Strategy," 197.

18. Daniel Markey, "How the United States Should Deal with China in Pakistan," *Carnegie-Tsinghua Center for Global Policy*, April 8, 2020, https://carnegieendowment.org/2020/04/08/how-united-states-should-deal-with-china-in-pakistan-pub-81456.

19. Michael Kugelman, "Pakistan's High-Stakes CPEC Reboot," *Foreign Policy*, December 19, 2019, https://foreignpolicy.com/2019/12/19/pakistan-china-cpec-belt-road-initiative.

20. Voice of America News, "U.S. Warns Against IMF Bailing Out Pakistan's Loans from China," *VOA News,* July 30, 2018, https://voanews.com/a/us-mike-pompeo-warns-against-imf-bailout-for-pakistan-that-aids-china/4506960.html.

21. Faran Mahmood, "Bumpy Ride on CPEC Road as People Cry for Transparency," *The Express Tribune*, March 12, 2018, describes a Senate committee's investigations and concerns, https://tribune.com.pk/story/1657399/unearthing-scandals-bumpy-ride-cpec-road-people-cry-transparency.

22. Miriam Berger, "An Investigation Found Pakistani Christian Women Being Trafficked to China as Brides. Then Officials Shut It Down," *Washington Post*, December 5, 2019, https://washingtonpost.com/world/2019/12/05/an-investigation-found-pakistani-christian-women-being-trafficked-china-brides-then-officials-shut-it-down; Sajjad Akbar Shah, "Chinese Workers Thrash Policemen in Khanewal," *Dawn*, April 4, 2018, https://www.dawn.com/news/1399531.

23. Madiha Afzal, "'At All Costs': How Pakistan and China Control the Narrative on the China-Pakistan Economic Corridor," *Brookings Institution Reports*, June 2020, https://brookings.edu/research/at-all-costs-how-pakistan-and-china-control-the-narrative-on-the-china-pakistan-economic-corridor.

24. Abhinandan Mishra, "GHQ Aggression Rises After China Floods Pak with Arms," *Sunday Guardian*, September 7, 2019, https://www.sundayguardianlive.com/news/ghq-aggression-rises-china-floods-pak-arms. The article is representative of dozens in the Indian press, most replete with statements from government officials.

25. Markey, *China's Western Horizon*, 65.

26. Gay Talese, "Aly Khan: Sportsman in New Role," *New York Times*, May 9, 1958, 31.

27. Gordon S. White Jr., "Second Pakistan Cricket Victory Indicates No Threat to Baseball," *New York Times*, May 12, 1958, 36.

28. Gay Talese, "Mayor Goes to Bat for Cricketers," *New York Times*, May 1, 1958, 38.

29. "Abdul Hafeez Kardar in Tell the Truth Show," YouTube video, 9:04, https://www.youtube.com/watch?v=P2nLDrebBe0.

30. U.S. Information Service Karachi, "People-to-People Program—Visit of Pakistan Cricket Team," July 25, 1958, https://eisenhowerlibrary.gov/sites/default/files/file/people_to_people_BinderD.pdf.

31. Tristan Lavalette, "Uncertainty Once Again Clouds Cricket in the U.S. After the Resignation of Chairman Paraag Marathe," *Forbes*, May 18, 2022,

https://www.forbes.com/sites/tristanlavalette/2022/05/18/uncertainty
-once-again-clouds-cricket-in-the-us-after-the-resignation-of-chairman
-paraag-marathe/?sh=ac2bfe27482d.

32. Tristan Lavalette, "As Focus Intensifies on Rising U.S., Cricket in China Remains a Work in Progress," *Forbes*, November 27, 2021, https://forbes .com/sites/tristanlavalette/2021/11/27/as-focus-intensifies-on-rising-us -cricket-in-china-remains-a-work-in-progress/?sh=44b988066beb.

4. Decolonizing a Sport

1. A great if grainy film, *Fire in Babylon*, ably captures the thrill of the late 1970s teams as well as their meaning to people of color around the world.
2. C. L. R. James, *Beyond a Boundary*, 50th anniversary ed. (Durham NC: Duke University Press, 2013), 94.
3. James, *Beyond a Boundary*, 50–51.
4. James, *Beyond a Boundary*, 125.
5. Stephen Wagg, *Cricket: A Political History of the Global Game, 1945–2017* (London: Routledge, 2018), 73–89.
6. Peter Oborne, *Wounded Tiger: A History of Cricket in Pakistan* (London: Simon and Schuster, 2014), 23.
7. Oborne, *Wounded Tiger*, 152–54.

5. Britain's Imperial Legacy

1. Simbal Khan, "Geostrategic Policies and their Impact on Human Security: Lessons from Pakistan's Peacebuilding Approach to Afghanistan," in *Conflict Prevention and Peacebuilding in Asia: Lessons in South-South Cooperation*, ed. Anthea Mulakala (Sejong City: Korean Development Institute, 2019), 73–75.
2. Zuha Siddiqui, "Protest and Purdah in Pakistan: How the Pashtun Protection Movement Became a Release Valve for Women's Anger," *Foreign Policy*, January 5, 2021, https://foreignpolicy.com/2021/01/05/protest-and-purdah -in-pakistan.
3. Aqil Shah, "Do U.S. Drone Strikes Cause Blowback?" *International Security* 42, no. 4 (Spring 2018), 47–84.
4. Imtiaz Ali, "Naqeebullah Was Killed in 'Fake Encounter,' Had No Militant Tendencies: Police Inquiry Finds," *Dawn*, January 20, 2018, https://.dawn .com/news/1384163.
5. Sadanand Dhume, "Pakistan's Pashtuns Take on the Army—And Terror- ists," *Wall Street Journal*, June 14, 2018, https://wsj.com/articles/pakistans -pashtuns-take-on-the-armyand-terrorists-1529018078.

6. Madiha Afzal, "Why is Pakistan's Military Repressing a Huge, Nonviolent Pashtun Protest Movement?" *Brookings*, February 7, 2020, https://brookings.edu/blog/order-from-chaos/2020/02/07/why-is-pakistans-military-repressing-a-huge-nonviolent-pashtun-protest-movement.

7. Simbal Khan, "Dynamic Militant Insurgency in Conflicted Border Spaces: Ferghana, the Afghanistan-Pakistan Border, and Kashmir," in *The Regional Security Puzzle around Afghanistan: Bordering Practices in Central Asia and Beyond*, ed. Helena Rytövuori-Apunen (Berlin: Verlag Barbara Budrich, 2018), 79–106. Khan notes that the left-leaning Pashtun movement of the 1970s stoked the establishment's concern about Afghan claims to territory within Pakistan.

8. Daud Khattuk, "Pashtun Tahaffuz Movement Comes Under Militant Attack," *The Diplomat*, June 5, 2018, https://thediplomat.com/2018/06/pashtun-tahaffuz-movement-comes-under-militant-attack.

9. Salman Massood, Mujib Mashal, and Zia ur-Rehman, "Time Is Up: Pakistan's Army Targets Protest Movement, Stifling Dissent," *New York Times*, May 28, 2019, https://nytimes.com/2019/05/28/world/asia/pakistan-pashtun-dissent.html.

10. Ayaz Gul, "Blasts Kill Soldiers, Shi'ite Muslims in Pakistan," *VOA News*, June 8, 2019, https://voanews.com/a/bomb-blast-kills-4-soldiers-in-nw-pakistan/4950405.html.

11. Afzal, "Pashtun Protest Movement."

12. Waleed Hashmi, "'Fierce and Warlike': Could the Baloch Separatist Movement Remain Pakistan's Longest Running Insurgency?" *Small Wars Journal*, August 21, 2018, https://smallwarsjournal.com/jrnl/art/fierce-and-warlike-could-baloch-separatist-movement-remain-pakistans-longest-insurgency.

13. Shakoor Ahmad Wani, "The Changing Dynamics of the Baloch Nationalist Movement in Pakistan," *Asian Survey* 56, no. 5 (2016), 807–32.

14. Arif Rafiq, "The China-Pakistan Economic Corridor: Barriers and Impact," *United States Institute of Peace*, October 25, 2017, 39–41, https://usip.org/publications/2017/10/china-pakistan-economic-corridor.

15. Rafiq, "CPEC Barriers and Impact," 39.

16. Kunwar Khuldune, "The Trouble with Modi's Balochistan Comments," *The Diplomat*, August 21, 2016, https://thediplomat.com/2016/08/the-trouble-with-modis-balochistan-comments.

17. Shuja Nawaz, *Crossed Swords: Pakistan, Its Army, and the Wars Within* (London: Oxford University Press, 2008), 29–31.

18. Oborne, *Wounded Tiger: A History of Cricket in Pakistan* (London: Simon and Schuster, 2014), 111–32.

19. Oborne, *Wounded Tiger*, 199–201.

6. The Challenges of Insurgencies

1. Stephen Wagg, *Cricket: A Political History of the Global Game, 1945–2017* (London: Routledge, 2018), 139–46.

2. Wagg, *Cricket*, 149.

3. Talat Masood, "Pakistan-Sri Lanka Relations and Exercise in World Class Diplomacy," *Arab News*, February 20, 2020, https://arabnews.pk/node /1630576.

4. Kumar Rupesinghe, "Sri Lanka: Tackling the LTTE," in *Insurgency and Counterinsurgency in South Asia: Through a Peacebuilding Lens*, ed. Moeed Yusuf (Washington DC: United States Institute of Peace, 2014), 257.

5. Rupesinghe, "Tackling the LTTE," 255–57.

6. Chalinda D. Weerasinghe, "From Postindependence Ethnic Tensions to Insurgency: Sri Lanka's Many Missed Opportunities," in Yusuf, *Insurgency and Counterinsurgency*, 244.

7. Stephen Tankel, "Beyond the Double Game: Lessons from Pakistan's Approach to Islamist Militancy." *Journal of Strategic Studies* 41, no. 4 (2018), 545–75.

8. "Pakistan al-Qaeda Leaders Dead," BBC *News Online*, January 9, 2009, http://news.bbc.co.uk/2/hi/south_asia/7819305.stm.

9. Al-Qaida's relative quiescence in Pakistan during the 2010s reflected both the legacy of U.S. and Pakistani policing actions and the organization's focus on using Pakistan as a place to clandestinely maintain its leadership and global command-and-control. Given the fuzzy lines between Sunni-oriented militants, however, it is likely that AQ operatives played a supporting role in myriad attacks attributed to other extremist organizations, including the Pakistan Taliban.

10. Stephen Tankel, "Ten Years After Mumbai, the Group Responsible Is Deadlier than Ever," *War on the Rocks*, November 26, 2018, https://warontherocks .com/2018/11/ten-years-after-mumbai-the-group-responsible-is-deadlier -than-ever/.

11. Hussain Haqqani, *Magnificent Delusions: Pakistan, the United States, and an Epic History of Misunderstanding* (New York: Public Affairs, 2013), 331.

12. Tankel, "Double Game," 555–57.

13. Pamela Constable, *Playing with Fire: Pakistan at War with Itself* (New York: Random House, 2011), 119–20.

14. Tankel, "Double Game," 554–55.

15. Jaffer Mirza, "The Changing Landscape of Anti-Shia Politics in Pakistan," *The Diplomat*, September 28, 2020, https://thediplomat.com/2020/09/the-changing-landscape-of-anti-shia-politics-in-pakistan.

16. Both the Bhutto assassination and the Marriott bombing generated persistent conspiracy theories. Some identified India or the United States as somehow involved. More frequent were suggestions that Benazir's widower and political and financial beneficiary, Asif Ali Zardari, was behind one or both. To this day, however, the most convincing suspects in both cases are anti-Pakistan extremists linked to al-Qaida or the Pakistan Taliban.

17. Zahid Hussain, *No-Win War: The Paradox of U.S.-Pakistan Relations in Afghanistan's Shadow* (Karachi: Oxford University Press, 2021), 98.

18. Hussain, *No-Win War*, 225–35.

19. Anatol Levin, "Counter-Insurgency in Pakistan: The Role of Legitimacy," *Small Wars and Insurgencies* 28, no. 1 (2017), 166–90.

20. Asfandyar Mir, "What Explains Counterterrorism Effectiveness? Evidence from the U.S. Drone War in Pakistan," *International Security* 43, no. 2 (Fall 2018), 45–83.

21. Levin, "Counter-Insurgency," 168–69.

22. Maria Kari, "No Sunset for Pakistan's Military Courts," *The Diplomat*, April 24, 2017, https://thediplomat.com/2017/04/no-sunset-for-pakistans-secret-military-courts.

23. Waseem Ahmad Shah, "View from the Courtroom: Military Courts–Related Legal Issues Far from Being Settled," *Dawn*, December 21, 2020, https://dawn.com/news/1596952.

24. Ben Farmer and Ihsanullah Tipu Mehsud, "Pakistan Builds Border Fence, Limiting Militants and Families Alike," *New York Times*, updated July 31, 2020, https://nytimes.com/2020/03/15/world/asia/pakistan-afghanistan-border-fence.html.

25. "Yearly Fatalities Data," South Asian Terrorism Portal (New Delhi), https://satp.org/datasheet-terrorist-attack/fatalities/pakistan.

26. Simbal Khan, "Geostrategic Policies and Their Impact on Human Security: Lessons from Pakistan's Peacebuilding Approach to Afghanistan," in *Conflict Prevention and Peacebuilding in Asia: Lessons in South-South Cooperation*, ed. Anthea Mulakala (Sejong City: Korean Development Institute, 2019), 72–74.

27. Abdul Sayed and Amira Jadoon, "Understanding Tehrik-e-Taliban Pakistan's Unrelenting Posture," *Nexus: George Washington University Program on Extremism*, August 16, 2022, https://extremism.gwu.edu/understanding-tehrik-e-taliban-pakistans-unrelenting-posture.

28. Author interview with retired senator Enver Baig, October 13, 2020. Baig led a parliamentary committee investigating the sport in 2009.

29. Denis Campbell, Kevin Mitchell, and Jason Burke, "Spies Trail High-Living Cricketers to Casino," *The Guardian*, June 27, 1999, https://theguardian.com/sport/1999/jun/27/cricket3.

7. Hostage Diplomacy

1. Stephen Wagg, *Cricket: A Political History of the Global Game, 1945–2017* (London: Routledge, 2018), 18–35.

2. Osman Samiuddin, *The Unquiet Ones: A History of Pakistan Cricket*, Kindle ed. (Noida, India: HarperCollins India, 2014); and Peter Oborne, *Wounded Tiger: A History of Cricket in Pakistan* (London: Simon and Schuster, 2014), 164–66.

3. Adam Goldman and Ian Austen, "Gunshots, a Cry of 'Kill the Hostages,' Then Freedom for Canadian-American Family," *New York Times*, Oct. 12, 2017, https://nytimes.com/2017/10/12/world/asia/american-canadian-hostages-pakistan-haqqani.html.

4. David Zuccino and Adam Goldman, "Two Western Hostages Are Freed in Afghanistan in Deal with Taliban," *New York Times*, Nov. 19, 2019, https://nytimes.com/2019/11/19/world/asia/afghanistan-taliban-prisoner-exchange-peace-talks.html.

5. Richard Whitehead, ed., *England's World Cup: The Full Story of the 2019 Tournament* (Cheltenham UK: History Press, 2019), 82.

8. A Dogfight over Kashmir

1. Telford Vice, "2003: Crossing Continents," in *The Official History of the ICC Cricket World Cup* (London: TriNorth., 2019), 136–37.

2. Boria Majumdar, *Eleven Gods and a Billion Indians: The on and off the Field Story of Cricket in India and Beyond* (London: Simon and Schuster, 2018), 347.

3. Reed, Adam. "India Is Already the Big Winner from the Cricket World Cup Even Before a Ball Has Been Bowled," *CNBC*, May 29, 2019, https://cnbc.com/2019/05/29/india-already-the-winner-the-cricket-world-cup-even-before-a-ball-bowled.html.

4. Reed, "India the Big Winner."

5. Yasmin Khan, *The Great Partition: The Making of India and Pakistan* (New Haven: Yale University Press, 2007), 100–103. Khan portrays the "fuzzy thinking" of all sides on the precipice of partition, including among Muslims in the middle of India, in predominantly Hindu states, imagining a future under Muslim rule in a "Pakistan" that would not require them to move. The massive movement of peoples across the two new countries' borders was underanticipated.

6. Khan, *The Great Partition*, 128–35.

7. Among many examples, Ajaz Ashraf, "India's Muslims and the Price of Partition," *New York Times*, August 17, 2017, https://nytimes.com/2017/08/17/opinion/india-muslims-hindus-partition.html.

8. Shuja Nawaz, *Crossed Swords: Pakistan, Its Army, and the Wars Within* (London: Oxford University Press, 2008), 57.

9. Nawaz, *Crossed Swords*, 67–73.

10. United Nations Security Council, "Resolution 47," April 21, 1948, http://unscr.com/en/resolutions/47.

11. Nawaz, *Crossed Swords*, 73.

12. Joshua T. White, "Why America Can't Escape Its Role in the Conflict between India and Pakistan," *Brookings*, March 6, 2019, https://brookings.edu/blog/order-from-chaos/2019/03/06/why-america-cant-escape-its-role-in-the-conflict-between-india-and-pakistan.

13. Marcus Hellyer, Nathan Ruser, and Aakriti Bachhawat, "India's Strike on Balakot: A Very Precise Miss?" *The Strategist* (ASPI), March 27, 2019, https://www.aspistrategist.org.au/indias-strike-on-balakot-a-very-precise-miss; and Nathan Ruser, "Were India's Airstrikes in Pakistan a Strategy for Public Approval?" *The Strategist*, March 1, 2019, https://aspistrategist.org.au/were-indias-airstrikes-in-pakistan-a-strategy-for-public-approval.

14. The USCENTCOM commander has served for decades as a key interlocutor with the Pakistan Army. During his three-year tenure, Gen. Joseph Votel exceled in the role, serving for a time in 2018 as one of the only working diplomatic channels to Pakistani leadership. During the Pulwama-Balakot crisis, however, Votel was on his way out, days from passing the command to a successor.

15. This policy of an intentional miss was communicated by the Pakistanis through our defense attachés and then seemingly confirmed in what can be considered Pakistan's official record of the events. Kaiser Tufail, "Opinion: Pulwama—From Bluster to a Whimper," *Defense Journal* (Pakistan), July

19, 2019, 35, https://defence.pk/pdf/threads/pulwama-from-bluster-to-a-whimper.621500.

16. Maria Abi-Habib, "After India Loses Dogfight to Pakistan, Questions Arise about Its 'Vintage' Military," *New York Times*, March 3, 2019, https://nytimes.com/2019/03/03/world/asia/india-military-united-states-china.html.

17. Mosharraf Zaidi, "Losing a Victory in an Abyss of Incompetence," *The News* (Pakistan), March 13, 2019, https://thenews.com.pk/print/443258-losing-a-victory-in-an-abyss-of-incompetence.

18. Lt. Gen. Deependra Singh Hooda (ret.), "Three Years After Balakot: Reckoning with Two Claims of Victory," *Stimson Center Commentary*, February 28, 2022, https://stimson.org/2022/three-years-after-balakot-reckoning-with-two-claims-of-victory.

19. "Irrelevant Whether Indian Planes that Violated LoC Were Targeted by F-16s or JF-17s: ISPR," *Dawn*, April 2, 2019, https://www.dawn.com/news/1473244. Tufail, "Opinion: Pulwama," states that an F-16 shot down a single Indian fighter aircraft, the MIG-21 flown by Varthaman, 36.

20. Paul D. Shinkman, "State Department Reprimanded Pakistan for Misusing F-16s, Document Shows," *U.S. News*, December 11, 2019, https://www.usnews.com/news/world-report/articles/2019-12-11/state-department-reprimanded-pakistan-in-august-for-misusing-f-16s-document-shows. The reprimand was over deploying the aircraft to alternative airfields where the U.S. contractors could not monitor them—not for Pakistan's use of the air assets in combat against India.

21. "Remarks by President Trump and Prime Minister Khan of the Islamic Republic of Pakistan Before Bilateral Meeting," The White House, July 22, 2019, https://trumpwhitehouse.archives.gov/briefings-statements/remarks-president-trump-prime-minister-khan-islamic-republic-pakistan-bilateral-meeting.

22. Sanjeev Miglani, "Trump Touches Off Storm in India with Kashmir Mediation Offer," *Reuters*, July 23, 2019, https://reuters.com/article/us-india-usa-kashmir/trump-touches-off-storm-in-india-with-kashmir-mediation-offer-iduskcn1ui0ii.

9. Lessons in Democracy Promotion

1. Stephen Wagg, *Cricket: A Political History of the Global Game, 1945-2017* (London: Routledge, 2018), 40-43.

2. Basil D'Oliveira, "The Basil D'Oliveira Affair," in Jonathan Agnew, *Cricket: A Modern Anthology* (London: Harper Collins, 2013), 100-108; and Wisden,

"The Obituary of Basil D'Oliveira," in Jonathan Agnew, *Cricket: A Modern Anthology* (London: Harper Collins, 2013), 110–15.

3. Princeton N. Lyman, *Partner to History: The U.S. Role in South Africa's Transition to Democracy* (Washington DC: USIP Press, 2002). Lyman provides a still-valuable description of the positive U.S. contributions during South Africa's transition, during the presidency of George H. W. Bush.

4. Albert Makochekanswa, T. James Hurango, and Prosper Kambaramir, "Zimbabwe's Experience with Trade Liberalization," *African Economic Research Consortium Research Paper*, no. 245, 2012, 18, http://publication .aercafricalibrary.org/handle/123456789/194. The parsimony of U.S. engagement in the 1990s was encapsulated in the mantra "trade, not aid," poorly disguising Washington's focus on a post Cold War "peace dividend." Zimbabwe was "graduated" from U.S. foreign assistance and offered the prospect of trade and private investment. Serving at the U.S. Embassy in Gaborone, in 1996, I was the local lead for a U.S. Department of Commerce trade mission to southern Africa that promised U.S. investors but delivered few of them.

5. Macdonald Dzirutwe, "Mugabe's Farm Seizures: Racial Justice or Catastrophic Power Grab?" *The Independent* (UK), September 6, 2019, https:// reuters.com/article/us-zimbabwe-mugabe-land/mugabes-farm-seizures -racial-justice-or-catastrophic-power-grab-iduskcn1vr156.

6. Alois Mlambo, "From an Industrial Powerhouse to a Nation of Vendors: Over Two Decades of Economic Decline and De-Industrialization in Zimbabwe, 1990–2015," *Journal of Developing Societies* 33, no. 1, 2018, 99–135.

10. The Best of the West

1. Stephen Wagg, *Cricket: A Political History of the Global Game, 1945–2017* (London: Routledge, 2018), 60–72.

2. Wagg, *Cricket*, 61.

11. Misadventures in the Great Game

1. Paddy Docherty, *The Khyber Pass: A History of Empire and Invasion* (New York: Union Square Press, 2008), 200–208.

2. Shareena Qazi, "How Afghanistan Fell in Love with Cricket," *Al Jazeera*, September 30, 2018, https://www.aljazeera.com/sports/2018/9/30/how -afghanistan-fell-in-love-with-cricket.

3. Stephen Wagg, *Cricket: A Political History of the Global Game, 1945–2017* (London: Routledge, 2018), 290–92.

4. Wagg, *Cricket*, 306.

5. Peter Della Penna, "Afghanistan Cricket Board Urges Patience with Women's Initiative," ESPN *CricketInfo*, November 10, 2020, https://www.espncricinfo.com/story/afghanistan-cricket-board-urges-patience-with-women-s-initiatives-1238928.

6. "Interview: Richard Armitage," PBS *Frontline Interview*, April 19, 2002, https://www.pbs.org/wgbh/pages/frontline/shows/campaign/interviews/armitage.html.

7. Shuja Nawaz, *Crossed Swords: Pakistan, Its Army, and the Wars Within* (London: Oxford University Press, 2008), 360–61.

8. Hussain Haqqani, *Magnificent Delusions: Pakistan, the United States, and an Epic History of Misunderstanding* (New York: Public Affairs, 2013), 276–77. Then-influential ISI chief Lt. Gen. Hamid Gul is often credited with institutionalizing the "grandiose" aspirations behind this strategy.

9. Pakistanis who lived in Islamabad and Rawalpindi at the time have indelible memories of the blast, which showered rockets and shrapnel over both cities and killed over one hundred. Many thought it was the opening salvo of an Indian invasion. There is still a wall at the International School in Islamabad scarred by the exploding ordnance 20 miles away.

10. Zahid Hussain, *No-Win War: The Paradox of U.S.-Pakistan Relations in Afghanistan's Shadow* (Karachi: Oxford University Press, 2021), 28.

11. Hussain, *No-Win War*, 16–31.

12. Alex Strick Van Linschoten and Felix Kuehn, *An Enemy We Created: The Myth of the Taliban-Al Qaeda Merger in Afghanistan* (New York: Oxford University Press, 2012), 243.

13. Van Linschoten and Kuehn, *Enemy We Created*, 246–54.

14. Pervez Musharraf, *In the Line of Fire* (New York: Free Press, 2006), 200–201. One can credit or not Musharraf's widely reported claim that deputy secretary of state Richard Armitage threatened to bomb Pakistan "back to the stone age" if it did not comply (Armitage denied it), but there can be no doubt that the persuasive tactics used in the immediate aftermath of 9/11 were heavy-handed. Melissa Block, "Armitage Denies Making 'Stone Age' Threat," *National Public Radio*, September 22, 2006.

15. Steve Coll, *Directorate S: The CIA and America's Secret War in Afghanistan and Pakistan* (New York: Penguin, 2018), 110.

16. Muhammad Amir Rana, "Taliban Insurgency in FATA: Evolution and Prospects," in Moeed Yusuf (ed.), *Insurgency and Counterinsurgency in South*

Asia: Through a Peacebuilding Lens (Washington DC: United States Institute of Peace, 2014), 118.

17. Zachary Constantino, "The India-Pakistan Rivalry in Afghanistan," *United States Institute of Peace Special Report*, no. 462 (2020), provides a concise description of Indian and Pakistani geostrategic preoccupations about their rivals' presence and role in Afghanistan.

18. Simbal Khan, "Geostrategic Policies and their Impact on Human Security: Lessons from Pakistan's Peacebuilding Approach to Afghanistan," in *Conflict Prevention and Peacebuilding in Asia: Lessons in South-South Cooperation*, ed. Anthea Mulakala (Sejong City: Korean Development Institute, 2019), 71.

19. Asfandyar Mir, "What Explains Counterterrorism Effectiveness: Evidence from the U.S. Drone War in Pakistan," *International Security* 43, no. 2 (Fall 2018), 45–83; David Kilcullen and Andrew Donald Exum, "Death From Above, Outrage Down Below," *New York Times*, May 16, 2009, https://www.nytimes.com/2009/05/17/opinion/17exum.html; "The Bush Years: Pakistan Strikes, 2004-2009," Bureau of Investigative Journalism, https://www.thebureauinvestigates.com/drone-war/data/the-bush-years-pakistan-strikes-2004-2009.

20. Hussain, *No-Win War*, 102.

21. Coll, *Directorate S*, 509.

22. Hussain, *No-Win War*, 120.

23. Craig Whitlock, "The Afghanistan Papers: At War with the Truth," *Washington Post*, December 9, 2019, https://washingtonpost.com/graphics/2019/investigations/afghanistan-papers/afghanistan-war-confidential-documents.

24. Coll, *Directorate S*, 415–62, provides a detailed account of the Obama administration's explorations of negotiation with the Taliban, based on a host of senior sources. For Pakistan's military leaders, despite consistent vocal support for a negotiated settlement, the idea of direct U.S. talks with the Taliban was anathema. They consistently sought to shape and manage any dialogue.

25. Coll, *Directorate S*, 537–39.

26. Jonathan Mahler, "What Do We Really Know about Osama bin Laden's Death?" *New York Times*, October 15, 2015, https://www.nytimes.com/2015/10/18/magazine/what-do-we-really-know-about-osama-bin-ladens-death.html.

27. Secretary of state Hillary Clinton said, "Cooperation with Pakistan helped lead us to bin Laden and the compound in which he was hiding." It implied

a degree of intentional cooperation not borne out in subsequent briefings and disclosures. "Clinton: Pakistan Cooperation Helped Find bin Laden," *VOA News*, May 1, 2011, https://voanews.com/a/clinton-stresses-pakistan -cooperation-after-bin-laden-killing--121092289/138824.html.

28. Eric Schmitt and Mark Mazzetti, "Pakistan Arrests CIA Informants in Bin Laden Raid," *New York Times*, June 14, 2011, https://www.nytimes.com /2011/06/15/world/asia/15policy.html#:~:text=washington%20%E2%80 %94%20pakistan's%20top%20military%20spy,Laden%2C%20according %20to%20American%20officials.

29. "Trump: Bergdahl a 'Dirty, Rotten Traitor'," *Wall Street Journal*, August 20, 2015, YouTube video, 1:00, https://youtube.com/watch?v=b3ci0S0RjXw.

30. Mujib Mashal, "Once Jailed in Guantanamo, 5 Taliban Now Face U.S. in Peace Talks," *New York Times*, March 26, 2019, https://www.nytimes.com /2019/03/26/world/asia/taliban-guantanamo-afghanistan-peace-talks .html.

31. Josh Smith, "U.S. Bombs Dropped in Afghanistan at Highest Since 2010, Under New Trump Strategy," *Reuters*, October 11, 2017, https://reuters.com /article/us-afghanistan-airstrikes/u-s-bombs-dropped-in-afghanistan-at -highest-since-2010-under-new-trump-strategy-iduskbn1cg0oo.

32. Hussain, *No-Win War*, 267.

33. "Trump Criticizes Pakistan for 'Lies and Deceit,'" *VOA News*, January 1, 2018, https://voanews.com/a/trump-us-aid-pakistan-got-nothing-lies -deceit/4187518.html.

34. Michel Ames, "The American Hostage Trump and Biden Abandoned in Afghanistan," *New Yorker*, September 7, 2021, https://newyorker.com /news/news-desk/the-american-hostage-trump-and-biden-abandoned -in-afghanistan.

35. U.S. diplomat Annie Pforzheimer, who was serving as deputy chief of mission in Kabul, describes a similar earthquake in Afghanistan, as Afghans (and the large American mission) grappled with the possibility that Trump would cut and run even without a diplomatic deal. *The Association for Diplomatic Studies and Training Oral History Project*, interview May 29, 2019, 111–12, https://adst.org/OH%20TOCs/Pforzheimer.Annie.pdf.

36. Constantino, *India-Pakistan*, 12.

37. Our ISI contacts were competent and civil and reminded me of the truth that even experienced diplomats (and spies) have trouble understanding foreign humor. I had to explain to an ISI contact that an article in *The Onion* about Osama bin Laden was satire.

38. Christopher Sandford, *Imran Khan: The Cricketer, the Celebrity, the Politician* (London: HarperCollins UK e-books, 2009), 268–70.

12. An Economic Divergence

1. Mahmood Hasan Khan, "Bangladesh and Pakistan: The Great Divergence," *Pakistan Development Review* 59, no. 2 (2020): 301–9.

2. Pervez Hoodbhoy, "Why Bangladesh Overtook Pakistan," *Dawn*, February 10, 2019, https:// https://www.dawn.com/news/1462757.

3. Shuja Nawaz, *Crossed Swords: Pakistan, Its Army, and the Wars Within* (London: Oxford University Press, 2008), 256.

4. Nawaz, *Crossed Swords*, 256. Nawaz puts the number at 5 percent in 1963, remarkably low given East Pakistan's larger population.

5. Gary J. Bass, "Bargaining Away Justice: India, Pakistan, and the International Politics of Impunity for the Bangladesh Genocide," *International Security* 41, no. 2 (2016), 140–87.

6. "The Report of the Hamoodur Rehman Commission of Inquiry into the 1971 War," quoted by Bass, *Genocide*, 156.

7. Peter Oborne, *Wounded Tiger: A History of Cricket in Pakistan* (London: Simon and Schuster, 2014), 182.

8. Oborne, *Wounded Tiger*, 195.

9. Oborne, *Wounded Tiger*, 209.

10. Stephen Wagg, *Cricket: A Political History of the Global Game, 1945–2017* (London: Routledge, 2018), 129–30.

11. Oborne, *Wounded Tiger*, 276.

12. Wagg, *Cricket*, 131–33.

13. Ishrat Husain, "The Bangladesh Story," *Dawn*, December 16, 2021, https:// dawn.com/news/1664104.

14. All trade data gathered from the Observatory for Economic Complexity, https://oec.world.

15. Abbas Uddin Noyon, "Bangladesh-India Trade Relations under Strain," *Business Standard* (Dhaka), July 5, 2020, https:// https://www.tbsnews.net /economy/trade/bangladesh-india-trade-relations-under-strain-102277.

16. William B. Milam, *Bangladesh and Pakistan: Flirting with Failure in South Asia* (New York: Columbia University Press, 2009), 195–97.

17. Sophia Saifi and Nectar Gan, "Almost 1 in 3 Pilots in Pakistan Have Fake Licenses, Aviation Minister Says," CNN, June 25, 2020, https://www.cnn .com/2020/06/25/business/pakistan-fake-pilot-intl-hnk.

18. Zuha Siddiqui, "In Pakistan, the Army Tightens Its Grip," *Foreign Policy*, July 8, 2020, https:// https://foreignpolicy.com/2020/07/08/in-pakistan -the-army-tightens-its-grip.

19. "Pakistan: History of Lending Commitments as of April 30, 2018," International Monetary Fund, https://imf.org/external/np/fin/tad/extarr2.aspx ?memberKey1=760&date1key=2018-04-30.

20. Kaushik Basu, "Why Is Bangladesh Booming?" *Brookings Institution*, May 1, 2018, https://www.brookings.edu/opinions/why-is-bangladesh-booming.

21. Afia Malik, Ejaz Ghani, and Musleh ud Din, "An Assessment of Pakistan's Export Performance and the Way Forward," *Pakistan Institute for Development Economics, Working Paper 153* (2017), https://pide.org.pk/research/an -assessment-of-pakistans-export-performance-and-the-way-forward.

22. Hoodbhoy, "Why Bangladesh."

23. Transparency International's Corruption Perception Index for 2019 Lists (from Better to Worse), India as 80th out of 198 Countries, Pakistan 120th, and Bangladesh 146th, https://transparency.org/en/cpi/2019.

24. Stockholm International Peace Research Institute, "Almanac: Armaments, Disarmament, and International Security," cited by the World Bank, https:// data.worldbank.org/indicator/ms.mil.xpnd.gd.zs?name_desc=true.

25. Siddiqui, "Pakistan Army Tightens Grip."

26. Nawaz, *Crossed Swords*, 253–54, 359–61.

27. Ayesha Siddiqa, *Military Inc.: Inside Pakistan's Military Economy*, 2nd ed. (London: Pluto Press, 2017), 138.

28. Siddiqa, *Military, Inc.*, 167.

29. Siddiqa, *Military, Inc.*, 256–82.

30. India's budget figure for 2020–21 from Anurag Vaishnav, "Demand for Grants 2020–21 Analysis—Defense," PRS *Legislative Research*, February 14, 2020, https://prsindia.org/budgets/parliament/demand-for-grants-2020 -21-analysis-defence.

31. United Nations Development Program, "Human Development Report 2020," 356–64, http://hdr.undp.org/sites/default/files/hdr2020.pdf.

32. Milam, *Bangladesh and Pakistan*, 212–25.

33. "Women, Peace, and Security Index, 2021," Georgetown University's Institute for Women, Peace, and Security, https://giwps.georgetown.edu/ the-index.

14. Legislating Blasphemy

1. Hashim Asad, "Explained: Pakistan's Emotive Blasphemy Laws," *Al Jazeera*, September 21, 2020, https://aljazeera.com/news/2020/9/21/explained -pakistans-emotive-blasphemy-laws.

2. A seminal description of the policy argument linking poor education in Pakistan to extremism and using U.S. assistance to address the challenge is contained in Lisa Curtis, "U.S. Aid to Pakistan: Countering Extremism Through Education Reform," *Heritage Lectures*, no. 1029, June 8, 2007, https://www .heritage.org/asia/report/us-aid-pakistan-countering-extremism-through -education-reform. Curtis acknowledges academic disagreement over the role of madrassas and notes that only a few madrassas are responsible for most anti-Western and anti-state militancy. USAID funding for education in Pakistan was in the hundreds of millions for two years, 2011–12, before dropping into the $50–60 million per year range through 2019 and then precipitously, along with all other bilateral assistance, by fiscal year 2020 (foreignassistance.gov).

3. On the divergent assessments of links between madrassa education in Pakistan and terrorism/extremism, see Nikhil Raymond Puri, "The Pakistani Madrassah and Terrorism: Made and Unmade Conclusions from the Literature," *Perspectives on Terrorism* 4, no. 4 (October 2010), 51–72; and C. Christine Fair, "The Enduring Madrasa Myth," *Current History* 111, no 74 (April 2012), 135–41.

4. Zain Siddiqui, "These 7 Points Explain the Supreme Court's Decision to Free Aasia Bibi," *Dawn*, updated December 21, 2019, https://www.dawn .com/news/1442634.

5. Jaffer A. Mirza, "The Changing Landscape of Anti-Shia Politics in Pakistan," *The Diplomat*, September 28, 2020, https://thediplomat.com/2020/09/the -changing-landscape-of-anti-shia-politics-in-pakistan.

15. U.S.-Pakistan Relations

1. Krzysztof Iwanek, "Imran Khan's U.S. Conspiracy Theory: A Close Examination," *The Diplomat*, April 13, 2022, https://thediplomat.com/2022/04 /imran-khans-us-conspiracy-theory-a-close-examination; Daniel Ten Kate and Khalid Qayum, "U.S. Denies Khan's Claim It Wants Him Ousted in Pakistan," *Bloomberg*, March 31, 2022, https://www.bloomberg.com/news /articles/2022-04-01/u-s-denies-imran-khan-s-claim-it-wants-him-ousted -in-pakistan.

2. On the mechanics of swing, see Rabinda Mehta, "The Science of Swing Bowling," ESPN *Cricinfo*, September 6, 2006, https://www.espncricinfo .com/story/the-science-of-swing-bowling-258645.

3. Unlike in American professional baseball, which replaces its game balls constantly over the course of every at bat, with the tiniest smudge grounds for early retirement, in cricket wear and tear on the ball is part of the game.

4. Christina Goldbaum and Salman Masood, "Pakistan's Parliament Ousts Imran Khan as Prime Minister," *New York Times*, April 9, 2022, https:// nytimes.com/2022/04/09/world/asia/imran-khan-pakistan-ousted.html; Faseeh Mangi, "Pakistan's Leader and Army are Locked in a Showdown at a Crucial Time for the Region's Geopolitics," *Bloomberg*, March 30, 2022, https://time.com/6163168/imran-khan-army-crisis-pakistan.

5. Lynne O'Donnell, "Afghanistan Regains its Crown as Terror Central," *Foreign Affairs*, April 20, 2022, https://foreignpolicy.com/2022/04/20 /afghanistan-taliban-terrorism-jihad-control; Center for Preventive Action, "Countering a Resurgent Terrorist Threat in Afghanistan," Council on Foreign Relations, April 14, 2022, https://www.cfr.org/report/countering -resurgent-terrorist-threat-afghanistan.

6. Joshua T. White, "Nonstate Threats in the Taliban's Afghanistan," *Brookings*, February 1, 2022, https://brookings.edu/blog/order-from-chaos/2022/02 /01/nonstate-threats-in-the-talibans-afghanistan.

7. United Nations Security Council, "Letter dated 3 February 2022 from the Chair of the Security Council Committee pursuant to resolutions 1267 (1999), 1989 (2011) and 2253 (2015) concerning the Islamic State in Iraq and the Levant (Da'esh), Al-Qaida and associated individuals, groups, under-takings and entities addressed to the President of the Security Council," February 3, 2022, https://digitallibrary.un.org/record/3957081?ln=en.

Index

Page numbers in italics indicate illustrations.

economic issues, 1, 7, 63, 120, 179, 180, 212, 213; education and, 187–88; impact of, 181; military spending and, 183–84

economic policy, 185; inconsistent/statist, 179, 181–82; pro-growth/pro-export, 181

economic prospects, 48, 176, 182, 222, 223

economic rights, 60, 133

Edgbaston Cricket Ground, playing at, 81, 139

education, 53, 79, 176, 183, 186, 189, 202; economic weakness and, 187–88; extremism and, 248n2; madrassa, 248n3; shortcomings in, 154, 202; terrorism and, 248n2; women's, 183

Eisenhower, Dwight, 54

elections, 4, 11–17, 230n8; flawed, 2, 13; secure, 5, 8

Electoral Commission (Pakistan), 12

Emergency Action Committee, 125, 205

Enduring Freedom operation, 91

England-Australia match, 193

England cricket, 20, 106, 107; rivalry with, xv; triumphs for, 193

England–New Zealand match, 193–94, 197

English Selection Board, 134

Entebbe Option, 109

entrepreneurship, 9, 112, 187, 189

equality: asserting, 59; economic, 12, 147; gender, 79, 172, 179; racial, 60

Erdoğan, Recep Tayyip, 212

Establishment Clause (U.S.), 209

ethnicity, 13, 66, 86, 174

ethnonationalism, 94, 178

European Space Agency, 123

extremism, 81, 201, 204; education and, 248n2, 248n3; Hindu right, 220; Pakistani-linked, 47; religious, 188, 199–200, 202; secular state and, 202; useful, 10–11; vulnerability to, 216

F-16 aircraft, 126, 127, 128, 241n19; U.S. providing, 218; withholding, 36

FATA. See Federally Administered Tribal Areas (FATA)

Fatah-e-Insaniat Foundation, 48

FATF. See Financial Action Task Force (FATF)

"fauji" companies, 183, 184

FBI, xx, 109, 129

Federally Administered Tribal Areas (FATA), 71, 74, 93, 96, 97

field hockey, 20, 24

Financial Action Task Force (FATF), 48, 128, 129, 221

Fire in Babylon (film), 235n1

First Amendment (U.S.), 209

foreign investment, 6, 34, 182, 223

foreign policy, 130, 155–56, 160, 161, 178, 214, 216, 220, 223; democratic criteria and, 5; human rights and, 2; Kashmir and, 118; U.S., 4, 135

Four Freedoms, 2

Free and Fair Election Network (FAFEN), 12

"Freedom Agenda," 4

Frontier Works Organization, 184

gambling in cricket, 33, 100

Ganges River, 114

Ganguly, Sourav, 112

Gates, Robert, 156

Gayle, Chris, 64

GDP. See gross domestic product (GDP)

gender bias, 179, 185

Gender Inequality Index, 186

Geneva Convention, 124

geopolitics, xiv, 52, 224

Georgetown University, 186

Ghani, Ashraf, 91, 109, 150, 165; diplomatic dustup and, 164; peace talks and, 166

Gilgit-Baltistan, 117

Pakistan-Afghanistan relations, 150; trade and, 166

Pakistan Air Force, 42, 115

Pakistan Air Force Museum, 124

Pakistan Army, xix, 41, 50, 73, 76, 96, 97; al-Qaida and, 151; anti-India militants and, 10; antiterrorism and, 14; assistance to, 14; Bajwa retirement and, 17; China and, 34, 52-53; counterinsurgency, 36, 37, 45, 70-74, 95-97; East Pakistan and, 87; economic demands of, 183, 185, 215; GHQ of, xvii, 9, 41, 52, 148, 151, 163, 218; IMET and, 46; Islamist militants and, 216; Kashmir and, 116-17, 118; nationalism and, 68; politics and, 5, 7, 17, 212; proxy policies and, 218; recruitment by, 69-70; religious extremists and, 200, 202; repression by, 70, 72, 174-75; Swat Valley and, 94; Taliban and, 15, 150, 217; Tora Bora and, 149; U.S. portrayal of, 38

Pakistan-Australia match, 104-5, 110

Pakistan-Australia relations, cricket and, 107

Pakistan-Bangladesh match, 174, 190

Pakistan-China relations: development of, 42-44; problems in, 47-52

Pakistan cricket, x, xiii-xvi, 20-27, 64-65, 81-83, 100, 102, 103, 110, 111, 189; attention for, 196; Bangladesh matches and, 176; in Melbourne, 105-7; transformation of, 112

Pakistan Cricket Board (PCB), 23, 24

Pakistan-England matches, xiii, 66-68, 84, 130

Pakistan-England relations, cricket and, 82

Pakistan Foreign Ministry, 76, 108, 123, 165; engagement with, xx-xxi

Pakistani Constitution, 97

Pakistan-India cease-fire, 125

Pakistan-India matches, 1, 111-13, 132, 172

Pakistan-India relations, 113, 119, 125; Bangladesh and, 116; cricket and, 111, 114, 115; trade and, 178

Pakistan International Airways (PIA), 179-80

Pakistani Parliament, 73

Pakistan military, 1-2, 223; action against, 221; bin Laden death and, 37, 157; Davis case and, 40; deployment of, 74; economic role of, 183, 185, 230n10; Indian threat and, 186; Khan and, 17-19; militant Islam and, 202; strategy of, 153; Taliban and, 92; terrorist attacks and, 75; western frontiers and, 68-76

Pakistan Muslim League-Nawaz (PML-N), 7, 8, 12, 16, 42, 210, 212, 215, 216-17; decline of, 11; election and, 14; government by, 96; leadership by, 10; in London, 80; transition and, 9; withdrawal of, 203

Pakistan Muslim League-Quaid-e-Azam, 213

Pakistan-New Zealand match, 139-42

Pakistan-New Zealand relations, 139, 141-42

Pakistan People's Party (PPP), 6, 8, 11, 12, 16, 24, 199, 212, 215; in London, 80; transition and, 9

Pakistan security services, 91, 157, 161; Afghan issues and, xxii; antidemocratic manipulation and, 14

Pakistan-South Africa match, 133-34, 137-38

Pakistan-Sri Lanka match, 85-89; abandonment of, 103

Pakistan Supreme Court, 24, 120, 205, 206; Bibi and, 204; Nawaz and, 10

Pakistan Taliban, 37, 71, 94, 151, 162, 168, 208, 224; attacks by, 214; insurgency of, 202; Pakistan Army and, 217. *See also* Tehrik-e-Taliban Pakistan

Pakistan-West Indies match, 59-65

Palk Strait, 88

Riaz, Wahab, 83, 110
Rizvi, Khadim, 203
Roosevelt, Franklin D., 2
Root, Joe, 83, 194
Roy, Jason, 196
Russia, 69; Ukraine invasion by, 181, 214, 223, 224

Saeed, Hafez, 129
Salafist school, 89, 203
"Salala Incident," 41
Samiuddin, Osman, 21, 23, 25, 104–5
sanctions, xxiii; economic, 9, 35–36, 44, 48, 128, 129, 135, 136–37, 155, 185, 222; limited, 221
Sandford, Christopher, 164
security, 13, 98, 100, 123, 204, 222; clearances, 163; concerns, xvii, xxi, xxiii, 52; diplomatic, xix; national, 4, 9, 220; nuclear, 126, 220; regional, 18
security establishment, 10, 162, 201, 221, 227; TTP threat and, 226
security forces, 39, 71, 72, 118, 222
security issues, 172, 177–78
security policies, 125, 221, 227
security relations, 47, 107, 219
segregation, 82, 133
Sehwan, attacks in, 91
Senate Foreign Relations Committee (U.S.), 40
separation, 70, 174. *See also* partition
separatism, 67, 73, 74
Serrano, Jorge, 3
7/7 attack, 79
sexism, theocratic/societal, 187
Shah, Aquil, 71
Shanghai, Pakistanis in, 46
Sharif, Nawaz, 5, 49, 80, 210, 215, 246n4; Bajwa and, 18; Chinese loans and, 42; government of, 9; PML-N and, 7, 8; political collapse of, 9–10; PTI and, 203
Sharif, Raheel, 18
Sharif, Shahbaz, 210

Sharma, Rohit, xv
Shia Muslims, 90, 91, 93, 209
Siddiqa, Ayesha, 183
Sikh Empire, 69
Sikhs, 114, 115, 116, 200
Silk Road, 43
Sindh Province, 8, 12, 91
Sindhis, 74, 94
Sinhalese, 86; Tamils and, 88
Sobers, Gary, 61
soccer, 27, 104, 193, 195; growth of, 55, 63; international, 20, 55; popularity of, 176
social conservatives, cricket and, 104
social developments, cricket and, 21
socialism, appeal to, 67
social media, 52, 70, 72, 159, 164, 207, 208; disinformation from, 2
socioeconomic development, 51, 154, 200–201
Sohail, Haris, 138, 142
South Africa, 112; ban on, 133, 134; cricket and, 20
South Africa cricket, 82, 106, 133–34, 136
South Africa–West Indies match, 137
South Asian Empire, 68
South Waziristan, 71
Soviet Union, 2, 78; collapse of, 35, 217
Special Representative for Afghanistan and Pakistan (SRAP), 154, 155
spot-fixing scandal, xiii–xiv, 64, 102
SRAP. *See* Special Representative for Afghanistan and Pakistan (SRAP)
Sri Lanka, 50, 99, 144; Australia and, 86–87; cricket corruption in, 102–3; match against, x, xv; Pakistan and, 85–86; political intrigue in, 88–89; terrorism in, 99; World Cup and, 95
Sri Lanka cricket, 86, 93, 95, 100, 103, 106, 196; attack on, 94; World Cup win for, 87
Sri Lankan military, LTTE and, 88, 89
Sri Lankan National Bank, bombing of, 87
Srinagar, 116, 117, 124

Trump, Donald, 16, 139, 141, 245n35;
Afghanistan exit and, 14, 160, 162,
166, 169; aid cut by, 46, 160; Bergdahl
and, 159; Coalition Support Funds and,
45; democratic criteria and, 5; Jones
and, 45; Kashmir and, 130; Khan and,
129–30, 210; retaliation and, 12; U.S.-
Pakistan relations and, 15, 44, 129–30,
160; would-be authoritarians and, 4
TTP. *See* Tehrik-e-Taliban Pakistan (TTP)
1267 Committee (UN), 225
Twenty-First Amendment (Pakistani
Constitution), 97

Ukraine, invasion of, 181, 214, 223, 224
ul-Haq, Imam, 172, 190
United Arab Emirates (UAE), 50, 77, 178;
matches in, 95
United Nations, 53, 161, 170, 200, 216,
225; Kashmir and, 117
United Nations Development Pro-
gramme (UNDP), 186
United Nations Security Council, 44;
Kashmir and, 117
United States Institute of Peace, 163
Unquiet Ones (Samiuddin), 21
Urdus, 72, 76, 80, 174, 206
Uri incident, 120, 122
U.S. Agency for International Develop-
ment (USAID), xx, 3, 5, 39, 248n2
USAID. *See* U.S. Agency for International
Development (USAID)
U.S. Army War College, 47
U.S. Central Command, 41, 123
U.S.-China competition, ix, 35, 52
U.S. Congress, 156; Taliban and, 14–15
U.S. Consulate, Lahore, 39
U.S. Consulate, Peshawar, xxi
U.S. Department of Commerce,
xx, 242n4
U.S. Department of Defense (DOD), xx,
127, 169; staff in Pakistan, xix

U.S. Embassy, Gabarone, 242n4
U.S. Embassy, Islamabad, xx, 54, 85, 108,
121, 151, 164; British High Commission
and, 77; construction of, xviii
U.S. Embassy, Kabul, 109, 165
U.S. Embassy, La Paz, 229n1
U.S. Embassy, New Delhi, 120, 121
U.S.-India entente, 218; China's rise
and, 217
U.S.-India relations, 121, 154
U.S. International Military Education
and Training (IMET), 46–47
U.S.-Pakistan relations, ix, x, 1, 54, 227;
achievable interests in, 218–19; Afghanistan and, 149–51; China's rise and, 217;
cricket and, 53; decline of, 37, 41, 44–47,
151, 156–58, 216, 218–19; drama in, 39–
42; intelligence cooperation and, 157;
maintaining, 34, 52–53; 9/11 and, 36–37;
reverse swing and, 215–23; sustainable
approach for, xxii, xxiv; Taliban and,
150–51; terrorism/nuclear proliferation
and, 38; Trump and, 129–30; war on terror and, 217; working on, xxii
U.S. Special Forces, 158
U.S. State Department, 3, 96, 154, 160,
163, 198, 210; Bibi and, 206; country
teams and, xix, xx; democracy commitment of, 5; human rights and, 5, 222;
IMET and, 46; Kashmir and, 130; Pakistan visitor program and, 45
Uyghurs, 38, 51, 96, 170
Uzbeks, attacks by, 96

Valentine's Day attack, 48
van Linschoten, Alex Strick, 148
Varthaman, Abhinandan, 124–25, 241n19
Veracruz, intervention at, 2
Vietnam War, 154
Votel, Joseph, 240n14

Wagg, Stephen, 86, 141, 142, 176

Wagner, Robert, 54

Wahhabism, 94, 202

Walcott, Clyde, 61

Wall Street Journal, 93

war on terror, 34, 105, 217

Washington Post, 153

Way, Lucan, 229n2

Weekes, Everton, 61

Weeks, Timothy, 107, 108, 109

welfare foundations, 184, 230n10

Wells, Alice, 160

West Indies cricket, 21, 59, 60, 61, 62, 64, 82, 87, 106, 112, 137, 138, 194; decline of, 63, 65; fast bowlers and, 104; Pakistan visit by, 22, 63; women's, 103

West Pakistan, 115, 175; abusive governance by, 116; cricket and, 22; independence and, 174; Muslim refugees in, 174

White, Joshua, 224

William, Prince, 77

Wilson, Woodrow, 2

Wisden, match description, 29

Women, Peace, and Security Index, 186

women's rights, 38, 153, 172–73; Bangladesh and, 182–83; decline of, 167; improving, 189

World Bank, 4, 135

World Cup (cricket). *See* Cricket World Cup

World Cup (soccer), 55, 193, 195

World Series (U.S. baseball), 198

World War II, 60, 69, 104, 105

Worrell, Frank, 61, 62

Wounded Tiger (Oborne), 21

Yao Jing, 48

Younis, Waqar, 211

Zahman, Fakhar, xv, 172

Zardari, Asif Ali, 8, 15, 238n16; Davis case and, 40; Kerry and, 41

Zawahiri, Ayman al-, 218, 225

Zero Dark Thirty (film), 41

Zero Light Seven, 156–58

Zhao Lijian, 52

Zia-ul-Haq, Mohammed, 18, 146, 183, 201

Zimbabwe, 135; hunger in, 136; trade unionists in, 136; trade/private investment for, 242n4

Zimbabwe cricket, 64, 102, 106

Zuma, Jacob, 136

Related ADST Book Series Titles

Terrorism, Betrayal, and Resilience: My Story of the 1998 U.S. Embassy Bombings
PRUDENCE BUSHNELL

The Mind of the African Strongman: Conversations with Dictators, Statesmen, and Father Figures
HERMAN J. COHEN

Born a Foreigner: A Memoir of the American Presence in Asia
CHARLES T. CROSS

Danger Zones: A Diplomat's Fight for America's Interests
JOHN GUNTHER DEAN

Diversifying Diplomacy: My Journey from Roxbury to Dakar
HARRIET ELAM-THOMAS

Behind Embassy Walls: The Life and Times of an American Diplomat
BRANDON GROVE

Nine Lives: A Foreign Service Odyssey
ALLEN C. HANSEN

Strangers When We Met: A Century of American Community in Kuwait
NATHANIEL W. HOWELL

The Incidental Oriental Secretary and Other Tales of Foreign Service
RICHARD L. JACKSON

American Ambassadors: The Past, Present, and Future of America's Diplomats
DENNIS JETT

The American Consul
CHARLES STUART KENNEDY

The United States and Pakistan, 1947–2000: Disenchanted Allies
DENNIS KUX

Vietnam and Beyond: A Diplomat's Cold War Education
ROBERT H. MILLER

American Diplomats: The Foreign Service at Work
WILLIAM MORGAN AND C. STUART KENNEDY

Witness to a Changing World
DAVID D. NEWSOM

Memoirs of a Foreign Service Arabist
RICHARD B. PARKER

The Craft of Political Analysis for Diplomats
RAYMOND F. SMITH

In Those Days: A Diplomat Remembers
JAMES W. SPAIN

Gifted Greek: The Enigma of Andreas Papandreou
MONTEAGLE STEARNS

Abroad for Her Country: Tales of a Pioneer Woman Ambassador in the U.S. Foreign Service
JEAN WILKOWSKI

For a complete list of series titles, visit adst.org/publications.